A FLICKERING LIGHT

A FLICKERING LIGHT
AN UNCONVENTIONAL VIEW OF WESTERN SCIENCE

MIGUEL OCHOA

A FLICKERING LIGHT
AN UNCONVENTIONAL VIEW OF WESTERN SCIENCE

iUniverse books may be ordered through booksellers or by contacting:

iUniverse
1663 Liberty Drive
Bloomington, IN 47403
www.iuniverse.com
1-800-Authors (1-800-288-4677)

ISBN: 978-1-4917-4104-7 (sc)
ISBN: 978-1-4917-4105-4 (e)

Printed in the United States of America.

iUniverse rev. date: 8/8/2014

INTRODUCTION

The technological explosion which we are witnessing around us has brought in its throes an enormous enhancement of the prestige and appreciation of modern science, which unqualified endorsement by the whole of humanity is a fact of major significance in the short history of civilization. Suffice is to mention the development of nuclear power and the trips outside our planet to understand why people behold with owe such achievements and why the reputation and notoriety of science and scientists has risen so vertiginously in the appreciation of the contemporary world. To question its premises and basic assumptions appears almost as sheer madness, and to explore its foundations an exercise in futility which has not been seriously attempted since the XVIII Century. After all, results are what matters.

Yet, I believe, it is precisely THAT what we should seriously attempt now for two fundamental reasons. In the first place science is, and has been for the last century, posed at the brink of a physical reality far removed and totally strange to us, a reality so remote from our cosmic level of existence as to defy the rules of understanding we commonly accept, the rules that had served us so well in our tackling of those scientific problems which had engaged, confronted and challenge man up to the turn of the XXI Century. Let me add that this is not 'idle theorizing'. If science is going to continue progressing and serving us in the future with the same fortitude and success of the past, it would need to dispense with obsolete and traditional ways of analyzing scientific data and, instead, plow along new and un-trodden paths once freed from the dead weight of our past, that is to say, of the cultural accretions of 3000 years of civilization.

In the second place, if machine intelligence is going to eventually replace many of the functions of the human intellect (perhaps all of them), it would be mandatory that we create a system of gathering and applying in a meaningful and productive way the relevant information and to that effect dispense with useless conventional notions of our minds, things that we take for granted and consider part of reality itself instead of what they really are: Cognitive frames rooted in the structural organization of our relational apparatus, the human brain.

It is impossible, however, to even begin to comprehend the ways we learn without a realization of the impact of knowledge itself in the attitude and behavior of humans in the further reception and elaboration of this knowledge. I believe that the complacent conformism, the almost religious reverence we assiduously display in the acceptance of scientific dogma (perhaps, in part the result of the enormous growth and ramification of all branches of scientific knowledge which render impossible for the human mind to master and understand all relevant information) is a perverse manifestation of our infatuation with modern technology. The extinction of the critical spirit, the blind acceptance of received dogma is the preamble to any totalitarian philosophy, and the reduction of every human being to the position of a docile automaton a mandatory necessity to its fulfillment. It is only ironic that such a glorious science which we all enthusiastically endorse in the hope that it will lead us to a paradisiacal state is, in actuality, reducing us progressively to a condition of functional illiteracy, a marginal existence in submissive dependence to the mercy of the all embracing god of modern technology.

Does this imply that we should advocate a total rejection of the efforts and achievements of several centuries of toiling humanity? Happily I don't think we have yet reached such a degree of sterile desperation. To understand the effect of modern technology upon the human psyche we need to analyze the perceiving and processing apparatus of the mind and above all the ways Man reacts to his environment, keeping all the time from forgetting our zoological affiliation as biped placentate mammals and therefore that we, as in the case of many other closely related groups, are social animals and consequently have the tendency of ACTING AS A GROUP.

We will also need to perceive the patterns of mass psychology, of how as Le Bon showed, man is influenced by verbal symbols which alluring power drives us mysteriously, and of how man can be compel, as Erich Fromm claims, by the need for security and the fear of standing alone to take refuge and solace in identification with the group, not underestimating how the persistent hammering of slogans and catch words terminates in the surrendering of our wills and the redirection of our behavior.

I maintain that in order to assess the influence of modern technology in the scientific community and in society at large we need to appreciate better the role of human motivation. But can the knower know himself? This ancient riddle going back to Plato is inextricably related to the structure of the perceiving and processing apparatus: The Nervous System and also to the nature of consciousness itself. The subject is one of the more confused in theory of knowledge and perhaps the one where the magnitude of our ignorance is more dramatically exemplified. How the brain learns and knows that it learns? How the information is sifted and stored? Is a computer basically a similar assemblage? What is the nature and function of language? How the need for self expression influence and modulates the received information? Is it possible to ascertain something more than has already been said in reference to human motivation and basic drives? How can we know that we know if we do not know the knower? Is this knowledge necessary or irrelevant?

Although obviously nobody today can give a semblance of an answer to these questions, I don't believe it is a useless platitude to speculate about them; particularly when it is realized that speculation is one of the functions of the human mind. In so doing we will, perhaps, develop a new respect for Nature and commence to discern the limitations of our understanding, even to the point of reverting our arrogant pride to meek humbleness when confronted with the mysteries of the Cosmo and the vagaries of the human condition. Possibly even, in conceiving better the way we perceive, learn and react, in other words, the modes by which we relate to the totality of our environment, we will be in an improved position to control and if necessary to redirect our behavior; or, at the least, be better qualified not only to realize the magnitude of our ignorance but maybe to improve the way we sift useful information.

It is my desire in the following pages to document that it is the association of events, not the 'visualization' of 'mechanisms' or 'causal' relationships what is important to Science; not the search for presumptive 'explanations' but the gathering of relevant and useful INFORMATION. The task, by its very nature, will demand an integration of evidence from diverse sources, some unfortunately quite technical, but nevertheless important in the clarification of my point of view and also mandatory in providing the proper perspective.

To this effect I had considered useful to begin with a brief historical review of Epistemology, in other words, of what Man had thought to be knowledge and the way to achieve it through the ages. The perusal is not intended to be exhaustive but only concerned with what is pertinent to the purpose and to the subject matter in question. This will be followed by a brief description of historical highlights into some basic scientific topics which will serve to illustrate my point. Then I will attempt the correlation of neurophysiologic facts with the fundamental premises of our understanding; those categories which we have viewed as mandatory if knowledge of a purported or assumed 'physical reality' is possible at all. In this regard I will try the difficult task of explaining why I believe that these basic preconditions could be transcended and are actually referable to something even more fundamental in our neurophysiologic make up, to some basic neuronal functional attributes which would, ironically, eventually allow us to cast away all hindrance to future scientific enquire and progress. The last chapters will be devoted to analyze epistemological problems peculiar to the Health Sciences, again preceded by a brief historical review followed by short biographical notes about some pioneers in science and technology.

CHAPTER I

There is a frequently repeated misconception among Western scholars which ascribed to the Greeks the 'invention' of science and philosophy. Although such opinion has a lot to do with how these disciplines are defined, philosophy, as a speculative activity preoccupied with the place of man in the Universe and all its ethical and political implications, did appear more or less simultaneously in China and Greece. Furthermore, science as a human endeavor seeking to discover relations among universal phenomena with the ultimate intention of procuring a better adaptation of man to its environment, certainly has a long tradition in civilized societies, preceding the Greeks perhaps for thousands of years in Babylon and Egypt.

What the Greeks truly pompously inaugurated was that peculiar belief of Western man to the effect that Nature 'ways' have a purposeful order, ACCESSIBLE to the analysis and understanding of the human mind after their fundamental components have been identified. What all this amounts to is a profound conviction and trust in the power of the intellect or 'Reason' to discern 'Truth' and 'Final Causes' and, consequently, to 'explain' away the 'mystery' of 'Creation'. This conviction, dramatically exemplified in the well known myth of Prometheus who stole the 'fire' (a well known allegory of 'Wisdom') from the gods, essentially represents an 'act of rebellion' and of affirmation of the power of man to 'conquer' Nature. Man was not only going to 'understand' his position in the World but to control and manipulate it; a hitherto divine prerogative. Fundamental in this regard was the prior apprehension of Nature as a 'Kosmo' or orderly whole, a prerequisite if any scientific or intellectual effort was going to be possible. It also needed the conception of this

1

'Kosmo' as something SEPARATED from Man, a significant development with no precedence in contemporary civilized societies, and finally also the belief in 'substance' and 'forms' as underlining 'facts' of ultimate 'reality'.

Reason, however, the divine fire stolen by Prometheus, was necessary to unravel the deceptive veil of appearances and behold the unambiguous face of Truth. The irreducible elemental constituent of things was assumed to be Water by Thales, Air by Anaximander, Fire by Heraclitus, all of the above plus Earth by Empedocles, an ethereal undefined 'wholeness' by the Eleatics, and finally 'atoms' by Leucippus. Behind the totality, and imbuing it with a deliberate purpose, was an ordering principle firstly mentioned in the West by Heraclitus as the 'Logos' and later on referred by others (like Anaxagoras for instance) as Nouns.

Rational thought then represents the firm belief in the power of human intellect to discern the unknown and so to discover the mystery of existence, in essence constituting a 'brake away', perhaps even an obliteration of the numinous in the human soul, coupled with a reaffirmation of a material 'cosmic' reality to be 'conquered' by that self promoted creature who robbed the fire from the gods.

Atomism was the final synthesis of Greek rationalism, a world view incorporating in each atom the attributes of the Parmenidian 'One', reconciled with the Pythagorean 'void' to explain multiplicity and change; therefore 'appearances'. The idea was that of solid, basic, regular 'corpuscles' also accessible to human intellect and consequently representing 'predictable' configurations. It was a mechanistic view of Nature, each atom being a single, indestructible and INERT body acted upon by 'external' forces, also accessible to human 'knowledge' and capable of being measured and quantified. The Universe, therefore, was not only orderly arranged but rigidly predetermined; an intuitive conviction of primitive agrarian societies which directly experienced, and were at the mercy, of the periodicities and regularity of meteorological changes.

But if the World was so constituted Man was not a 'free agent', a precondition to any 'conquering act'; Reason would have been useless and any scientific endeavor rendered impossible. Man needed to extricate himself from these fetters and it is precisely such reflective act, this 'emancipation' of Man from the rest of Nature, this 'pulling away' and above IT what is characteristic of the Western ethic and could be traced back to the Greeks. The power of Reason was to be employed not only to 'understand' and 'know' the Kosmo but also to 'control' and manipulate it. These intentions are implicit in the platonic dialogues (particularly in the early ones) where life purpose becomes the perfectibility of Man thru knowledge and in Aristotelian cosmology; in fact representing the purpose of Western Philosophy.

The ambiguities and contradictions of this dual ethic of 'free will' and 'determinism' has, since then, haunted the fabric of Western thought. It is apparent in the works of the late stoics, who were prompt to assume personal responsibility and to take the blame for their own wrong doings, while graciously forgiving others for their mistakes and sins on the grounds that humans were nothing but 'play things' of Fate. The explosive issue was later on taken by the early Christian Church, provoking numerous conflicts and controversies of doctrine which cost the life to more than one 'heretic'. After the Reformation, however, the Calvinist embraced the banner of 'determinism' making it central to their dogma which, however strangely, still holds Man accountable for his actions. The concept of 'free will' finally emerged victorious from these disputes and was uphold by most Christian denominations as a sacred gift to Man from God, the basis of all virtues and source of human dignity and responsibility.

If in the West Man was viewed as a quasi-divine free agent who was to use his 'Reason' to 'know' and ultimately to control Nature, an entirely different outlook took hold in Eastern lands. There, within the nucleus of agrarian societies in the gangetic planes and in Southern China, a completely different conception of Man and Nature evolved among the displaced and uprooted survivors of nomadic invasions to the earlier bronze-age civilizations of the Indus and Yangtze River valleys. For them there was no question as to the place of humans in the cosmic order. Anybody foolish enough to oppose Nature's designs was to meet only with disgrace and utter defeat. The Indian ascetic of the forest believed that the world of the senses was an illusion (Maya) created by a generative principle (Karma), a veil impeding us to reach the sublime abode of the Soul beyond all descriptions and images: The ineffable

3

primordial immanent principle of Brahma. The access to him was not thru any 'reasoning' by the thinking mind but only by way of meditation, a 'closing', so to speak, of the physical eye and concomitant opening of the inner one of Atman, the divine element of the human soul which, as such, allowed the revelation of the ultimate 'truth'. Mystic introspection rather than Reason was the 'main tool' or devise of the ascetic 'mind'.

Likewise, the Chinese sagas of the VI Century B.C. developed an anti-rationalistic attitude and a mystic approach to the understanding of Nature: The Tao. For one thing, they considered futile and useless to act 'against' the basic order of Nature. Taoism developed a dynamic view of Life which was understood as the interplay of polar opposites, that is, of a receptive, yielding, passive, cool and feminine Yin and of an aggressive, active, fiery and hot, masculine Yang. These dynamic notions possessed an intriguing similarity to the philosophy of Heraclitus, who was roughly contemporary with Lao Tzu and whose ideas constituted a temporary 'dead end' in Greek thought; only to eventually resuscitate and be integrated by the early stoics in their speculative system.

Be it as it may, it can be safely stated that the oriental mind, ever since its inception, conformed to a mystic anti-rationalistic course and, furthermore, conceived Man AS PART OF NATURE. It would have been inconceivable for them any attempt to seize or conquer IT; something they would have considered as vein, futile and even absurd. Their science had only a practical character, devoid of theorizing or struggles to 'understand' the World order.

In this regard, I think, it is very revealing the complains of Yuan Yuan, a historian of Chinese science and technology who claimed that Western man was obsessed with explanations rather than merely considering the simple facts (S.F. Mason 'A History of the Sciences'. Collier Books. 1962, P. 88).

The reliance in the power of the human intellect to discern and analyze the Cosmo with the ultimate aim of understanding, controlling and manipulating the World is a typical Western trait completely alien to other civilized men of comparable cultural development. Yet, an streak of the mystic outlook, probably an early oriental influence of dubious origin, had undeniably permeated the fabric of Western thought creating an undercurrent with diverse ramifications, better expressed in Central

Europe since the Early Renaissance, where it arose an speculative, vitalistic, intellectual tradition which, firstly realized in alchemy and the biological sciences, have had profound repercussions even in modern physics. We shall now try to trace the roots of these two cultural traits and some of their branches.

The ways and means of how man 'learns' or acquire 'knowledge' of his environment has preoccupied Western Man at least since the time of Plato. It should be clear to anybody that such marvelous speculations presuppose the awakening of an analytic reflective mind, as well as an availability of time and leisure away from the daily toils of mankind, only possible in a fairly advanced civilization capable of affording this kind of 'luxury'. But it also requires more: At least it demands an attitude freed from a numinous content in addition to a tolerant social milieu.

Once this is realized it appears hardly surprising that such inquires were first undertaken, as far as we can tell by the historic evidence, in the Greek city-states where all the above preconditions were fulfilled; particularly in the ingratiating and propitious atmosphere of Athens. Here free men could congregate, during the Golden Age at least, to argue and discuss abstract and 'esoteric' subjects without worries and fears.

To a layman and indeed to anybody when first confronted with these problems, it sounds strange that so much discussion and argument could have resulted from quite apparent 'trivialities', and even more shocking that a voluminous literature could have been written and compiled in such epistemological matters. Our 'common sense' tell us that we know the 'outside' reality by means of our senses, and learn to differentiate the various objects and creatures by observing them and their behavior. No wonder the sense of bewilderment and surprise experienced by a person when first confronted with the conclusions arrived at in the dialogues of Plato. Sense perceptions, we are told, are not to be trusted because appearances are deceptive; a theme maintained previously by the Eleatics and implicit in the theorizing of the Miletians. (First Parmenidian fragments according to Simplicius as quoted in John Burnet 'Early Greek Philosophy'. Meridian Books. 1967, P 172.)

The learning by 'argument', the admonishment against the 'wandering eye or sounding ear or tongue' is typical of this line of reasoning which culminated with the 'ideal' platonic realm. There is some historic evidence, stemming from the second part of this poem, suggesting Pythagorean and perhaps early Miletian features in Parmenidean cosmology (even some authorities maintain that he was a renegade from their sect).

His negation of the possibility of empty space, a precondition for the denial of fragmentation and diversity, was the basis for his monistic approach and unitarian world view; which set him apart from others and necessitated, clearly, a rejection of sensory perception as a precondition for ascertaining the true nature of the Universe.

Although the Eleatic system was essentially sterile from the scientific point of view it, nonetheless, had great influence in antiquity, probably because of the wandering habits of Parmenides himself and the force of his personality. Despite of been finally overcome, eleaticism, nevertheless, had great impact on ancient Greek thought and its influence is clearly visible in Plato's insistence about the impossibility of knowledge in a state of 'flux'. Nothing that was continuously changing could be adequately discerned and understood by the mind, in other words, it transformed into something else before it was capable of being studied and analyzed, rendering us forever ignorant. The essence of this line of reasoning was unfolded by Plato in the Theaetetus and subsequently, in a more elaborated and mature form in his immortal Timeus. (Plato 'Timeus' .Translation of Desmond Lee. Penguin Books. 1971, P. 28-29.)

Because of the transient nature of perceived phenomena the perceptual world could not be an object of knowledge. Only the immutable realm of ideas could be studied and understood by man with the help of Reason; the light of the intellect. As Frank Magill commented pointedly, it was not unheard of to dismiss the observations as deceptive. (See 'Masterpieces of World Philosophy'. Salem Press. 1961, P 20.)

The true incorruptible reality lies in the eternal Forms accessible only to the mind, while what we capture of the fleeting ever changing Nature is only an inferior reproduction, a shifting incomplete reflection, as so vividly expressed in the popular and well known cave allegory of the Republic. All that exist including the ethical categories did have an ideal Form, the Real one, perceived solely by human understanding of which individual instances known thru the senses were imperfect manifestations. Only intense cultivation of the intellect and training of the mind in philosophy could eventually permit a given person to 'see' distinctly by means of the eyes of his understanding, to behold directly and unambiguously the 'ideal' shapes, of which everything sensual were poor imitations.

Greek Reason, the conclusion seems inescapable, was A TYRANT OF THE SENSES, a sieve where all sensory impressions became purified, a supreme judge which issued the final verdict as to the reality of the knowable world or perhaps an 'inner light' that directed our conscience in the search for 'truth'.

By far the most influential of Greeks philosophers, however, was Aristotle. He was the first logician as well as, in natural sciences, the first system builder, a man of a prodigiously productive mind who exerted a dictatorial influence in Western thought for more than 2000 years. In epistemology Aristotle endorsed resolutely traditional Greek rationalism and, throughout his voluminous writings, stressed that true knowledge was knowledge of 'final causes' and that superior knowledge could only be obtained by demonstration of what is necessary and universal.('The philosophy of Aristotle', R. Bambrough. Trans. J.L. Creed and A.E. Wardman. Mentor Book.1963, Posterior Analytics: Book I. Entry 20)

Aristotle, it is well known, was the first to describe formally the syllogistic method in Logic, something that had been used without explicit realization by many Greek geometers and philosophers before him. It is, as he explains, a system of finding conclusions from valid premises, whether necessary or conditional, universals or particular, according to the necessity, conditionality, universality or particularity of the premises themselves. He, however, following the mainstream of Greek thought conceived ' true knowledge' as knowledge of 'universals' and 'final causes'. The existence of 'ideas', in the platonic sense, he resolutely rejected, but then introduced to replace them the ambiguous category of Primary Substances, Forms or Essences which, for all practical purposes, replaced the platonic universals with other kind of his own; although he never tired of emphasizing that those Forms were inextricably associated to the particular and individual, and therefore that they did not possessed an independent existence. Yet, it is difficult to see how Essences or Forms did not have a sort of independent existence, particularly when he discusses the process of 'coming into being' (Ibid. Metaphysics, Book VII. Entry 7) and introduces what he calls formal nature, something of the same form as 'the thing itself' and thru which agency they came into being; a kind of template allowing things of certain class to exhibit the same form of their predecessors.

For Aristotle then if knowledge was at all possible it needed a preliminary ordering of everything that exist in classes with similar properties, allowing generalizations to be made and relational patterns to be 'discovered' in order to achieve true knowledge of 'universals'. Causes and conclusions in demonstrative syllogistic logic pertained to already identified or 'known' things or classes. Even concepts like 'good' or 'health', which the Greeks ascribed a 'reality' difficult to understand to a modern Western mind, were so classified.

It is impossible to deny a degree of circularity and contradiction in Aristotle's Logic as, for instance, when he places as one of the preconditions for perfect knowledge the 'knowledge of causes', a way of using a definitional term to explain itself (for all their psychologism the Greeks never solved the problem of 'how we know that we know'), or Aristotle account of inductive knowledge (which he called intuitive) when, after denying the possibility of knowledge from perceptions he follows with an account of how perceptions are capable of affording universal knowledge; an obvious contradiction. (Ibid. Book I, Entry 31).

The perplexity stems from the fact that Aristotle first states that we cannot 'perceive' universals and therefore obtain 'true knowledge' thru perceptions, and later on claiming that universals 'become clear' from a number of 'particular instances'. The difficulty could be a semantic one (we are trying to understand what somebody wrote 2500 years ago in an already extinct language). Perhaps for Aristotle the term 'perception' applied only to perception of particular objects or phenomena and universals were CONCEPTIONAL TERMS arrived at by intuiting from sense experience. Nevertheless, at least indirectly even by his own admission, it appears a necessary precondition to all definitional categorization the singular individual perception; thus it seems unjustified his obstinate rejection of perception as a source of knowledge.

The platonic influence here is clearly manifested. As Aristotle tired of repeating, to 'know' that something is the case is not to 'know why', in other words, is not knowledge of final causes; which for the Greek intellect was the sine qua non of true absolute knowledge. Perceptions only provided the material from which our minds 'intuited' (he probably meant what we call 'induction') general characteristics, ABSTRACTIONS of a sort from where the intellect derive the 'Universals'.

Perceptions, then for him, appeared not to allow ultimate knowledge but only knowledge of those characteristics that subsequently served as the basis to acquire, by applying the syllogistic demonstrative logic, the understanding of final causes (nothing but a revelation of relational attributes), considered by the Greeks the only true and complete knowledge. Causality, induction and abstraction underline not solely the works of Aristotle but the entire scientific and cultural enterprise of the originators of Western Civilization. Classification of natural phenomena, because it searched for fundamental patterns (Universals), was a kind of inferior (intuitive) knowledge from which the promethean light of Reason would attain final 'Truth'. Knowledge, consequently, was the result of a round trip proceeding from the individual to the universal (inductively) and then, after discovering the relational causal laws between these universals, by way of the application of them to 'explain' the particulars.

It is difficult not to ascribe, despite of Aristotle vigorous and repeated denials, some character of 'substratum' to his 'universals', in other words, that they represented for him an existing underlining reality pervading the entire group of things of which they constituted the essences. Their platonic flavor was distinct and after the medieval attempt by the scholastics to utilize Greek Reason in a futile effort to 'prove' the existence of God, it gave rise in the early Renaissance to a 'reaction' perhaps first embodied in a most unlikely figure: A disgruntled Franciscan friar once accused of heresy and who ended his days as an exile in Germany, where he flew to escape the persecution of his enemies after turning away from his religious order and the Pope himself.

William of Ockham is better known in popular circles for his 'razor principle': The notion that from several explanations of a given incidence, that one necessitating fewer assumptions is best. His approach to epistemology was eminently empirical, as could be sensed from the above principle, a tendency to simplify matters by dispensing with superfluous causal attributes.

Ockham was the first thinker in the West to unambiguously declare, as far as I know, the superiority, even better, the absolute primacy of empiric knowledge and in fact to indicate the impossibility of any other kind of it. He is important to us, above all, for valiantly repudiating medieval 'dogmatic rationalism' and for resolutely challenging the Aristotelian tyranny by denying the validity of universals. They, he claimed, were the product of 'abstracted cognition' and therefore a concoction of our minds: A view that introduced in philosophy a kind of 'psychologism' which sounds surprisingly modern for its times (he was writing in the XIV Century).

After Ockham death the stage was set for the next frontal attack upon the imposing and venerable bulwark of rationalism. This time was the turn of a refined English gentleman who was interested in influencing King James I about a new concept in learning. He despised the speculative theorizing conceived as 'reasoning' by many of his contemporaries and, needless to say, by most of the medieval scholars, referring to their errors as pure 'idolatry'. According to Francis Bacon the mistakes of his predecessors fell into four distinct classes: The idols of the tribe were fallacies proper to humanity or race in general, such as the inclination to assume in Nature greater order than actually was, prompting people to wild unjustified generalizations or conclusions. The idols of the cave were errors stemming from individual predispositions, what we perhaps can define in modern terminology as 'personal bias'. The third were the idols of the marketplace, the errors resulting from the influence of language upon the mind of man, something which can be called the tyranny of words (as we will see very pertinent in the field of Medicine),thought by him to be the worst source of human mistakes. Finally the forth category of errors was the idols of the theater, the consequences of opinions accepted on the basis of the reputation and authority of their promulgators. Here of course he was primarily referring to the scholastics and to Aristotle who Bacon, I think unjustly, accused of sophistry because he considered syllogistic premises arbitrary speculations and fictitious definitions.

Bacon had been credited by history with the honor of being the first man who clearly enunciated the inductive method in Science, but in the fertilized soil of his Middle Ages there were some predecessors, like his namesake Robert Bacon, William Conches and above all Robert Grosseteste, who is reputed to be one of the first to use truly experimental methods. Bacon thought it possible to arrive by the thorough study of all universal phenomena to the basic Forms, which according to him was the true purpose of Science. The method he proposed was to utilize tables of comparative instances, in other words, the tally of cases when a given 'nature' was present, then of instances when it was absent and finally of occasions when it was present in greater or lesser degree.

The classical example he used was that of 'Heat'. In order to arrive at the Form of heat, he pointed out, we need to find out 'that' which is present or absent when heat is present or absent, or changes when 'it' changes. The mechanism was essentially a process of exclusion of unnecessary characteristics based in an exhaustive study of all positive and negative cases. Following his method he thought that 'ultimate truth', that is, the essential Form of what was being studied, would be infallibly found once all pertinent examples had been studied.

The greatest problem in any attempt to judge the excellence of Bacon's method, in my judgment, is the ambiguity surrounding precisely the meaning of the term which apprehension he considered the true goal and justification of Science. Forms are described as 'the very thing itself', differing from sensual things 'as the real differed from the apparent' or 'the internal from the external'. In these quotations it is difficult to avoid the feeling of similarity between Baconian Forms and the conception of the same term hold, intriguingly enough, by the man whose logical system he most despised: Aristotle.

In other passages of his Novum Organum the semantics of the term appears to change. 'When I speak of Form-he states- I mean nothing more than those laws and determinations of absolute actuality which govern and constitute any simple nature, as heat, light, weight'. Here the meaning seems to be akin, for instance, to Newtonian gravitation, a term for a purported 'force' capable of being given a mathematical expression. Be it as it may, Bacon's inductive method strove to arrive at generalizations (Forms, Laws etc) from the detailed analysis of particulars (the World's phenomena), permitting the enunciation of 'general laws of activity' capable of predicting future incidences of same phenomena, with the explicit utilitarian purpose of controlling and manipulating Nature for the betterment of Man; a very British ideology and approach.

Bacon has been criticized for failing to understand or emphasize the importance of hypothesis in scientific inquire, or the inherent selectivity of appropriate facts and phenomena germane to any enterprise in Science. In fact, if 'natural laws' before being discovered needs an exhaustive enumeration of all instances where they are applicable, they would then lack predictive value. Likewise, if before we arrive at the understanding of a notion like 'heat' (to use Bacon's example) we need to know all cases where the term is applicable, then we would have to investigate all natural phenomena; something evidently beyond the capacity of any human and, as such, the significance of the term would itself be forever hopelessly unknown.

For all his detestation of Aristotle Bacon failed to perceive how much prejudice and mistaken judgment plagued his own system. If Aristotle was unable to see how shaky the epistemological foundations of his universals were, Bacon was equally wrong in assuming that his forms rested in more solid grounds. Again, if Aristotle was mistaken in thinking that many of his definitions applied to 'real things' rather than to fictions of the mind, Bacon deceived himself into considering that an exhaustive survey of all instances of a kind of event would lead, without further elaboration, to 'know' its Nature or even to be possible at all. In actuality he even failed to appreciate how much enmeshed in the fabric of human thought were his own 'idols of the market place', the fact that many of man's 'objects' of scientific inquire are fabricated notion, categories of the imagination embodied in tyrannical words, even including the same term he used as example in the quest for Forms: 'Heat'.

Francis Bacon was fond of quoting his entomological version of intellectual human types. He said there were those who, like the spiders, would construct from their 'insides' their own webs of 'speculations'. Others, who, like the ants, would take things from outside and give nothing in return, and finally some who he considered the true embodiment of the scientific spirit because, like bees, would transform within themselves what they collect into something new like honey.

I think he was wrong in all counts. Neither it is possible to evolve 'something from nothing' (not even the spider can), nor does the ant refrain in producing something from what she takes (we only needs to look inside an anthill to convince ourselves of that). But above all, the quality and kind of honey depends of the type of flowers the bee chooses! The process of scientific inquire implies a SELECTION of facts to suit the aims of the investigator.

The next 'corner stone' in the Western pageantry of epistemological evolution corresponds to a disenchanted young man who fell victim of skepticism after seen his high school hopes crashed in the Jesuit college of La Fleche, where he had enrolled with youthful enthusiasm. Soon after such momentous event the youth developed the conviction that all the tedious efforts spent in studying ancient tongues, philosophy, jurisprudence, theology etc., were stupendous but redundant ornaments of the personality, incapable of advancing the only cause he considered meritorious: The quest for knowledge. Thoroughly disgusted with his academic endeavors, upon graduation, he decided to travel and to come into contact with practical men, that is to say, with humans devoid of the stuffy and pedantic scholasticism of his teachers. The high hopes that these new acquaintances would instill fresh vitality and interest into his life were, however, totally and equally disappointed. As he soon found out, practical men are as much subject to err and disagree as scholars. Their wisdom was certainly relative and not the avenue leading to 'true knowledge'.

Rene Descartes, perhaps because of his profound disenchantment with external circumstances or because he was by nature an introverted soul, took refuge into himself. In early life his considerable mathematical skills had led him to discover Analytical Geometry, and always held a special admiration for what he considered the queen of sciences. The impeccability and infallibility of its method did exert thereafter a profound fascination in the lad, who became allured with the possibility of modeling all sciences in its exact and conclusive example. Often also he wondered from where such quasi-divine knowledge came and, invariable, arrived to the same conclusion as his chain of predecessors, including Plato more than 2000 years hence, did before him: Mathematics could not be learned by looking into Nature but only by searching into oneself. Its laws were somehow engrained into the human mind; there was no need for 'external' experiences. Chocked and enticed by his discovery Descartes wrote: "I resolved at length to make myself an object of study and to employ all the powers of my mind in chasing the paths I ought to follow".

The path he set for himself was that of searching for something that had already been a source of preoccupation to numerous philosophers before: What is the True and how do we arrive at that which should be the 'object' of our inquire; above all how do we know that we know something at all. To achieve his goal there was need to separate the true from the false, and what was novel in the Cartesian method was his approach, the way he fulfilled this purpose.

Descartes commenced by methodically questioning how he came to the idea of a physical world around him, and concluded that there was really no reliable way one could completely rule out the possibility that sensations like touch, sounds, smell, etc., were nothing but illusions of the mind. Existence, then, could not incontestably be proved by resorting to items of sense perception, in view of the fact that all this information could be unfounded. In so proceeding systematically he finally arrived at one thing he could undeniably and positively assert. If I think, he contended, 'something' has to do this thinking and 'that' underlining substratum of my mental activity had to be me, BY DEFINITION is me: 'Cogito ergo sum"; which could be translated as "I think, therefore I am".

From the basic premise of his own existence, from this rather solipsistic position, Descartes recovered the entire physical world following a devious route plagued in many respects with logical figures strongly reminiscent of St Anselm ontological argument (the most notorious medieval attempt to 'prove' the existence of Almighty God).

How could it be, Descartes proceeded, that an imperfect being like me could harbor the 'idea' of something so sublime? From where such a concept came? Certainly from no external perception inasmuch as they were, in the grand platonic tradition, not to be trusted. Such a concept, he told himself, like the case of mathematical knowledge, can only come from a seed planted in the soul. Now, these conclusions, he claimed, were very 'clearly' seen by his mind, just as much as mathematical proofs, and therefore he conceived this 'clearness' as the precondition for his acceptance as 'truth' the postulates and presumptive facts that his mind had to address in its quest for real knowledge.

But his repertoire of 'proofs' for the existence of the Supreme Being was not yet exhausted; another modality of a sort also occurred to him. Imperfect bodies, he pointed out, by their imperfections manifest the need for the existence of a 'Supreme Builder'. Also, the idea of a Perfect Being implied the reality of this being, because 'existence being one of his attributes the lack of it would indicate imperfection'. Utilizing a similar logic he 'proved' the validity of the physical world.

Characteristic of 'rationalistic' minds since Plato and the Eleatics, as we had seen, was the notion that sensory perception could not be the source of 'true knowledge', and Descartes was no exception in this regard. The senses, according to him, only provided a hopelessly confused picture of the World from where we can learn nothing. He thought that only terms that we can CLEARLY CONCEIVE could be the source of knowledge. Now, these terms, again, were not 'perceptions' but rather those properties in what we observe which are PERMANENT, in other worlds, that will not change with time. A body shape, color or direction of motion, for instance, was not INSEPARABLE, intrinsic and specific attributes of it, only 'extension' and 'mobility' were essential and clearly conceived. Because God is omnipotent and perfectly veracious, error and deception could not be part of his Nature, so then, he concluded triumphantly, the Supreme Being would not allow us to suffer from mistaken 'clear' conceptions, or to deceive us into such monstrosity as the belief in a non-existent physical world. In fact, if God did not place those distinct notions about an external reality in our minds, how else could they have found a way into the recesses of our souls? The 'existence' of the World was then 'proved'.

It was the youthful ambition of Descartes to postulate general laws of reasoning applicable to all sciences once the basic and fundamental terms of these sciences, their 'simple natures', were 'clearly' identified. To understand what these basic laws of reasoning were he analyzed the thinking process that led the intellect in the operations of the prototype of exact sciences: Mathematics. The first and more important one, he thought, was 'intuits', a direct non-inferential act of 'single', momentary and infallible apprehension of reality. By this means we obtain information as to the basic terms mathematics deals with, things like the sphere, ellipse, and triangle; all notions we 'clearly' understand and subsequently define.

The next operation the mind avail itself of is 'deduction', indicating as such the identification of the relations distinctly demonstrable between the different 'intuited" terms. In order to arrive at the discovery of these relations there was need to proceed analytically and synthetically, from complex to simple terms and then in the opposite direction (what we can in modern mathematical terminology call the demonstration of the relational terms of a theorem). Lastly came the 'enumeration', a mental process of recounting the steps of the 'deduction' to improve the relations, and if possible to eliminate unnecessary steps.

Descartes thought that a similar mental gymnastic was applicable to all the different sciences. Once their 'simple natures' were 'intuited' by Reason the terms would then be related, in the same fashion that words are arranged from letters, to discover the texture of 'complex natures' and in fact to deduct and comprehend the entire world. Mathematics once applied to these 'natures' would, he thought, logically produce the unraveling of all physical animated and in-animated things, in the same way that letters and laws of syntaxes allows the deciphering of written language. The world was reduced to parametric terms amenable to be quantified by universal relational laws, formulated numerically and capable of being applied to the entire realm of universal phenomena. These conceptions, of course, implied the belief in a pre-determined Cosmo accessible in its entirety to mathematical description and understanding; biological beings were like machines.

Descartes rationalism by its emphatic affirmation that the deductive method was the only capable of ascertaining the true facts and laws of Nature intuited and identified by the 'light' of our minds, was in effect a tacit endorsement of an epistemological line typical of the Western mind, a line already envisage in the pre-Socratics. Notwithstanding the novelty of his 'doubting method' in providing an answer to the existence of the individual thinking mind, the run-about course he followed in 'demonstrating' the reality of a physical world, clothed in an scholastic jargon as it was, could have not please or satisfy the new spirit of enquire. His ontological premises were suspected and a reaction to his ideas did soon take place in the opposite side of the British Channel.

John Locke, credited by history with being the first major exponent of the British empiricist view point, was a refined bourgeoisie gentleman who studied at Oxford and eventually, significantly enough, became a physician. Although he practiced little of his profession, was nevertheless greatly influenced by the observational approach of Medicine and the biological sciences. After the 1688 revolution Locke returned to England from Holland, where he temporarily had taken refuge, and was one of the great advocates of those traditional libertarian values which found their way not only into the parliamentarian system of his nation, but also into the American Bill of Rights and the canons of the French Revolution.

Commencing by denying the existence of 'innate ideas' championed, not exclusively, by men of other epochs as Plato, but also by many of his contemporaries like Descartes and specially Hebert of Cherbury, Locke went on to articulate one of those concepts that because of their graphic expressive power become immortalized for future generations. The mind, he manifested, is a white sheet of paper, a 'tabula rasa' (a statement strongly reminiscent of contemporary Rousseauan ideas, like the opinion that man at birth was a 'noble savage' devoid of any innate malevolence) where we imprint our experiences, the sole source of knowledge.

These bourgeoisie XVIII Century notions perhaps articulated a deeply felt social need to give away with the past and start fresh anew 'from scratch', but we could not be detained in these unnecessary speculations. Locke claimed in his 'Essay concerning human understanding' that there were three ways of how man could acquire knowledge: 1)-By intuition of the mode of achieving knowledge of self existence, something in general similar to the Cartesian position. 2)- By demonstration, (the method of knowing God's existence), again an approach with similarities to the scholastic and Cartesian method which he so much criticized, and 3)- By means of sensations (the only true empiricist kind) of a putative external world. Yet, this knowledge only referred to 'ideas' or even to the perceptions of agreement or disagreement between these 'ideas'. Pervading the system of Locke there is a basic ambivalence as to whether knowledge refers to something external or not. We are told, on the one hand, that knowledge is and could be only knowledge of 'ideas' by whatever means we obtain them (intuitive, demonstrative or sensorial), and on the other that ideas are a 'real' character of things. Tied in with this concept is the further subdivision of ideas as those referring to 'primary quality' and those of 'secondary quality'. Locke called primary qualities those which were inseparable to the object of knowledge, like solidity, extension, shape, mobility and number. Secondary were things like colors, tastes, etc., actually depending on the perceiver rather than on the 'objects themselves'; a view immediately bringing to mind the

Cartesian differentiation between 'simple' and 'complex' natures . 'Real' were the primary qualities only; the kind uniquely deserving to be single out and behold for study by the human intellect.

This reliance of true knowledge in man's power of relation introduced a profound contradiction in Locke's theory of knowledge because, if as he claims, there are no innate ideas, how and resorting to what mysterious standard of reference could the mind conclusively ascertain what is true? As his critics were fast in replying, his 'primary' qualities could be as much a figment of his imagination as the 'secondary' kind.

It is difficult not to conclude that as a philosopher Locke was not too original despite of his immense influence in Anglo-American philosophy. The entire corpus of his epistemology was debased by inconsistencies and imbued by surreptitious and ill disguise rationalism. Intuition and demonstration for him were the only two sources of certain knowledge, and his distinction between 'primary' and 'secondary' qualities represented a grossly arbitrary notion for any kind of empiricism, a search after immutable universals in the comfortable Platonic tradition. His work, it seems to me, is instilled with a distinct Cartesian flavor, with a change of emphasis to stress the empiric viewpoint.

The weaknesses in Locke's system were rapidly seized and manipulated by his detractors who uncompromisingly led empiricism to its self consistent but baffling and not too profitable end; in fact an epistemological 'blind alley'. Bishop George Berkeley set out in a very ambitious project, a project more ambitious than any ecclesiastic had ever attempted before, so far reaching in consequences as to appear to possess a taste of insanity and yet having an undeniable importance for the future of Science: Namely THE NEGATION of matter. 'Reality' was not to depend on it, but rather in perceptions which became the supreme arbiter of 'existence'. An 'object', he categorically stated, had no more veracity than the perception we have of it, in actuality IT CONSTITUTED THE PERCEPTION; they were both the same thing.

Now, such a thesis demands that the existence of 'outside' reality be an invalid preconception of the mind; even more, a true absurdity or contradiction in view of the fact that all we know are ideas of our perceptions (as Locke previously postulated) and, therefore, there is nothing external to them. This assertion, of course, conveys the serious consequence that material objects would not have an existence INDEPENDENTLY of the perceiving mind; a notion that became the source of scorn and ridicule by his contemporaries. But our good bishop would remain undisturbed and challenge the offender to mention any quality in the presumptive 'object' that would not refer ultimately to the perceiver mind. Using 'Ockham razor' this devoted man expertly, and efficiently, disposed of all unnecessary attributes and superfluous concepts.

One of his favorite targets became the Cartesian, and also Locke's, classification of qualities (we should recall that in the opinion of these authors primary or simple were those qualities' inseparable' from the objects of Nature, like extension and mobility for Descartes, shape and solidity for Locke. Secondary or complex were those like 'color', 'odor' etc. that were dispensable and therefore did not represent intrinsic properties of bodies) which, however, for Locke seemed to referred to ambiguous attributes of 'ideas' while for Descartes, after his acceptance of the an 'external reality' referred to 'objects' of a material world.

Berkeley adamantly denied the validity of these inferences. The problem, he claimed, is with the notion that qualities could be abstracted from a group of other qualities and what is common to all then 'behold' in our minds as a separate entity in its own right. Could properties such as extension, size and shape be separated from the specific objects of scrutiny and, for example, conceive with them a triangle? How anybody could have a distinct idea of such a thing? Was this triangle simultaneously equilateral, isosceles and scalene? Yet, Berkeley did not deny the propriety of the notions of universals. These ideas, he explained, were 'generalities', not abstractions. Primary qualities (abstractions) for him, therefore, were one thing and universals, the symbols used in necessary calculations, like in mathematics, were another. The former he called 'conceptions' and the latter practical 'functions', no more than conventions needed for demonstration. Primary qualities, consequently, represented empty terms and were as arbitrary as those so-called secondary qualities; it was illusory to think that they afforded a 'proof' of the existence of 'material substances'.

I must embarrassingly confess my incapability to clearly comprehend what the true difference is in Berkeley's notions of 'abstractions' and 'generalities', but evidently he felt the second pertained to 'something real' while the first represented complete arbitrary notions. Be it as it may, he was making a serious and vigorous effort to deny any externality to the qualities of ideas, rejecting, in other words, the notion that they provided any indication as to the existence of a material Universe.

A curious result of Berkeley opinions was of immense epistemological importance, not only to philosophy but even for science in general. If ideas were neutral they did not possessed any 'activity', and therefore were totally devoid of any capacity to influence other ideas. Causality then was an INVALID ASSUMPTION, a worthless hypothesis lacking any meaning. We can only, he insisted, be aware of the succession of phenomena or events, but nothing else. This succession essentially was what we construe as causality, but there was nothing in the 'ideas' to suggest the possibility of any influence of one upon another, nor was it contradictory to dispense altogether with this concept.

Quite characteristic of Western Philosophy up to the XVIII Century was the obligation felt by most thinkers to advance 'proofs' for the reality of God, and Berkeley was no exception. Forgetting his own method he argued that we could REASON the existence of other spirits by the 'effect' they produce in Nature, and by analogy established that we could 'conclude' the existence of God by its effect: The Universe (conceived of course not as matter but as a set of ideas placed in our minds by the Supreme Spirit). But how was it possible that if, as he tired of repeating, we can only know our own ideas, could we then surmise the existence of something EXTERNAL to us, as God had to be? If causality was a myth or a plain mirage, how could an assumed 'cosmic' Being INFLUENCE us in any way? This inconsistency among other discrepancies which are beyond the scope of this assay to detail, proved fatal to Berkeley metaphysics. Our devoted bishop seemed to have fallen in a trap of his own creation, but an entirely different fate awaited his epistemology which was subsequently elaborated on its own merits. His dispensation with categories like 'matter' and 'causality' as unneeded redundancies was to have a lasting effect, as the history of modern physics sufficiently displays. (See Chapter II)

It took the efforts of another great man to divest British Empiricism of the metaphysical inconsistencies of his predecessors and to elaborate its central themes into a cogent, articulate and mature corpus with a surprisingly modern outlook which has been enormously influential in shaping the future course, not only of Anglo-American philosophy but of continental thought as well. In the title page of his ambitious 'A Treatise of Human Nature' David Hume indicated that his aims were 'an attempt to introduce the experimental method of Reasoning into Moral Subjects'. By detailed observation of human nature he considered entirely possible to discover 'general laws' as to the manner that man thinks and behave, as well as the presumptive limits of human knowledge in scientific areas: Such as mathematics, social sciences etc.

The attempt to find these 'limits', of course, was not a novel 'desire' in the history of mankind. Skeptics had existed since remote antiquity, but ever since the decline of the Roman Empire the stronghold of 'anti-rationalism' (and ironically enough also of rationalism) had been the Christian Churches in any of its different denominations. Hume approach, however, was novel and different, among other things because it was not based in any theological presupposition and was, therefore, devoid of the scholastic jargon which plagued the works of his immediate predecessors.

He began by agreeing with them in what referred to the non-existence of 'innate ideas' and, consequently, that sense perception was the only source of knowledge. He also agreed with Bishop Berkeley as to the fact that universals were inconceivable, and that ideas were only about individual things to which generic names were applied.

In the Empiricist tradition Hume considered that all our information of reality consisted basically of impressions and ideas. The difference between these two categories, he explained, is that the former were more 'vivid' than the latter and ordinarily preceded them in our minds. Furthermore, he elaborated, both, impressions and ideas could be simple or complex, the second formed by the first which were also indivisible.

The simple ideas, except for their 'vivacity' exactly resembled the impressions, but the complex type did not need to do so. We could imagine or have an 'idea', for example, of golden apples without ever having seen one if we already had the simple ideas of 'golden' and 'apple' based in truly 'real impressions'.

When it came to the processing of our perceptions Hume differentiated between two 'mental' functions: Memory and imagination. Memory was to preserve ideas in the order in which they were received, while the imagination was free to organize these ideas in any arrangement the mind desired. But the imagination did not acted arbitrarily; it was subjected to some limitations. Certain ideas were inextricably associated in such a way that the recalling of one will necessary elicit the memory of the other. These associations, Hume thought, represented a kind of attraction among groups of ideas. Their importance became clear later on in his work when addressing the subject of causality; by far the best contribution of his theory of knowledge to later generations.

Before embarking in a full development of his views, however, Hume considered important to attack the foundations of what had been, up to then, considered demonstrative 'a priori' knowledge; namely Mathematics. Arguing not too convincingly, perhaps because of his lack of expertise in this field, he asserted that arithmetic and algebra deal with quantities, and consisted of demonstrable relations between their terms.

Now, these terms were not 'fictions' of the imagination, something innate in the mind, but resulting from WHAT WE SEE, in other words, ultimately were based in perceptions. Here he made use of a notion first advanced by Locke, and explained that the discovery of the quantitative relations among these terms, or ideas, by means of intuition was what represented 'real' knowledge and what in essence consist 'a demonstration' which, consequently, ultimately could not dispense, and actually depends on perceptions, that is to say, possessed an empiric root. The case of geometry and spatial science, he thought, was even simpler to dispose of. Undoubtedly this branch of mathematics did have an empiric origin in view of the fact that it dealt with observable points, although there was a limitation in our capacity to clearly identify and count these points. Therefore, he claimed, geometrical postulates always had some degree of inherent incertitude.

I believe that Hume's views in relation to the empiric nature of mathematics deserve more credit than had been granted. We will expand in this theme later on but we should presently continue with the exposition of the central and more influential, maybe more felicitous, aspects of his epistemology. If bishop Berkeley refuted the existence of a material 'substratum' of phenomena, Hume denied the possibility of a spiritual substratum of the Self. He pointed out that whenever a person thinks of himself it was impossible to disentangle such a notion from that of the impression or ideas crossing the mind at such an instant. We are in essence inseparable from our thoughts, impressions and ideas. In fact the Self was nothing more than 'a bundle of perceptions', assorted in certain orderly sequence and in such a manner that the consciousness of one would invariably elicit the other with which it was associated.

Hume, as Berkeley before, searched meticulously into the nature of ideas to see whether he could discover in them something supportive of the universal concept of causality, that is, of an 'influence' of a given event upon another but, as his predecessor before, he was unable to detect any 'reasonable' necessity or obligatory inference for its validity. The belief in causality, he concluded, being neither intuitively evident nor demonstrable in any sense is then completely irrational, something inconsistent with the ascertainable 'facts'. Just as the concept of an underlining Self was not present in any idea we could conceive, causality was not obvious in the analysis of phenomena; there was nothing intrinsic in them capable of rendering absurd the hypothesis that they were not causally related. In such a case, he logically concluded, there was no way to deny the possibility that causality was a fiction of the imagination.

But if causality was not demonstrable or a discoverable property of phenomena, how comes that we conduct our lives AS IF it were one of the most essential properties of perceptions? Psychological insight, he claimed, determines that if, in our experience, two perceptual events are temporally related, our minds automatically infer that the first is the 'cause' of the second. Now, such an act of inference was actually nothing less than an instinctive subconscious trust in the regularity of Nature, the belief that the future will resemble the past and the association of events about which we have had no previous experience will inexorably imitate those of which we have; a peculiar trait of the mind that Hume was completely at a lost to explain.

Although there was nothing in our impressions or ideas to justify our beliefs in causality and induction, we act, he claimed, in a manner implying an automatic inference of their reality. His only comments were that such an inference was a sort of 'habit' with no fundament in Nature. Cause he then define as "An object precedent and contiguous to another and so united with it in the imagination, that the idea of the one determines the mind to form the idea of the other, and the impression of the one to form a more lively idea of the other". I think that anybody would agree this is a psychological rendering and a definition completely devoid of any precondition or non-empiric category.

Hume had been frequently criticized and accused of inconsistency because of these views in causality. When he states that one idea 'determines' in the mind the form of the idea of the other he is saying nothing less than one idea 'causes' the mind to form the idea of another. In fact, he appears to be resorting in the realm of 'the mind' to the same explanation he questions in an assumed 'physical world' to explain its own invalidity. We either would have to postulate two different sets of rules for 'mental' and 'material' phenomena or else admit the contradiction inherent in such an explanation. But is this criticism valid?

I believe that Hume's detractors had misunderstood his position in this regard. He had not claimed that causality did not exist, but rather that it IS the invariable precedence to some phenomena upon others, and that is ALL. Evidently an ordering of such perceptions, he thought, corresponded to a similar group of ideas in our mind. If there was not any correspondence of terms between a putative external reality and the mind, there would be no possible way we could use our intellectual faculties to help us in the act of surviving and reproducing the species. That he was convinced about the usefulness of causality so redefine (as invariable precedence) is clearly portrait in his opinion, later also shared by many other empiricist, that the role of science was to organize experience into laws of predictive value. Evidently if we would have chosen not to believe in the 'regularity of Nature' it would have been impossible to harbor 'reasonable expectations' as to future events. These predictions, Hume affirmed, rather than the search for 'causes' and 'explanations' were the true tests of Science.

Admittedly Hume was a skeptic who definitely thought that all conclusions about the World were only tentative and based in probability. An element of incertitude was inherent in all nature's phenomena. Causality (as influences) and induction were un-demonstrable categories of our understanding. The illusion that Man could advance uncontestable 'proofs' for the existence of an external World and of God had completely dissipated with the empiricists. With them philosophy had reached a point diametrically opposed to the Scholastics. An anti-rationalistic seed had been planted which was destined to grow into a robust tree which exuberance Hume would have never dreamed of.

Radical Empiricism, as much as 'pure' Reason, appeared to be epistemological dead ends. If philosophy was to preserve its relevance for the Natural Sciences there was need for a fresh and novel approach to the theory of knowledge. The stage was set at the end of the XVIII Century for such a reformer. It came in the unlikely form of a methodical man so regular in his habits that the citizens of Konigsberg, where he lived and taught, used to set their clocks in when they saw him appear for a daily evening walk assiduously assisted by his servant of many years, who followed close on his steps. Reputedly awoken from his 'dogmatic slumber' by Hume's Treatise, Emmanuel Kant intended to realize, according to his own ambitious worlds, 'a Copernican revolution in philosophy' to vindicate and revived metaphysics, and in the process reconcile both, the empiricist and rationalistic view points in a coherent and credible system. He confronted his monumental task with Teutonic fervor.

Kant commenced by postulating that grammatical statements could be grouped into three different types. Firstly, there were those which he called 'analytic', when the predicate was included in the subject and consequently are frivolous and provide no knowledge of any kind. To this general group belonged phrases like 'Quadruped animals have four legs' or 'Fishes live in water'. Secondly were the phrases when the predicate was not incorporated in the subject and therefore truly provided knowledge or information of some kind, which he called synthetic. These belonged to the class of empiric statements, those from which we can learn something, as for instance 'Lincoln was a president of U.S '. There is absolutely nothing intrinsic in 'the president of the U.S.' that refers to the name 'Lincoln'.

But Kant did not stopped with the classification of these two types of possible grammatical statements. He proceeded with the claim that there was another kind of phrases ALSO capable of providing knowledge, but that nevertheless were not empiric: This he called 'a priori synthetic', implying that the predicate here also was not included in the subject, therefore fulfilling his definition of knowledge, but accessible only by means of deductive reasoning. As example of this possibility Kant selected, not surprisingly, mathematical theorems. In effect, therefore, Kant attempt was a valiant effort to reconcile Reason with Empiricism, and concluded that both were capable of providing 'true knowledge'. His position, however, failed to resolve the epistemological quandary already encountered by his predecessors, and although he believed in the existence of an external world (the Itself), he admitted the impossibility of knowing directly about it. Knowledge could only be of 'ideas', whether mathematical or not. Nobody was able to pretend nothing beyond this point.

After Kant philosophy in continental Europe became the domain of 'professionals', university professors of obscure prose (at times undecipherable except to themselves and a close circle of associates) who inaugurated a rigid, systematical attack against Reason, effecting an idealistic reaction and system building culminating with the Hegelian and Marxist dialects, which became preponderant trends of thought up to the early part of the XX Century, only to be followed by the limited focus and highly academic approach of the Logic-Positivists and Linguistic Analysts; also professionals who devoted their efforts to small audiences of adept students.

In spite of his failure to reconcile Reason with true knowledge of a putative 'external world' Kant was the first to point out the enormously important fact that the mind cognizes in terms of specific 'categories of understanding', in other words, that sense perceptions are organized in certain way by the human mind before they acquire meaning for us. Although his selection of categories appears today rather arbitrary, I believe that modern scientific findings seem to support these contentions. What all this amounts to is that THE FORM OF REALITY CONFORMS IN SOME MANNER TO THE INTERNAL ORGANIZATION OF THE NERVOUS SYSTEM, that is to say, although according to him we are denied 'direct access' to the external world we receive impressions from it which, when elaborated by the brain, are converted into recognizable perceptual data by the intellect. (See Chapter III)

A particular vexing, and to many unappealing, aspect of his system was Kant's affirmation that space and time were 'forms of intuition'. Such statement is taken by some to mean the falsity and subjectivity of the 'framing' of phenomena in Nature by our minds and, in fact, the denial of dynamic notions such as 'motion'; something abhorrent to scientists even prepared, in principle, to go along with his idea about categories of the understanding.

It will not be farfetched, I think, to declare that Kant's was the last serious attempt to give philosophy a meaningful content for science. After his failure to provide for a 'bridge' between 'Intellect' and 'Nature' Philosophy lost all relevance to the scientific effort, dissipating its vigor in sterile semantic enquires far removed from practical application to vital questions in Epistemology. By being unable to conclusively 'prove' the existence of a knowable 'external world' philosophy did become a veritable dump of empty argumentations detached from the needs of everyday life.

After concluding this brief recount of the highlights in the history of epistemology in the Western World, I think it is proper to ask ourselves what points, if any, are shared in common by the different views expressed by the diverse thinkers whose philosophical systems we had touch on. When the two main currents of Western Thought in this subject, the rationalist and empiricist traditions, are careful scrutinized it is possible to discover a great number of similarities between both schools; something, ironically enough, surprising when it is recalled that the main actors in the historic drama considered their systems of thought as irreconcilable positions.

Let us take first the case of Rationalism. Its central theme is that 'real knowledge' could only be obtained by the use of the intellect, that is to say, by the application of a system of innate rules to general terms or abstractions of the mind; a process of analysis which would allow a demonstrative proof of 'final causes' giving rise to general laws applicable then to specific particular cases of the real world for the purpose of predicting future happenings of the same kind. This in essence, with some modifications from author to author, was the general claim of the advocates of this system.

How much truth there is in such belief? Let us consider momentarily the case of the science which constitutes the epitome of rationalism: Mathematics. Can we truly accept, as Hume pointedly rejected, that without having any previous information about a 'material world' (or our ideas of it) we could conceive the science of mathematics as we know it today? I think it is fallacious to endorse such assumptions. If when we place together two apples we would end up with one, three or none, a very different type of mathematical rules would have evolved. In the same way, without sense perception the Platonic notion of geometrical 'forms' separate from our experiences appears hardly conceivable. Lines, triangles, squares and circles are all in actuality notions abstracted by the mind from the observation of a putative 'physical world', and consequently possess an empiric basis. If we now proceed into an study of what truly represent a mathematical proof or demonstration, we necessarily will have to conclude that it consist solely in a ' revelation' or 'discovery' of hidden, or not immediately obvious, relations between the various terms in question, which we then proceed to associate by means of equations (an assortment of symbols and operational rules which are not 'innate', as we want to believe, but based in the way that events associate in Nature). Looked in this way geometrical 'proves' are tautologies based primarily in concepts of the human mind, generalities based in fabricated notions of the intellect which we assume to have universal validity. These concepts are based on abstractions like the platonic ideas (innate prototypes of the intellect) or in formulations resting in static or dynamic processes we observe in Nature.

But something else results as a consequence of the application of deductive logic, something of upmost importance to our purpose: The conclusions to which it arrives, we are told, have the force of 'absolute conviction'; they lead us to think that proofs and demonstrations confer absolute and uncontestable validity to their postulates, that is to say, afford for their EXPLANATIONS. This, I think, is a very important point to which we will return to shortly.

Let us now consider the case of Empiricism. If we exclude the case of those thinkers who denied sense perceptions relates to any outside reality, and instead accept the possibility that they do, then the premises upon which conclusions are based disclose a surprising similarity to the method of Rationalism. Like its opposite, it has first to abstract from the maze of perceptions the 'elemental' components, followed by an attempt to study their relations by observation or experimentation before framing the results in general laws (induction), often implying the formulation of a working hypothesis before finally applying the result to specific instances of the phenomena under investigation, for the ultimate purpose, here like in the case of Rationalism, of PREDICTING future configurations or clustering of similar events.

In summary therefore, in both, the cases of Empiricism and Rationalism, there is first a search for common terms of the phenomena under study, followed by an attempt to relate them in equations, laws, etc. (which the rationalists believe are innate while the empiricists consider they are a product of experience), in order then to utilize the discovered relations in the prediction of future instances of said phenomena.

Yet, we think of both systems (Rationalism and Empiricism) as completely different in their methods. We consider the former as 'deductive', that is to say, as proceeding from general rules or truths, 'discovered' solely by the mind, to the particular and individual, while in the case of Empiricism we believe to move in the opposite direction, because the formulation of the general laws follows the observation or experimental manipulation of individual cases.

I believe that pure rationalism, as originally postulated by the Greek mind, is a gross misrepresentation of facts that for obscure reasons we had been unable to shake off. ANY GROUP OF ABSTRACTIONS INTERRELATED BY A 'DEMONSTRATION' OR 'DEDUCTIVE ACT' (WHETHER WE CALL THEM ELEMENTAL FORMS, PRIMARY QUALITY OR SIMPLE NATURES) IS, TO START WITH, A GENERALIZATION FROM PARTICULARS, and not resulting from 'innate ideas' or 'a priori' categories including, as we had seen, the analytic queen of sciences: Mathematics. We should ask ourselves what is the validity of the numerical rules serving as the basis for 'demonstrations' in this most 'exact' of sciences [1].

To dramatize the postulated difference of what is considered deductive (Rationalistic) and inductive (Empiricist) knowledge let us resort to an elemental geometrical theorem. The empiricist method would postulate that we should MEASURE the angles in a number of triangles, and then, if in every case they add up to 180 degrees it should be reasonable to conclude, inferentially, that in ALL cases it will be so. The empiricist will be happy and content with these findings which he will then proceed to formulate as a general principle. Not so the rationalist. As we have seen, he instead would insist that the empiric method still lack 'absolute certainty', which could only come about by way of a 'demonstration'. At first glance this claim appears valid, but if analyzed in more detail, such assumption seems to be completely unfounded.

The original 'demonstration', referred to the Pythagoreans by Eudemus, needs the previous acceptance of naive notions borrowed from our immediate experience. (See 'A history of Greek mathematics' by Sir Thomas Heath. Dover Publications Inc. 1981, P. 143). Ultimately, when the analysis is carried to the very end we, in all cases, encounter that the entire edifice of Classical Geometry (and also of any branch of mathematics deductive logic) is supported by some UNDEMONSTRABLE basic assumption (called the 'axioms' in Geometry) which we take at face value, and justify this acceptance with the claim that they are 'obvious realities' striking the mind as absolute and unequivocal certainties. Precisely here resides the fallacies and weakness of deductive logic.

Let us consider the case of the 'axiom' serving as the basis for the 'demonstration' of the above mentioned theorem: The Euclidian parallel postulate. It is implied in it that we already 'know' what is meant by 'distance', 'point' and 'straight line'. They all relate to conceptions ultimately derived from our sense perceptions and taken to be true representations of physical realities. But how much can we rely in those perceptions of a putative inferred 'existing' world? Straight line is a notion of plane geometry, a geometry which assumed that space is flat. As modern physics has attested, space actually is curved and the curvature varies from place to place according to its relation to matter in neighboring space. What we call 'straight line', therefore, is nothing but a convention of the mind, a fiction based in our perceptual limitations and erroneously conceived as unassailably truth. In our world the real shortest distance between two points IS A GEODESIC, which curvature do vary from place to place. Innate ideas (Kant thought that Euclidean geometry was an 'a priori' concept), we inescapably have to conclude, are invalid inferences of an assumed real world, fantasies of the imagination incapable of supporting any kind of absolute knowledge; at best definitions providing no more certainty in their conclusions than our incomplete conception of reality. We will never comprehend what a line, point or distance is until we 'experience' them.

Returning to the above example of the simple geometrical postulate, we delude and deceive ourselves when we think that our 'demonstrations', pertaining the three angles of a triangle adding to 180 degrees, represents a more SOLID KNOWLEDGE than simply inferring so from the empiric procedure of measuring directly the angles, summing them and, if in many instances they add up to 180 degrees, inductively postulating the universal validity of our conclusions (which, by the way, also will be wrong for the same reason than in the case of the Rationalist). In fact as it was shown by the works of Nikolai Lobachevski and Janus Bolyai in the XIX Century (after their rejecting the forth Euclidian postulate which states that from a 'point ' outside a 'straight' line only one parallel to it could be drawn), depending on the 'shape' of space the angles of a triangle would add to more, equal or less than 180 degrees. The comfortable geometry we inherited from the Greeks then did not have universal applicability, conforming only to our immediate cosmic neighborhood, therefore representing at best an approximation to 'reality'. The discovery of 'curved' space-time was a refutation of the universality of classical rationalism. (See the Conclusion)

A 'demonstration', therefore, is nothing more than A REVELATION OF HIDDEN RELATIONS BETWEEN TERMS (SYMBOLS) ABSTRACTED FROM SENSE PERCEPTION AND LIMITED ONLY TO OUR COSMIC PLACE IN THE ORCHESTRATION OF UNIVERSAL EVENTS. KNOWLEDGE, IN THE LAST ANALYSIS AT LEAST, DO HAVE IN ALL INSTANCES AN EMPIRIC FOUNDATION, AND THE EXISTENCE OF INNATE IDEAS IS NOTHING BUT A DECEPTIVE ILLUSION OF THE MIND, an illusion which gives rise to the feeling of 'absolute certainty'. Mathematics, after all, is only A SELF CONSISTENT SYMBOLIC LANGUAGE.

But now we have to ask ourselves what is common to both the empiric and rationalistic traditions in Western thought other than this recognized or unrecognized reliance in sense perception.

Undoubtedly, the most notorious characteristic of Western enquire into Nature is the feverish search for fundamentals, a 'dismantling' of complex events into their elemental constituents, a separating and singling out of phenomena for further study and measurement. To 'know' is an 'act' needing of a basic 'dichotomy' between something called the 'knower', who perceives, and the object of knowledge, the perceived target of our enquires.

Pertinent to this matter are the studies conducted by the Swiss psychologist Jean Piaget in relation with the intellectual development of the human child (See 'The Origen of the Intellect' by J. L. Phillips Jr., W.H. Freeman Co. Second Edition). Once it is granted that many of his stages and criteria, perhaps unavoidably, are afflicted with a great dose of arbitrariness, the work is revealing in the sense that it points to an essential dynamic process of continuous inter-action of the mind with the environment as the determinants in the growth and evolution of the cognitive faculties. The child, who originally is only capable of reflective responses to environmental stimulus, progressively develops the capacity to more complex non-automatic behavior coupled with the gradual organization and systematization of the 'sensorial input' into identifiable constellations of events (the objects), and later on of abstracting concepts or symbols which manipulation allows the formulations of speculative 'reasoning' and the achievements of logic-mathematical thought.

Piaget's theories based in interpretational aspects of his research activities are important, I believe, because they point out to a mutual feed-back between the sensorial stimuli and the mind, where the percepts are modified by the cognitive structures of the intellect which in their turn are changed by them, an interface of the processes of assimilation and accommodation striving to achieve an state of 'equilibrium', a sort of dialectic. New environmental experiences are incorporated into the pre-established cognitive frames but not without eliciting changes in them. There is a progressive, ever more complex, integration of patterns of activity and cognition with the ultimate acquisition of the abstract symbolic expressions of our cultural heritage (things like weight, density, number etc.), a necessary prolegomena to scientific logic-mathematical thought. Very little is credited by Piaget to innate ideas as the basis of our knowledge other than the elemental survival reflexes. The process of learning, according with his investigations, is a slow painful one of continuous testing, by trial and error, of ever more elaborated mechanisms of perception and action.

It follows that for him knowledge, even abstract analytic-mathematical constructions which the Rationalists viewed as the epitome of the a priori 'demonstrative' type of 'truth', is solely possible after a prolonged period of mental training based in THE EXPERIENCE provided by our senses. The growth and maturation of our intellectual faculties appears, therefore, according to Piaget's observations and experiments, to be inextricable associated to the continual rapport of the mind with the external world and are what provide the stimulus, in a sense the necessary guidance, for its eventual full development.

The pattern of this development, the potential avenues it can take, are of course limited by the internal framework of the nervous system, that is, the wiring of our relational apparatus (borrowing a cybernetic term we might say by the 'hard ware' of our brains which constitute a limitation impossible to overcome). But knowledge of the world other than very elemental reflex acts, it is apparent, can only be acquired after prolonged interaction with our environment, in a gradual fashion, a sifting process mediated and conditioned thru channels plowed by the architectural blue-prints of our relational apparatus, which modulates and imposes insurmountable constrains to cognitive development.(See also Chapter III)

Yet, learning from Nature is not limited or circumscribed to the human species. Animals,as we will see, also can be thought of as undergoing a similar, although perhaps more primitive, type of cognitive development with the creation of concepts corresponding to constellations of 'sensations' capable of identifying conglomerate of events needed for survival. If an animal is unable to adequately recognized the 'objects' representing his food or enemy there is no possibility he could survive long (See also Chapter IV). Animal species in order to survive in Nature necessarily need to be able, as much as it is possible, to separate or individualized 'phenomena', or group of them if self-preservation is to be achieved. They have to 'know' what to eat as well as to identify other harmful or beneficent creatures. They also should be able to 'recognize' another member of their own species, whether for protective or mating purposes and to run away from danger, as the case might be.

By extension it might be assumed that man's relational apparatus, the human brain, in order to 'know' its environment necessitates the 'analytical' power of the nervous system, of the capacity to categorize and individualize MEANINGFUL constellations of perceptions. Now, it does not follow that WHAT IS MEANINGFUL TO US AS BIOLOGICAL BEINGS OBLIGATORILY HAS PARAMOUNT VALIDITY IN THE

COMPLEX TOTALITY OF TRUE NATURE. If we were of the size of an ant, or even less, like that of a microbe, it would be irrelevant if a 'truck' runs over us or an 'earthquake' demolishes 'our town'. As a matter of fact, 'reality' then would seem completely different and the Universe to us would appear as a strange place with a radically novel set of associated phenomena.

What is typical of Man, however, is the capability to COMMUNICATE his experiences and 'knowledge' to other members of the same species; something allowing him to create culture and civilization. This is the function of language.

It is widely accepted the premise that the prelude to any classificatory task, in itself basic to 'knowledge', is the naming of whatever is being classified. Language, however, is well known also to have another surreptitious quality clearly spelled already in the Old Testament: IT EFFECT WHAT IS UTTERED (Isa. 1. v, 10-11), judges, destroys and delivers (Jer. v. 14, Ps. cvii,20). It has a quasi-independent existence and power as in blessing and cursing (Zech. v, 3-4); even more, is capable of CREATION (Ps. xxxiii, 9) as also dramatically exemplified in Genesis when God created the World by 'name calling' in six days.

These passages of the Old Testament attest to the deep rooted ancient belief that language, besides being a means of communication among humans, also represents an agent for the deliverance of God Will and, as such, possess AN INTRINSIC GENERATIVE POWER. As a matter of fact, this magical quality of the uttered word was already anticipated in an Egyptian Stella from the Old Kingdom found in the temple of Ptah, where it is explicitly stated that "Every divine word came into existence by the thought of the heart and the commandment of the tongue". The Word of the Lord, during the Hellenistic period came to be identified, as seen in the gospel of the 'forth evangelist', with the Greek Logos, which has also in the West a long and rather confused tradition traceable to the works of Heraclitus of Ephesus, who, as it was mentioned before, saw in the universal harmony the activity of a 'Logos', that is to say, of an intrinsic immanent ORDERING REASON clearly implicit in the Greek conception of 'Kosmos' (ordered whole).

Now, this Logos for Heraclitus did not consist of anything immaterial separated or transcending the 'Kosmo' although, as he claimed, nothing material could be conceived without it. Logos was INSEPARABLE from the tangible world and its existence had not preceded it; the soul of man was one of its manifestations. It hardly needs to be added that such a Logos was in essence a quiet introduction of God in Heraclitean cosmogony, easily identifiable with the immanent, all-encompassing deity of the agricultural bronze-age Middle Eastern ancient societies. The 'Reason' of man reflected the universal Reason and his Logos was a small part of it. Man, for them as for Heraclitus, was in itself a MICRO-COSMO, a conception, as we will see, also shared by the German Mystics.

Heraclitus's ontology was ultimately superseded, in the evolution of Greek thought, by the conception of a supreme presiding principle separated from the existing material world. This kind of notion was first manifested in the works of Anaxagoras and later on incorporated into Platonic and Aristotelian world views. Logos, for these thinkers, came to represent merely 'final causes', 'energies', 'entelecheia', 'morphe', etc; words connoting material causes. The term 'Nous' meant for them what 'Logos' was for their predecessors. Only with the advent of the Stoic School, with its oriental influences, did the old meaning of Logos recover its original status; although this trend of thought distinguished between the Logos of 'reason" (endiathetos) or 'ratio', and the Logos of 'oratory' (prophorikos) or 'oratio', a conception very close to that of the Old Testament, something extremely revealing in relation to the intriguing opening statement of the 'Forth Evangelist' where Logos (as oratio) becomes indentified with the Word, in actuality representing a divine hypostasis; an obvious manifestation of the cultural syncretism of the Hellenistic World.[2]

There has been a progressive modification in the connotation of the term Word (Aramaic menira) from the Targamus of the Old Testament, where it was nothing more than a device to avoid mentioning the divine name, to the hypostasis of the Johnnaine opening remarks. The 'Logos' of the Fourth Gospel, therefore, is understandable only when viewed with the perspective of shifting religious grounds in Late Antiquity where Christianity was born. The identification of the biblical Word with the Hellenistic Logos transformed the meaning of the term eventually from a divine 'effector' to a sacred 'principle' and perhaps was precipitated, ironically enough, by the abhorrence of the ancient Jews for uttering the name of God.

But there were also some other less orthodox currents within Judaism coming nearer the position of the gospel of John than the writers of the Targamus. There is some inkling to this in the voluminous and disorganized writing of Philo of Alexandria, where Logos sometimes seems to acquire an Stoic flavor ('seminal' or immanent and 'expressed' Logos), but is more clearly identified in the 'Gospel of Truth', a Gnostic work dating from the First Century A.D. discovered in the Jung Codex, where a long speculation of the divine name as an hypostasis is explicitly undertaken. Interesting in this regard is a Second Century Gnostic work where a mythological figure, appearing diversely under various guises such as 'Son of God', 'Image of God' etc. (among which was 'Logos'), functioned as a mediator between an unknowable God and Man, bringing 'Gnosis' to humanity. This clear link between Logos and Gnosis still pervades the semantics of the term in Western language and thought today.

The Logos of the Stoics eventually became in Christianity incarnated in the figure of Jesus Christ, the epitome of 'grace and truth', and was subsequently upheld by the apologist fathers; but for our purpose it is sufficient what had been said up to here. The evidence then seems undeniable: The uttered Word has a long and distinguished tradition in Judeo-Christian societies, being imbued with generative power and in essence represents a manifestation of God himself. It transcend the confines of a mere descriptive or communicative device to become an effector imparting being and knowledge. Indeed, language in general, even from primitive times, was instilled with the magic power of conjuring and actualizing whatever is uttered. This power akin to the biblical enchantment of the Word was not possessed by everybody in the tribe or clan but only entrusted to some selected persons; ordinarily a holly man or witch doctor. Diseases were usually attributed to the intrusion of demons into the fabric of the body and the act of caring or treating a patient was conceived as an exorcism brought about by divine intervention; to which was naturally ascribed the eventual restitution of health, if that took place.(See Chapter V)

The fact, therefore, is that by persistent emphatic repetition words force upon the mind the impression that whatever is uttered is true. What kind of reality could be credited to terms like 'spirit'? Is it a personification of the intellectual processes of man or rather a true ethereal component of humans animated with consciousness and capable to outlive our bodily component? Examples of the 'reality rendering' potentiality of language are so prevalent as to hardly need to be mentioned. From the opinion manipulation of demagogues of all kinds to the achievement of advertisement techniques, we all are aware of the 'influences' of language in the psyche of man. Much in the cyclical rationale of the, already mentioned, notorious medieval ontological argument of St Anselm was based in this type of pervasive power of words; until Kant pointed out fittingly that 'existence' was not a predicate but a precondition of ALL predicates.

But the other related and also strong attribute of language is its relevance to 'knowledge'. In naming something it is essential to identify whatever is named, and consequently somehow to 'know' what that something is. Names have the economic function of replacing a more or less elaborate description of an object, and constitute a necessary prelude to any classificatory attempt; which truly is no more than a system of rules to order objects according to a given set of specific qualities. A name, therefore, refers ordinarily to a concrete and discernible thing identifiable by those who speak the same language. As long as this 'something' is a tangible material thing, an 'object' is other words, there is usually no difficulties; it will correspond to a percept seen by all and easily identified. Although we can never be sure that our perceptions are identical to those of someone else, the fact is that, as far as language is concerned, we can always agree in what constitutes a given percept. Once the notion of 'a table' is understood we can all agree in what kind of properties to look for when a perception of such alleged object strikes our consciousness.

Obviously, if in every occasion we want to signify 'a table' there will be need to refer to it as 'the flat surface supported by rods placed vertically on the floor', speaking will be not only a draining effort but outright impossible. Any object identification presupposes the usage of language WHICH, AFTER ALL, IS NOTHING ELSE BUT A SYSTEM OF PHONETIC AND WRITTEN CONVENTIONAL SIGNS PERMITTING COMMUNICATION AMONG PEOPLE. Here resides the compelling need to ascribe names to 'things' if there is going to be any kind of communication at all.

But difficulties arise when we try to fit names into classificatory configurations design by man to arrange 'existing things'. Let us take for the sake of illustration the botanical and zoological examples. A 'mammal', for instance, is defined as a warm blooded viviparous vertebrate provided with specific types of readily accessible secretory glands design to feed the off-springs during the early defenseless period of extra-uterine development, and equipped with lungs for respiratory purposes. A bird, likewise, is a warm blooded beaked oviparous vertebrate provided with wings and likewise equipped with lungs. A fish is a cold blooded oviparous vertebrate, which because of his aquatic habitat, utilizes gills for respiration. Finally, a reptile is also a cold blooded oviparous vertebrate, but, again, provided with lungs for respiration. These characteristics could be interpreted as minimal definitional criteria for assigning and grouping vertebrates into broad easily identifiable and remembered categories. We further think that this classification is 'natural', in other words, based in multiple characteristics. [3]

Such compartmentalized view of Nature, however, will fail to accommodate or 'explain' transitional, or rather intermediate, living forms which defied any classificatory attempt. Where, for instance, are we going to place the Australian Platypus and Equidna? Are they egg laying mammals or reptiles provided with mammary glands? The existence of these oddities serve us as a reminder that life on Earth is a morphologic spectrum and consequently any effort to fit living creatures into tight, neat compartmentalized categories is arbitrary, only justified as a way to facilitate recall or possibly as a means to render analysis of presumptive phylogenic relationships feasible (for which we will have to accept beforehand the assumed reality of that possibility).

Because of these magical properties of language, this strange generative power, the mere fact that we name something creates often the subjective illusion of 'reality' for whatever we so refer and, therefore, seems to imply a 'knowledge' of a sort. The mystification becomes grievously magnified, however, when names are assigned to concepts or processes, for example, things like 'storms', 'thunder', 'fire' etc. It is precisely here that there is more clear danger of creating false, imaginary categories resulting from arbitrary ordering of perceptual impressions, which we nonetheless instill with resolute 'existence'. (In no place other than in the field of Medicine this dangerous human pitfall has been and still is, better manifested). (See also Chapter VI). Perhaps behind that mistaken assumption of the Greek mind, the belief that Reason alone unaided by the senses could provide ' true knowledge', is this strange reality rendering of language; the conviction that 'verbalized' abstractions constitute not only real BUT THE MOST REAL THINGS that could ever be.

What transcend the epistemological rationalistic-empiricist duality of Western man, however, is the passionate search for fundamentals, those basic 'building blocks' of the World capable of allowing a clear understanding of the associative 'laws' of the 'Kosmo'. But there is another basically different epistemological position, one emphasizing the indissoluble interpenetration of universal events, the merging and blending of all phenomena: The great oriental mystic tradition, a tradition which made inroads also in Western thought. We will now turn to trace its historic roots and the relevant epistemological repercussions.

According to the ancient Taoist and Hindu religions there is an underlining undetectable 'Reason' behind the sensorial diversity of the World, which is merely an illusion. The polarization of opposites is also only a false impression, a deceptive conviction of our conscious understanding. The multiplicity of forms in Nature has arisen, according with this belief, from an undifferentiated state or principle called Brahma in Hinduism, and 'The One' or ' The Way' for the Taoists in China. (See the Chandogya Upanishad 3.14 and 6.12. Trans. of Juan Mascaro. Penguin Classics. 1969)

In the West, as we had said, we find echoes of such views as early as the Pre-Socratic's. Heraclitus 'the dark' had said that 'the ways up and down are the same' and championed a philosophy of 'flux'. It was not until the IV Century B.C, however, that a distinct mystic streak appeared in Greek thought. (See also Chapter II)

On 323 B.C. Alexander the Great, after conquering more than half of the known World, was prematurely dead and his vast empire found itself without a firm head. The period of turmoil, confusion, division, progressive cultural decay and transformation that followed was, nevertheless, precisely because of the incertitude, hardships, and personal insecurity, fertile soil for practical beliefs capable of serving as inspiration, guidance and consolation in troubled times. But the geographic locus of the civilization which 'discovered' philosophy was not ready to divorce itself from its cherished consort and give up so easily one of its dearest traditions.

The only possible way, we might surely say, of assuaging the Greek spirit in times of tribulation was by resorting to philosophy which had been since the early Pythagoreans, not only an attempt to understand the Kosmo and man's place in it, but itself a cultural trait and 'a way of life'. Predictably, humanity in the Hellenistic World resorted in these difficult times to its sagas for an answer and solution to their plight in order to console their sufferings.

From the four major philosophical schools proliferating and evolving during this period the one that primarily interest us here are the Stoics. Epicureanism was a late development of atomism and the Cynics, in thought and action, were akin to the Stoics and in fact their founder Zeno of Citium was a cynic for a while, in such a vein writing his first important treatise: 'The Republic', which he wrote for the explicit purpose of refuting Plato. Finally Skepticism, as Rex Warner pointedly argues, 'became a parasite upon the Stoa in the sense that its life consisted fully in combating stoic doctrine'('The Greek philosophers' by Rex Warner. Mentor Book. 1958, P. 165).

Stoicism, however, not only introduced fresh oriental ideas into Greek thought but perhaps, because of its stern character and discipline, flourished unhindered and matured in the Roman Empire. Of their founding fathers, however, little is truly known. Zeno himself was, apparently, originally from Phoenicia and, therefore, of Semitic extraction; although he lived for many years in Athens where, we are told, he preached vehemently his ideas. Zeno recaptured the great Heraclitean insight of 'flux' and attempted to explain why it was so. He, following Plato, considered that matter was all that is capable of acting and be acted upon, boldly concluding that this category included ALL THAT IT IS. His ontology was materialistic, based in the solid ' substantiality' of matter, and the agency of activity was 'Force'; a physical principle giving rise to all the changes suffered by the Primary Substance, explaining thus the multiplicity of 'Forms'. 'Forces', however, were not random or erratic principles but thoroughly guided by 'Reason'; another conception, as we have seen, firstly expounded in the West by Heraclitus.

Now, up to here, except for his 'resurrection' of Heraclitean ideas (and its intriguing similarities with Taoism), nothing un-Greek appears to stem from Stoic conceptions. Cleanthes, however, went one step further and claimed that the source of 'Reason' for the ever living fire causing the eternal flux were imbalances or 'tensions' in the all pervading fundamental 'Substance'. An original ethical conception was therefore extended and applied to Physics.

Here, in this notion of an intrinsic tension residing in formless substance, thus explaining change and becoming, is found the great resemblance of Stoic Doctrine to oriental mystic philosophies. The forces acting upon matter were not external but, on the contrary, internal, actually integral part of this primary substance which, therefore, was not inanimate and purposeless but exactly the opposite; that is, imbued with a 'life of its own' propitiated by this inner tension or 'internal force' guided by the universal Logos, which prompted growth, differentiation and decay. In the speculative physics of the Stoics we finally find a challenge, and an alternative, to traditional Greek mechanistic atomism and perhaps, deep down, this represents the true profound reason for the natural antagonism between them and the Epicureans or Late Atomists.

The Stoics were also the first to explicitly formulate in the West the belief in a 'World Spirit', an immanent principle permeating the Cosmo and coextensive with it, of which each individual soul was nothing but a particular manifestation, a condensation of the ubiquitous 'Pneuma' or 'Breath of Life' which tensions gave purpose and form to existence; yet as 'substantial' as any other piece of matter.

We will not be concerned here with the ethical precepts of the Stoics except in so far as to affirm that their teachings, if nothing else, reinforced the oriental flavor of its basic ideas. Their 'outlook' of life was fatalistic; man should discharge his duties in this world according to the dictates of Nature inasmuch as it was useless to struggle against the divine will. As it was said before the resemblance to ancient Chinese thought was truly remarkable. The advice of the latter to follow the 'way of nature', the Tao, and to refrain from acting against the pre-established order curiously resembles the Stoic 'apathia', the detached and unemotional manner they recommended in the fulfillment of one's mundane tasks always following the dictates of wise Nature, which ultimately was a manifestation of the divine principle from where everything evolved and eventually will return, only to repeat the entire cycle again in an eternal recurrence akin to that proclaimed by Hinduism (Samsara).

The trail of the mystic trend in Western thought that has been named 'vitalistic' can be picked up again in the Neoplatonists; the group of philosophers who represent the final identifiable distinctive intellectual refulgence of the Greek genius. The root of their doctrines apparently originated with The Middle Stoic Poseidonius and can be followed thru the so-called Middle Platonists and Neopythagoreas to Plotinus himself. The Neoplatonists expounded considerably in the stratification of 'reality' and devised a plurality of hierarchical arranged 'spheres', each evolved from its superior, of which it was an image and from where it derived its being. The lowest of all was the material spatio-temporal sphere where we conduct our lives.

Plotinus, who history credits with being the founder of this school, lived and learned the basis of the doctrines destined to constitute his philosophical theories in Alexandria, reputedly from a man named Ammonius Saccas early in the Third Century A.D. It is also known, perhaps significantly, that he traveled to the East with the Roman Emperor Gordian in the ill-fated expedition that cost the Caesar his life. How much philosophy Plotinus learned from the Asiatics nobody really know, but the oriental elements, as we have seen, were by then already enmeshed in the fabric of Western thought.

Plotinus was not as complicated in his hierarchical categories as some of his successors, especially Iamblichus. He was intellectually mercifully frugal and only conceived of few superposed levels of stratifications: The highest was Nous or Intellect; where the archetypes of all that exist resided, including not only the universal Forms but also the individual ones. This level, roughly corresponding to that of the Platonic ideas, was that of intuitive thought, the 'cause' of the immediately succeeding lower strata: That of Soul, the source of rational-discursive reasoning. Soul, however, although possessing 'reason' and, therefore, evolving its activities in the spatio-temporal Universe, was capable of transcending his condition, whether to ascend into the intuitive 'intellectual' level, and perhaps beyond to reach idyllic identification with the ineffable 'One', or else to descend into the inferior level of the material World which was formed and animated by it, or even below into the deep morass of unanimated matter.

Neoplatonic metaphysics undoubtedly displayed an unmistakable oriental flavor and in that it differed from Platonic doctrines. The 'One' was indescribable: In fact transcending Being although itself the origin of all that existed. From him everything was created by an 'outgoing' impulse and to him everything was supposed to return by an 'ingoing' natural tendency. Furthermore, because this 'One' was not an 'object', no predicate could be applied to it, consequently being inaccessible to the rational mind. There was no way we could 'imagine' or 'picture' this truth; according to their creed the mind could only hope to reach it by 'mystical' insight. Here lays the great departure from traditional Greek thought, that is, from the worship of 'Reason' and, therefore, the great similarity with Oriental philosophies. The immanence of the One reminds us of the all pervading universal principles of Hinduism and Buddhism. Furthermore, as in these religion-philosophies, the ultimate aim of life was the return to the One and the road was that of renunciation, the 'closing' of the eyes to material appetites and worldly desires (matter for them was a source of evil). Rigorous moral discipline was a necessity but, in opposition to the Indian Ascetic, they did not preached a policy of withdrawal from the world of the senses but rather of contemplation of physical beauty, as it would lead the soul back to identification with Intellect of which it was a 'reflection'.

Neoplatonic notions, particularly ethical and metaphysical, found their ways into early Christian Doctrines, although during the Middle Ages there was not a clear cut differentiation as to the contribution of Plato himself and his successors. It is one of the ironies of fate that the religions (Christianity and Gnosticism), which they attacked and fought so vigorously, did already, in the case of the Gnostics, or would eventually, in the case of Christianity, come to resemble, or at least to incorporate, so much of their conceptions in their ethical doctrines.

The 'trinity' of Father, Son and Holy Ghost is striking in its similarity to the Neoplatonic of One, Nous and Soul. The hierarchical ordering of angelical spheres of beings, originally an Aristotelian conception, reached the scholastics by way of the Neoplatonists. Likewise their condemnation of matter as base and evil, as well as, their advise to 'turn the eyes' on the spiritual sphere as a means of return to the One, resembles the Christian admonition to resist the sinful bodily 'temptations' and resort to God for salvation by acts of prayer and virtuous behavior (the latter also a path of attunement for the Neoplatonists).

More interesting for our purpose, however, is to analyze and compare Neoplatonism with the central themes of their great predecessors the Stoics. At first sight, perhaps superficially, there appears to be rather vast differences between both philosophical schools. The Stoics, for instance, considered that everything that 'existed' was 'material' including even the soul of man, which was coextensive with the body. This type of 'substantiality' was revolting to the Neoplatonists and for them thoroughly evil. On the other hand the Stoics advocated a moral conduct that was actually defined, as we have seen, as 'apathia'; the total unemotional disregard with personal destiny in those things where Will could not intervene. Such pattern of behavior would also have been repugnant to the Neoplatonists, in many ways conceded and insolent, a proud ill disguise contemptuous, almost defiant, aloofness.

"I must die. But must I die groaning? I must be imprisoned. But must I whine as well? I must suffer exile. Can anyone then hinder me from going with a smile, and a good courage, and at peace? 'Tell the secret'. I refuse to tell, for this is in my power. 'But I will chain you'. What say you, fellow? Chain me? My leg you will chain-yes, but my will-no, not even Zeus can conquer that".

Life, as this passage attributed to Epictetus discloses, must, according to the Stoics, be lived in resigned indifference, something strange to the humble submissiveness of the Neoplatonists to the Will of God. For the Stoics the notion of 'substance' and 'matter' was a DYNAMIC one, they were the 'vehicles' of activity (those condensations and rarefactions of 'pneuma' resulting from the tensions and explaining the flux of Nature.)

An all pervading 'element' was the WORLD SOUL of which the individual souls were the parts that animated the bodies with an inner Reason eventually stemming from the universal 'Logos'. On the other hand, in many respects the Neoplatonic metaphysical and immaterial 'principles' represented an 'spiritualization' of the stoic 'Reason', the postulation of an ultimate ruling Mind which, we can cogently argued, followed almost 'naturally' from the Stoic notion of this 'Logos' in view of the fact that it implied the existence of a 'reasoning something', a subject to the predicate, which has been identified by some scholars with the Neoplatonic 'Nous' or 'Intellect' (inasmuch as the ultimate indescribable 'One' could not even be called 'Being'). This is something with no parallel in Western thought, perhaps only comparable to the Hindu Brahma of Buddhist Nirvana.

Be it as it may, and as it is the case with many early philosophical enterprises, the Stoics abstract principles represented a SECULARIZATION of religious categories which were surreptitiously 'recovered' by the Neoplatonists, who removed the 'facticity' and substantiality of the Stoics with a new other-worldly attitude, essentially representing a rediscover of the Platonic realm of the Mind. The trend to this end is already evident in the Stoizising Platonists of the First Century B.C., like Antiochus of Escalon and the prolific Poseidonius; followed later on, as we have already mentioned, by the Middle Platonic and Neo-Pythagorean traditions immediately preceding Plotinus.

There was, therefore, a gradual merging and slow transition between these two late great philosophical traditions of the ancient world, facilitated by their very similar ethical precepts. Man, both preached, should live virtuously as a means to achieve inner peace and self contentment, a way of reaching ultimate reconciliation with the universal World Soul or the One. Certainly the Neoplatonists were more reverent than the early Stoics, although no traces of apathetic contempt remain in some of the works of the late representatives of this school, particularly Marcus Aurelius.

The Western mystic tradition that emerged in late antiquity incorporated, therefore, material from multiplicity of sources. It endorsed, by way of the Stoics, the concept of 'flux' and change of Heraclitus and of a physical world evolved as a manifestation of a World Soul or ineffable One, directed according to the 'intentions' of a Logos or Nous to give purpose and order to Nature. Man was supposed to live in 'agreement' with the intentions of these infinitely wise designs of fate, even if his limited intelligence not always was able to discern its good aims. He was to conduct an honorable and virtuous existence because, although the world of events was predetermined, man was a rational being and as such free to WISH good from evil; at least to his own spiritual gratification.

45

The Pythagorean early themes of transmigration of souls as a mean to attain progressive spiritual perfectibility, and the concept of the body as a tomb of the soul from where it had to escape with death (something also inherent to some oriental beliefs), were also wrought in the fabric of their doctrines, serving as a frame to some 'spiritualist' heretic undercurrents, even within Christianity, which survived up to our present era.

What is not clearly formulated in this 'Greek' mystic tradition, it seems to me, is the explicit postulation of the principles of good and evil found in oriental philosophy; but the Stoics already postulated the polarization of opposite tendencies as underlying all natural phenomena or change (as in Taoism). Their Pneuma itself was the active principle while matter was the passive quality-less one. From their interpenetration or 'krasis' (total mixture) new substances would come into being. Cleanthes 'tensions' provided the basic source for the dynamic interplay of these tendencies, their 'flux' accounting for everything that existed. These beliefs are important components of the mystic Western tradition as it evolved in the Post-Medieval years.

The Early Church, it hardly needs to be mentioned, adopted an 'official' Rationalistic dress. It viewed with concern, fear and disgust any mystic tendency, in other words 'any experience of one-ness with ultimate reality', as mysticism is often defined. God for them was a transcendent ordering Soul 'out there', the supreme 'maker' and 'judge', only to be approached by humble prayers and submissive acquiescence to his divine Will. Nevertheless, and despite of the hostility from the official Church many, more or less, disguised mystics flourished during this period providing evidence of the power of such religious trait in the life of Man.

The Early Christian Mystics, perhaps befitting a 'Hellenized' religion, were often labeled as heretics, something that happened without question in the case of the Gnostics. The early fathers, like Origen and Clement of Alexandria, had to couch their language very carefully in religious matters to avoid being likewise categorized. Dionysius the Oreopagite is reputed with the feat of being the first who gathered and arranged the disparate mystic elements of Christianity in his 'Mystical Theodicy', where he described the threefold paths to deification or union with God by 'way of negations', after discarding the Empirical rational mind.

In the West the mystic Christian tradition was uphold by Hugh of St.

Victor and his followers, who blended some of the elements of Dionysian theories with Augustinian notions. Two important documents of the Late Middle Ages represent the final form this tradition was to take: 'On the imitation of Christ' reputed to Thomas a Kemp and the other, particularly pertinent to us, is the anonymous 'Theologia Germanica'. This last document, firstly published by Martin Luther, contains many of the mystic insights subsequently appropriated by the early Reformation and which appeared to have influenced him powerfully, at least during his formative years.

Now, Luther was a profound and militant anti-rationalist who even had once defined this most cherished of Greek and scholastic virtues with the vilifying epithet of 'a whore'. The Reformation was prompt, and happy, to seize and manipulate any weapon or resource against the hated traditional Christianity, and mystic undercurrents were undoubtedly appealing to the troop of reformers who held sway over Christian revolution in Central Europe: Particularly men like Kaspar Von Schoenckfelt and Sebastian Frank. Their emphasis in 'immediate' union with God, the 'given away' with intermediaries like the array of sacraments institutionalized by the Medieval Church, represents one of the main themes and weapons of Luther followers. But mystic outlooks in the High Renaissance by no means were exclusive patrimony of the Reformation, as the Spanish Mystics like Teresa of Avila as well as John of the Cross exemplified. Be it as it may, the importance of Central European mysticism for us results from the unbridled influence the Reformation exerted in the German Romantic Movement, the outlook of an epoch with enormous repercussions, not only in the arts and literature, but also socially, philosophically and even in the scientific development of Central Europe.

The roots of this trend can be traced to the medieval theologians Meister Eckhart and Johannes Tauler. Their teachings strongly influenced the life and works of such pivotal figures of reformation as Johann Arndt and Jakob Boehme. In the speculations of the latter we can already discern, in an identifiable form, the essential components of the metaphysical themes exposed in German Nature-Philosophy and the elaborated dialectic of the Idealistic School which saw its pinnacle in the XIX Century.

For Boehme, as for the Neoplatonists before, man was essentially a microcosm; a 'copy' of the Universe. As such, man followed 'privately' a developmental course resembling entirely the evolution of the World; his psychology, so to speak, provided him with a clue as to this development. Boehme postulated that Man behavior is the result of the interaction of two opposing tendencies or 'forces': One centripetal, egotistic, of self possession, urging the satisfaction of his body, and another centrifugal of self-denial or extinction. Man behavior was then determined by these opposing 'drives' and he considered natural to extrapolate them to universal dimensions and so to explain the existence of the Cosmo.

For Boehme then, at the beginning of time, there was a 'principle' which represented, at the same time, everything and no-thing (another Neoplatonic idea), animated however by opposite 'desires' of self-possession and self manifestation. In the 'flux' created by this conflict the possessive component assimilated the impulses for self-manifestation and controlled its 'expression' as Nature.

His triadic law of growth and development speaks of a reconciliation of opposites effecting a 'resolution' of conflict. The germ of the great German dialectic school is here clearly expressed, serving as anticipation to the system building of Hegel and later Marx, who so profoundly influenced the societal dynamics and economy of the XX Century. But Boehme, perhaps influenced by Paracelsus, used to shroud his dialectic in the symbolism of the Iatrochemists. (See below and also Chapters II, V, VI). Sulphur was the expansive desire of the Spirit for self manifestation (comparable to the Chinese Yang), while Mercury, on the contrary, was that of self possession (Chinese Yin). On the other hand the interaction of both substances was the 'salt', a new product that magically 'combined' and superseded the original two(by this time Paracelsus himself was already expounding an alchemical system using terms in many ways identical to the Chinese and this, it seems to me, hardly could be a coincidence).

The Reformation movement, therefore, constituted in Central Europe a fertile soil where mystic conceptions, using frequent alchemical symbols, flourished quite freely; coming truly to form part of the traditional character of the people. Another point in common between Oriental and Western mystics is their similar beliefs in the evolutionary advance, or improvement, brought about by death and regeneration. Life, after all, was a process, a dialectic movement brought about by 'conflicts' which resolution eventuated in the 'creation' of something new. The comparison of this life with a chemical reaction was warranted by the conception of man as a microcosm, a mirror of the universe. Death was a new beginning, a way to a higher stage of being.

The birth of Nature-Philosophy in Germany properly began with the school of Iatrochemists. Closely related with the alchemy of Paracelsus, who can be considered a true predecessor or perhaps even a founder father of this discipline, the school attempted to explain the chemical basis of biological processes; in a sense an application into Medicine of alchemical principles, which was also an early hope and aim of the Chinese. Van Helmont, from Belgium, maintained the opinion that every object of the World was an autonomous entity, each driven by its own inner force in a process of generation, growth and evolution. Besides, each being was self-directed by its own free will. Even the constituent parts of a whole, like the organ systems of the human body, were individually driven by this inner impulse or, as he called it, its own 'archeus' or propelling soul (See also Chapter II and V)

Now, these ideas, it should be obvious, are elaborations from a theme already touch on and developed by the Stoics, who considered each object was permeated by 'pneuma' which 'tensions' explained the directed and purposeful activity in everything. The internal individual driving force of this pneuma could be equated to the Iatrochemical archeus, and both were intended to express the inner source of any activity, a belief in complete contradiction to the Western mechanist tradition of atomism with their 'inert bodies' and 'external forces'.

Contemporaneous with Van Helmont, and fittingly enough an acquaintance of him thru his son, there was a man widely reputed to be one of the greatest talents ever to walk on Earth, one who gave metaphysical content and consistency to the speculations of the Iatrochemists, a man who integrated Western Logic and mysticism conceptions in a comprehensive, and surprisingly consistent, system and whose genius besides all these achievements also gained the rare distinction of being a co-discoverer of the calculus: Gottfried Wilhelm Leibniz.

Leibniz achieved a remarkable syncretism of 'rationality' with 'mysticism'; maybe as no other human being had, not only achieved, but even ever attempted again. He is popularly known primarily for having coined the notion that 'this is the best of all possible worlds' (a belief which intentionally or unintentionally could only had pleased his sponsor the Duke of Brunswick) and also for his best known metaphysical work 'The Monadologie' (a short manuscript written during a sojourn in the French capital, where he was sent in a diplomatic mission by the elector of Mainz to convince Louis XV not to attack Europe).

Leibniz, above all an eclectic spirit, not only did try to bring together the two main intellectual traditions of the West but also, in a different plane of discourse, endeavored to unify Europe and also of effecting a reconciliation between the two main branches of the Christian faith evolving after the schism of the Reformation. In Logic he attempted the impossible task of trying to devise a universal symbolic language that will give away with semantic ambiguities, and even reached the point of wanting to quantify emotions. In any matter of litigation, he thought, all the parties to the dispute needed to do was to sit down and by means of this abstract idiom arrive at a 'logical' truth; a naive hope revealing some wanting in his understanding of the human soul.

Nevertheless, that intent was meritorious and his frequent conciliatory activities betrayed the yearnings of a well motivated eclectic mind. Leibniz, as can be easily surmised from the quotation above cited, belonged to the philosophical affiliation defined by Bertrand Russell as the 'mathematical party', together with such illustrious names as Plato himself, Pythagoras, the Atomists and, more recently, men of the stature of Descartes, as well as, many Rationalist Philosophers. Yet, as we know, the large majority of these men were mechanists, particularly those of the Post-Medieval period who treated matter as something inert subject to 'outside forces', which explained the world of continuous change and becoming.

What is surprising about Leibniz is that, notwithstanding his deeply rationalistic tendencies and mathematical approach to Metaphysics, he did not shared many of the beliefs of his great contemporary rationalist philosophers. Taking from the Iatrochemists the concept of a reality composed of self-propelled individual units he gave this idea a central position in his scheme, yet arrived at its postulation in a traditional Western fashion, that is, by means of a logical process of 'reasoning' rather than by means of an 'intuitive vision', as a mystic would.

Leibniz took the age old Greek dispute of whether or not an extended body could be divided 'at infinitum' and concluded, as Anaxagoras did before, that anything 'spatial', at least in theory, could be still subdivided no matter how small. Because all material bodies occupied a place in space they, he concluded, had to be a complex 'thing'. Now, he proceeded in a rigorous rationalistic grand-manner, if there were complex (compound) things it implied THE LOGICAL EXISTENCE of simple units from which they were derived. Furthermore, these 'units' could not be material things and thence partake of the property of extension and complexity, but by necessity needed to be metaphysical, yet real; the equivalents of the spatio-temporal material world of phenomena.

The monads, as he called these units, were something similar to 'a point' where a number of lines with diverse angles converged, a dimensionless counterpart of the extended lines and angles, centers of organization for the seemingly chaotic contingent material world. The monads, on the other hand, also had a dynamic character; they were the locus of directional activity giving rise to all universal phenomena. This activity, therefore, was purposeful, even if we might be unable to discern what this purpose was in many cases; a mysterious transcendental 'goal' in fact representing a 'resurrection' by Leibniz of the Aristotelian concept of 'entelechy', a self striving for more elaborated and refined mode of organization or degree of perfection.

The monads, so to speak, were like the 'seeds' which include the entire 'plan' or blueprint of an adult plant; at the same time CODES AND TEMPLATES of the multifarious physical world, and no less real than it. The monads then included all possible aspects of 'existence', which therefore was cast in a rigid deterministic mold.

Now, if the physical Universe was a MANIFESTATION of the monads activity, an expression or unfolding of a pre-established immanent program, of a FATE that could not be modified, then, clearly, there was no possibility of one monad influencing another, something which would have introduced contingency and unpredictability into the 'order' of things, an untenable contradiction. So much was so that the soul monad could not 'act' upon the body monad. How then could it be that we feel 'in control' of our bodies? Leibnitz answer in this respect anticipated Hume. His explanation was simple: The soul and the body monads were

SYNCHRONIZED in their activities since the beginning of time, set at the same pace by God who, in his wisdom, regulates all the monads in a harmonious totality. But how then were perceptions of an outside reality (which Leibniz did not deny) possible at all? Were they not AN ACTION of this external world upon our minds thru the mediation of our sensory system? No, he claimed, we only perceive an 'image' of this reality by looking inside of ourselves because 'each monad is a mirror of the Universe'.

Monads then formed by the 'Divine Grace' a system of self-contained units, true Universes in themselves mirroring each other and the totality in a pre-established harmony, but with no hope for intercommunication except by the 'inner light' provided by Providence to render us aware of our surroundings.

Leibniz logico-metaphysical system appears, therefore, not only to be a rationalization of the Iatrochemists 'intuitive insight' into nature, but also to include in its enunciation material from several other sources. Firstly the debt to Plato is not only evident but rightly acknowledged by him in some of his letters. The positing of two paralleled 'real' worlds, a material factual one and an ideal metaphysical realm only accessible to the intellect, is present in both cases. There is one difference however: Leibniz monads were more than 'ideas', actually they constituted dynamic 'centers of activity' from where stemmed the world of multiplicity and change. The apparently contingent material world had an ordered and measurable essential Nature.

Less well known, and certainly not admitted by Leibniz, was a debt to the frequently underestimated Stoics. The material bodies, we should recall, were all energized by the 'tensions' of the inner pneuma in accordance with the mandates of a universal 'Logos'; a dynamic conception very close to the world of the monads. Nature, in both systems, consisted in the unfolding of a preordained program of self propelled units which also continuously strived for self improvement, thus explaining material change and evolution. Equally present in both philosophies there is also an intriguing contradiction between the prearranged Cosmo and the freedom of Man, a fact difficult to reconcile with a predetermined fate and which, in the case of Leibniz, arose questions about his sincerity.

Finally, and not surprisingly because of his relations with the

Iatrochemists, Leibniz's world view had strong points of similarity with Oriental beliefs. As a matter of fact, in his mature years he was known to have studied Chinese Thought (which he defined as anti-West), probably by way of translations by Jesuits monks of texts from the neo-Confucian school of Chin Hsi; a philosophical trend having apparent roots in Mahayana Buddhism(See 'The Tao of Physics' by Fritjof Capra. Bantam Books. 1975,P. 289). Granted that Leibniz 'atomism' had no counterpart in Oriental notions of reality and betrays his Western intellectual roots, but his 'fundamentalism' does not refers to the physical material Universe, but rather to its metaphysical counterpart. As it was said before, for him material objects, which 'appeared' to interact, in actuality constituted 'synchronous systems' set in such a fashion by Divine Providence from the start.

Leibniz rationalism provided a 'logical' solution to the mystic insights of the Iatrochemists and a metaphysical foundation for the German Nature -Philosophers, who developed a 'vitalistic' theory of Biology and Medicine. His exquisite blending attempt of often antagonistic philosophical positions has not been realized or accepted for what it is: A rationalization of mystic insights into Nature, perhaps a futile eagerness to immortalize what is personal and individual. Notwithstanding opinions to the contrary it is hard to deny certain solipsistic flavor to his whole epistemology.

Again, if the monads are 'window-less', how could we really 'know' the existence of an 'outside world'? His arguments in favor of such a view displayed a circularity akin to the Scholastic Ontology, and maybe this is one reason why his doctrines had not been more influential in the West. Leibniz died alone and forgotten. His strange mixture of Platonism, Atomism and Oriental Mysticism was not fully understood or appreciated for nearly three centuries, but nevertheless he was highly influential, still within the same century of his death, in the ulterior history and evolution of German scientific thought.

The characteristic and peculiar evolutionary theory of the Nature-Philosophers was advanced, originally, by Johann Herder in the later part of the XVIII Century. He postulated that for living forms to increase in complexity and organization there was need for a previous annihilation of the lower creatures, because they were constituted by the same constant pool of organic substances. (Similar thought had been held previously by Leibniz in his speculative metaphysics. The monads, he explained, coalesce in aggregates which totality strives for the perfection of the group that eventually dissolved; the monads then entering new associations.)

Typical exponents of this school were Friedrich Schelling and Lorenz Oken. These two men followed the general trend of the German Mystics and Alchemists in postulating, as Leibniz did before, that the Universe was animated by a purposeful drive under the commands of a World Spirit. Man, they also claimed, was the epitome of this universal order, a belief, as we had already seen, shared by the Neoplatonists and by Leibniz himself, who maintained that the human soul-monad was the highest pinnacle of monad evolution; followed by the animal, vegetative and in-animated types, in that order. (See Stephen Masson 'A history of the Sciences'.Collier Books. 1962, P. 356)

Lorenz Oken concepts are heavily indebted to Boheme and Leibniz and the influence of Paracelsus, who had developed before the theory that chemical elements which reacted to form a compound 'attracted' each other like the manner of a 'man and a woman', is also obvious (this concept, we had already seen was also central to the speculative beliefs of the Chinese alchemists). But Oken also made a new emphasis clearly derivable from the monad concept.

If a man was an epitome in an evolutionary line, and, therefore AT THE END OF IT, it follows that he must, per force, 'comprehend' everything that HAD PRECEDED HIM; like Leibniz monads which 'encoded' the universal and individual fate. If that was the case, then, each man development represented a recapitulation of that line from the beginning of biological time.

Oken replaced with his biological muco-vesicles the logico-metaphysical monads of Leibniz. Following Herder he concluded that, if in order for new and more perfected living forms to come into being it was necessary the previous dissolution of the earlier type of organisms, then, he 'logically' asserted, organic matter had to be built of fundamental units that would survive the continuous biological process of death and rebirth. Again, significantly, Oken expounded a cosmology with intriguing similarities to the Stoic System. The World, he explained, was created from an 'ethereal' chaos while organisms, likewise, arose from a primeval mucus which ultimately gave rise to all living creatures by a similar organizing and polarizing 'activity'. The similarity with the organizing tendencies of the 'tensions' in the primeval all pervading Stoic 'pneuma' is obvious. (Ibid P. 359)

These notions eventually gave rise to the 'idea' that ontogenic development was a recapitulation of the phylogenic evolution and, so to speak, fathered the biologic discipline of 'Embryology'; a thoroughly German science. Even the field of modern physics was not inconsiderably influenced by their conceptions; in fact it owes much to the mystic Centro-European outlook of life, as we will see in later chapters.

CHAPTER II

After this brief recount of the general philosophical positions which are at the root of Western Epistemology as we know it today, we shall now analyze specific examples of how they have modeled, guided and actually determined the progression and evolution of our science and technology up to the present time.

There is a popular, commonsensical, widespread conception of Science which assumes its progress to represent an objective and detached accumulation of 'knowledge' about man's endeavors (called variously Nature, World, Cosmo or Universe), with the ultimate purpose of discovering causal 'laws' guided by hypothetical working models, which will allow us to understand, predict and control events, or perhaps in the last analysis, to discover the primordial 'truth', 'reason' and 'cause' of IT all. Such an 'ideal' view, without any doubt encouraged and proclaimed rigorously and uncompromisingly by scientists as the corner stone and basic creed of their trade, is disarmingly naive, unsupported by facts and pathetically distorted. To many this statement, I am sure, will be utterly arbitrary and entirely unjustified from every point of view. It is more than natural that it be so when we realize the enormous prestige and miraculous accomplishments of modern Science and Technology.

This is neither the place, nor it is my intention, to engage in a detailed historic exposition of the evolution of notions like 'science' and 'technology', which lies well beyond the scope of the present work. It becomes imperative, however, to emphasize one fundamental and little appreciated characteristic of scientific activity: That contrary to the opinion of many, the social 'milieu' and historic circumstances, in other words, the totality of the human environment and experience at a given time and place, exerts a powerful influence in shaping scientific theories, which in the last analysis represent our 'view of reality', that is to say, what we consider 'existential truth'. This remarkable fact, undoubtedly, results from the complicated character of much that is accepted in our culture as knowledge, something which not only is deeply rooted in the structure of the human mind, in the way we think and relate to our world, but also in historic cultural and social factors.

With the collapse of Scholasticism in the Early Renaissance two fundamentally opposed 'world views' evolved in Europe. In the Western region, following the main stream of Greek thought, mainly in England, France and Italy, a mechanistic philosophy, as typified in the Cartesian and Newtonian systems, as well as in the works of Galileo and Leonardo, evolved. This philosophy considered Nature as composed of essentially inert matter controlled in its totality by external forces (giving rise to the Deist conception of God). In living beings it established a dichotomy between the 'lower forms', equally animated by external 'forces', and man himself who possessed a soul; although in no way was it clarified or generally accepted that this soul 'energized' or 'propelled' matter. Some like the French philosophers of the Enlightenment even completely dispensed with such notion of a 'soul' and became 'materialistic' while others, like the bishop Berkeley, completely abolished the relation of sensations to an outside World and became 'empiricists' in the British sense. (See also Chapter I).

As was already mentioned, in Central Europe an entirely different, actually completely opposed belief took shape during the same period. There was not, so it went, such a thing as 'inert' matter. Every particle, it was claimed, was imbued with life in its own right and its activity represented a 'revelation' of its potentialities and inner spirit. This vitalistic outlook, defended by Leibniz and Boehme, was an elaboration of the earlier Iatrochemical School which more notorious champion was, of course, Paracelsus. Every universal particle was alive and empowered by a self unfolding principle giving expression to its independent inner necessity; this was the conception of the Mystic. [1]

It can hardly be claimed that such opposing world views could be the result of careful un-bias analysis and search into Nature. The first would appeal to sea-fearing people and merchant societies deeply rooted in the materiality of things and the whims of the surrounding elements, which solely determined their successes or failures. It perhaps has its religious roots in the extroverted Near Eastern patriarchal divinities that created the World variously by self-mutilation, ejaculation and 'name calling', or by a monumental act of craftsmanship. God, the supreme craftsman, 'built the Cosmo' in one way or another.

The second conception would appeal to land-locked agrarian societies, an Oriental, mystic introverted outlook which held Creation represented an unfolding, an actualization of a self expressive urge; an act of INTROSPECTION, of recovery of inner potentiality. It is in the context of these opposing world views, based ultimately in religious 'attitudes', that the development of biological and physical theories should be understood. Also it should be obvious that personal experiences, based in the realities of the cultural and social milieu where men grew and/or lived tainted the interpretation of the gathered facts.

A fairy typical example of how the social milieu and historical circumstances model scientific views is the Theory of Evolution. Fundamental, and central to its development, was the notion of 'progress' which was 'in the air' at the turn of the XVIII Century, whether in Germany with the dialectical notions of their mystics, or in coastal Western Europe, as exemplified in the system of The Philosophes where it took a social character, and in England where it was mainly materialist, largely mediated by the Industrial Revolution.

Once accepted, progress was also conceived as a 'drive' determining the chain of beings revealed in the fossil evidence; but the INTERPRETATION of the facts took different direction in each of these different territories. German Nature-Philosophy viewed biological evolution as resulting from a progressive unfolding or manifestation of an specific pattern of development originating with the most rudimentary in-animated condition where all inert matter was classified, followed then by an intermediate state as chemical substances when the different components were capable of specific reactions, to a final state as living organisms, when matter acquired the capacity of independent self determination. The final culminating state was Man, in whom the World Spirit had produced the most perfected Being, the highest reachable point of the self unfolding pattern.

Strangely enough Man, after destroying the medieval hierarchical descending order of angelical beings, substituted that for an also graded, but ascending material order concluding in Man. Yet, as we have just seen in the German conception of the ascend, the entire process owed its 'progression' to the Will of the 'World Spirit', with each biological species struggling in its own way to reach the highest grade of perfection allowed by its potentialities. Typical theories of evolution originating in France and England clearly reflected the religious views of Christianity in their diverse manifestations but they also, as we have already claimed, reflected the social milieu and idiosyncrasies of those lands.

In France, for instance, evolutionary ideas were firstly entertained by men like Ribonett but, subsequently, became refined by Jean Baptiste Lamarck. Central to their thought was the affirmation that species transformed one into another in an unbroken chain, again culminating in Man. (It should be noticed, however, the difference between this alleged transmutability and the private, individual 'progression' in the Germanic theories where each stage SUBSUMED the lower one.)

But in addition, the Lamarckian point of view established that the 'mind controlled the body', a curious counterpoise to the mechanistic Cartesian system. According to Lamarck, in the early rudimentary stages of biological evolution environmental stimuli certainly determines the fate of organisms, but subsequently they acquire an independence, an inner drive which ultimately self-determine the 'advance' of living forms thru their particular line of descend. It is important to note the absence, in these speculations, of any metaphysical entity like the Germanic 'Spirit'. The biological forces determining the progression of living forms in their multiple transformations, although peculiar or 'sui generis' were, nevertheless, material and earthy.

Lamarck, who was also called the last of the philosophes, is better remembered by his hypothesis about the inheritance of acquired characteristics. According with his views the latter were evolved by the desire or urge of living forms to satisfy a need, or perhaps even a caprice. Giraffes, for instance, developed their long necks so they could feed in the high trees of the open savannah. Birds grew wings because their ancestors 'wanted' to fly. All this amounted to an 'influence' of the Mind over the physical environment, which is precisely one of the central postulates of the French Revolution and was also of paramount importance in shaping, later on, the Bergsonian system with its central conception of the 'elan vitale'.

Lamarckian theories, however, did not go unchallenged. Even in his time Geoffrey Hilarie embraced a more traditional, and classical, view in postulating that the organs were what defined the bodily functions. For him morphology compelled and predetermined the fate of living creatures. This notion of an entirely mechanistic flavor relegated the Mind to become a prisoner of the body and subservient to its shape.

Hilaire was strongly influenced by the Okean conception of archetypes, and could be considered one of the forefathers of comparative anatomy. For him all zoological groups partake in a general common morphologic plan, as attested in the uniformity of design of anatomical parts (like vertebras or limbs in vertebrates), as well as, in the correspondence of internal organs. It was to the search for this general blueprint that he dedicated his energies, inasmuch as Hilaire considered all conceivable anatomical characteristics as variations of the same prototypical 'master plan'.

Georges Cuvier, professor of Comparative Anatomy at the Paris Museum of Natural History, upheld a theory exactly contrary to that of Hilaire. According to him the functional needs is what predetermine and channel the organic differentiation. The animal need to move around, for example, demanded the necessity for locomotive organs (legs, wings, fins etc.) and also sensory organs for spatial orientation.

This mutual interdependence of organic characteristics, which he called 'the principle of subordination of characters', led Cuvier to conclude that the life history of an animal, that is to say, his habits and behavior, even his organic blueprints, could be 'rationally deduced' from one of his parts. Given a paw with a set of sharp claws one, for example, could deduce that the animal was a predator carnivore and consequently 'predict' other anatomical characteristics. Cuvier proposals had great practical impact in the field of Comparative Anatomy, and his theorizing about functions as permanent organic pre-determinants (he did not believe in evolution), did have a great impact in mechanistic France; particularly during the post-revolutionary Napoleonic Period when the aim and purpose of the State was supposed to justify the political 'shape' of its government. Predictably

Cuvier became powerful and worldly successful. Under Napoleon he was Inspector General of the University of France, Professor of the College of France, and perpetual secretary of the Academy of Sciences.

At the end, then, the mechanistic point of view prevailed in French evolutionary theorizing. The organic species were highly structured and immutable, their characteristics being such that they could be 'deduced' analytically one from the other; evolution was OUT OF QUESTION. Of the other two theories, Lamarckism was based in the idea of progress extolled by the philosophes, whose notions became the rallying logic of the French Revolution. According to him, as we had seen, biological species, like societies, formed a graded evolving chain of beings, continuously 'improving' themselves in agreement with a general plan activated by means of a mysterious 'vital force' or elan that served simultaneously as its cause and justification. This evolving progression was mediated by the inheritance of acquired characteristics, a mechanism which provided ' the explanations' for the step-ladder evolutionary ascent. These ideas obviously became 'unpopular' after Napoleon seized power.

Hilaire views, who's conceptions of archetypal designs, the derivation of function from morphology and the mutative 'jumpy' character of evolution (which according to him was only minimally, if at all, influenced by the environment) had, like is the case with Lamarck views, strong similarities to German Nature-philosophy, and were destined to ultimately be forgotten in France. Man, who sees and understand Nature as modeled after human society could not, in this period of post-revolutionary expansion when the country needed the most internal stability, accept the 'idea' of evolution, even less of a mutational 'jumpy' type or a notion of structure as defining function; something which would have deprived of meaning and validity the French Revolution and subsequent Napoleonic wars.

In England, where because of historical and cultural affinities with France the bourgeoisie conception of progress became also a popular belief, the theory of 'evolution' germinated fruitfully but developed a peculiar British 'flavor', again borrowed from prevailing opinions as to the dynamics of social change. I am referring, specifically, to the commercial consideration of 'competition' as the active energizing 'principle' behind Man continuous increase in material wealth and worldly powers. This most cherished premise of laissez faire capitalism, revealingly, couldn't have failed to influence powerfully their views of nature and biological matters.

Evolutionary theorizing in Britain commenced with men such as Erasmus Darwin who were well acquainted with, and strongly influenced, by contemporary French thinkers; particularly Lamarck. His grandson Charles was, however, to give together with Alfred Russell Wallace, the final shape to British evolutionary views. Of central importance in this respect was the faithful voyage of 'The Beagle', which gave Charles the unique opportunity of broad exposure to an enormous array of facts and ample time to brood upon them. What he saw throughout South America and the Galapagos islands convinced the young man as to the truth of evolution. Upon his return he had the opportunity of conversing extensively with skillful breeders and, according to his own words in an autobiography, then 'perceived' that selection was the key stone in the evolutionary process. Darwin nonetheless, by his own admission, still was at a lost to explain how this selective mechanism could be applied to Nature as a whole. He did not shared the Lamarckian belief in an inner driving force (as his grandfather did) and was puzzled over the matter until he gave a relaxed cursory read to Malthus works on population, from where he seized upon the idea of the 'struggle for survival'. Darwin hesitated and procrastinated for many years before deciding to publish his conclusions. Apparently he feared the repercussions of his theories but finally was prompted to it by the draft of a paper that Russell Wallace sent him with a plead for its publication. Remarkably, and independently, Wallace had also arrived to identical conclusions after reading the works of Malthus!

It would not be difficult to imagine the surprise, chagrin and disbelief of Darwin when he received the correspondence from Wallace. Yet, he was honest enough to submit the manuscript together with his own paper for publication. The theory of "Natural Selection', although opposed by the Church and the entrenched conventions of contemporary Science, became, notwithstanding the formidable controversy it engendered around the civilized world, finally accepted and popular; firstly in England and eventually almost everywhere. The fears of Darwin were proved largely unfounded.

Now, we may ask, could it be considered a mere coincidence that two bourgeoisie Englishmen from the Victorian Era should have almost simultaneously, and independently, arrived at identical biological insights as to the workings of Mother Nature? It seems extremely unlikely that the dynamics of evolution should have been considered by both workers the principle of 'competition and struggle' providing for the 'survival of the fittest', if they were not mirroring the cherished ideal of the society of traders and merchants from where arose laissez faire capitalism. When analyzed carefully the facts appear to be an example of how Man sees and understand Nature in terms borrowed from his physical and social milieu, which provides the 'explanation' of how 'things works'. This is not a new concept or revelation, but rather a view that has already been advanced since long before them by sociologists and political scientists.

If the betterment of a society was, according to contemporary Victorian English view, achieved under conditions allowing the maximal personal freedom thru spontaneous 'natural' check and balances by the competing individuals, it was only logical that the Almighty, following the same principle, would likewise organize the living World. The weaker creatures would perish while the stronger, or more resourceful and prolific, would survive to perpetuate its kind. Thus Nature 'selected' the best; a wise mechanism accounting not only for the success of Man on Earth but, as well, for the triumph of the bourgeoisie over the preceding aristocratic order. The selection of the fittest provided a mean and justification, not only for an entire social class but also for Nature itself.

The works of Darwin and Wallace, appearing before the experiments of Mendel, provided for a 'mechanism' to clarity phenotypic variations and certainly, as we will see, furnished an speculative base for the ulterior theories of Wiserman and Nageli in Germany, which laid the groundwork from where the Science of Genetics became neo-Darwinian dogma as we know it today (See also Chapter V). Natural selection acting upon random mutations, by increasing the 'genetic pool' of a given characteristic, eventually gave rise to the 'fixation' or universal prevalence of its corresponding phenotypic expression.

Revealingly, the XX Century with its explosive development of Molecular Biology, had brought to us a new evolutionary concept at the molecular level, a concept in keeping with the fatalistic, perhaps aimlessness, post- Second World War society: That of the 'genetic drift' or fixation of neutral variations, in other words, the ultimate prevalence in a genetic population of random mutational changes with no noticeable useful SURVIVAL ADVANTAGE. This theory uphold by Motoo Kimura and collaborators (Scientific American, Nov. 1979, P. 98), utilized a mathematical analysis to reveal the possibility that these 'neutral' (not evolutionary advantageous) mutations could occasionally, and predictably, prevail in the genetic population. Although the authors do not claimed the possibility of extrapolating their results to phenotypic macroscopic evolution, the implication for the whole field of evolution is easily understandable. The World might not be necessarily populated by the 'fittest' but by the 'lucky', by those who occasionally statistics favor. A meaningful purposeful Universe suddenly vanishes from sight.

This, it should be emphasized, is not the coincidental chance of 'selectionist' theories pertaining the random mutational events (to be preserved or discarded according to their 'survival advantage'). On the contrary, 'genetic drift' proposes the preservation, and ultimately prevalence, of mutations in no way providing any potential survival benefits and in essence representing a statistical chance (the drift) superimposed in another chance (the mutation).

The theory, totally in keeping with the emotional makeup of the modern soul, is a vigorous indictment of rationality or of a logical ordering of natural phenomena (the Aristotelian entelechy), and in a sense it is a glorification of the absurd so much in vogue in the XX Century; a century which witnessed the mass imbecility of two world wars and lived and toiled under the constant threat of sudden annihilation or the, maybe even worse, present possibility of progressive spiritual impoverishment and/or the subjugation of man to the overwhelming demands of the 'machine'.

Just like evolutionary theories in Western costal Europe were based in the merchant-bourgeoisie ethic of progress, genetic drift is based in casual, fortuitous events with no reason for their occurrence other than the fulfillment of an statistical eventuality surrounded by a degree of incertitude and indefiniteness; perhaps much in tune with the ethic of the modern technocrat or organization man. Chance becomes the winner.

If evolutionary theories in biology provide a good example of how scientific theories are modeled after ethico-social factors as well as the uselessness and waste of speculation in human thought, I believe that Chemistry, of all disciplines invented by man, perhaps is the one conveying better the meaning of what that signifies. If closely followed, and impartially studied, the history of its development clearly displays the needless additions and monumental wastage of time and effort brought about by the urge to 'understand' causally, or to 'visualize' unseen relations and proportions rather than contenting oneself with the simple tabulations of facts and analysis of mutual relationships. It is my contention that such efforts to 'explain the unseen' have been of absolutely no help in the growth and development of this science which, I think, would have reached the same degree of modern complexity anyway.

This, I admit, is not easy to document and requires a careful selection of what is established fact from theory. To start with, the origin of Modern Chemistry in Alchemy is a well known fact mustering sufficient historic documentation; its cultural groundwork was being well fertilized since Early Antiquity. In the West, we had seen that, the Stoics are credited with an animistic belief. They thought that 'all things are alive' and reactions between material substances were considered logical manifestations of this inner life. Each object arouse and grew from a seed including its Form, sustained and energized by the universal all-pervading principle of 'pneuma'(See Chapter I).

Intimately associated with this belief was also that of the transmigration of the vital essence or Spirit from one material body to another by a process of death and resurrection. These convictions probably had a source in the fertility cults of ancient agricultural bronze-age civilizations, when frequently an emperor or king was immolated with his entire entourage as the eternal universal symbol of fertility; renewing itself every year and growing anew with each crop. Early manifestations of such associations are found in the manufacture of metals by the Assyrians, who considered the process a birth ritual. A Persian myth, dating back to approximately 500 B.C., also viewed the 'birth' of metals as the consequence of the death of a divine being which, when killed, cooper flowed from his bones, steel from his flesh, silver from his marrow, tin from his blood, lead from the head and, significantly, gold from his soul. Even in this early myth we can see the ancient, almost primeval, association of gold with the noblest attributes of Man and the World.

How and from what specific source these alchemical conceptions reached the West, or whether they were an autochthonous product, is not yet known with certainty and we can only speculate about that. Traditionally, Western alchemy has been considered a concoction of Greek metaphysics, Egyptian metallurgical expertise and Middle Eastern religions. Unquestionably its place of birth was the Hellenistic World at the time when the conquests of Alexander the Great had opened to the Greeks new cultural horizons and profited from the intercourse of other civilized people. Although the purpose of all alchemists was the transformation of base metals into gold, the Chinese version was more interested in the healing qualities of their products, so they mixed their metals with some 'medicine' seeking to produce gold; reputedly capable of bringing about eternal life.

Yet, and despite of these early differences, both the Eastern and Western versions of alchemical traditions came to develop similar metaphysical symbolisms and practices, probably resulting from the dissemination to the West of Chinese ideas when Arab culture 'wedge in' geographically between them, apparently assimilating from 'renegades' Nestorians refugees basic Western Alchemy, and from the East the concept of 'Medicine'; initiating a development that crystallized with the medieval 'philosopher stone'.

From the Chinese these Arabs apparently also acquired the reductionist approach of conceiving only two fundamental substances, sulfur and mercury, and perhaps with it the mystical duality of the Taoists about the dynamic dialectic of the Yin and Yang which appeared, although not explicitly, to have influenced the speculations of German Mystics and XVI Century Alchemists. From cannibar, a red substance, upon heating, two formative elements did separate; one silvery and stable (mercury), the Yin, and the other fiery and volatile (sulphur), the Yang, corresponding to the Aristotelian 'murky exhalation'.

Both in China and the West mercury and sulphur came to be considered as the generative principles of all substances, entering in a hidden form into the composition of everything. Also in both extremes of the civilized world there aroused a great preoccupation with the obtainment and transmutation into gold of base metals. Given the universal religious and mystical origin of alchemy, and considering the spiritual symbolism ascribed to the material properties of all substances, it is not difficult to surmise why this is so. Gold, the metal which could be 'melted a hundred times without being spoiled', as Ko Hang, the Chinese alchemist said, maintain the purity of its yellow splendor despite of all attempts to transform or debase its magnificence. No physical or chemical assault would corrupt its essence and therefore this metal became, for alchemists throughout the World, an allegoric representation of durability and incorruptibility. As such it was cherished for conferring immortality and became an obligatory component in every elixir, allegedly imparting these blessings upon their 'consumers'.

The mystical and practical aspects of alchemical processes, its numinous content and useful counterpart, were progressively separated and by the Third Century of our era (as exemplified in the Leiden and Stockholm papyri which were eminently practical, or the works of Zosimus eminently mystic and religious in content) they had completely done so. By the High Middle Ages alchemical practices were widespread in Europe and in the Muslim world, where they became further elaborated by a sect of sufists from Bactra: The Brethren of Purity.

So strong became the influence of alchemical notions in the West that it was proscribed by a bull of Pope John XXII in 1317. By then the quest for the elixir of immortality and for a reliable method of transmuting other elements into gold was in full swing. A system centering in mercury as the basic element was developed by Raymond Lull, in regard to the possibility of isolating 'the spirits' of terrestrial things thru the process of distillation. By heating, an intangible invisible vapor was separated from the liquids to be further condensed in the convolutions of the distilling apparatus, a concentrated elixir possessing all the essential attributes of the heated substances: its 'spirit'. This magical character, the portentous capability to reveal 'the hidden' composition of things, was what gave Alchemy its alluring quality, an appealing mysterious aura attracting millions of followers and precipitating the intervention of the Church; which immediately sensed the threat posed by such strange discipline to its basic institutions.

Lull thought that alcohol, one of the first 'spirits' so to be prepared by distillation from wines and beers (originally described in the XII Century by Magister Salernus) and widely regarded as the 'water of life', was actually an impure spirit because, upon distillation, it would separate into two different portions, an upper blue layer and a turbid lower one; similarly to the case of mercury which, he thought, did separate into Heavens and Earth at the primeval generation of all things. According to him one spirit would attract another, so he utilized distilled alcohol to 'extract' the spirits of other substances like plants and herbs, which were then widely used as beverages, perfumes and medicines.

The late alchemists became increasingly involved in the treatment of diseases and, in a sense, developed the apothecary tradition which collided more and more with the entrenched medical dogma of the day represented, above all, by the tyrannical everlasting authority of Galen and his followers. (See Chapter V). Forbidden by the Church, resented by physicians, bypassed or proscribed from the medieval universities and in the 'official' view considered a practice associated with black magic and devilish enterprises, Alchemy, nevertheless, survived the attrition of the High Middle Ages to, ironically enough, 'transmute' into the fruitful seed of Modern Chemistry.

The place was Switzerland, a land-locked country notorious for its mystical tradition, more precisely the well known town of Basle, the occasion an innocent enough student bonfire in the patio of the university and the 'culprit' a voluminous forceful man which we had met before: Aurelius Theophrastus Bombastus Von Hohenheim who, on that fateful date, had the audacity of symbolically commit to the fire the works of Avicenna and Galen.

Now, Theophrastus Bombastus was not small town alchemist. He literally honored his name by 'bomblasting' the fabric of medieval dogma and in the process antagonized so much the political, religious and academic establishment of the day that his tenure as professor in Basle did not last long after he commenced to invite apothecaries and surgeons to his lectures. Paracelsus (as he liked to be called) fame, however, was well deserved. He is supposed to have refurbished the old Hippocratic theory of disease as a 'dis-balance' of body humors, also introducing inorganic chemicals as Medicines because he insisted that the animal body contains salt besides the old alchemical elements (sulphur and mercury).

Above all, his view of life as a sort of chemistry and of therapeutics as an art of treating individual diseases with specific drugs (instead of the old panaceas) have a surprising modern ring. As we have already seen Paracelsus was also a mystic in the Central European tradition and his doctrines were imbued with vitalistic assumptions and the belief that he was divinely inspired. (See Chapters I,V)

Paracelsus lived and toiled during a period of revolutionary ferment in Central Europe (when Luther shocked the foundation of the Western Church and Copernicus unfolded his heliocentric system). His rebelliousness was well received by the youth in many places and at times he seems to have lived a dissolute life, almost as an errant mendicant. His enemies accused him of being a charlatan or quack and, it is true, that his prodigious intellect generated exuberantly wild speculations without the faintest scientific foundation. Little useful serious work could be ascribed to him, and yet, his inconformity appeared to have had a salutary influence, contributing to the rekindling of an intellectual mood which, after remaining dormant in Europe for almost 2000 years, was to spread as wildfire in the next two centuries.

The Iatrochemical School, which more forceful proponent was Paracelsus, was further pursued and developed by another man we already have met before: John Baptist Helmont from Brussels. (See Chapter I). As in the case of his predecessor and followers Van Helmont scorned the rationalists, particularly the deductive logic of mathematics, which had commenced to take force in England with Bacon and later in France under Descartes. He continued to maintain the primacy of mystic insights into the works of Nature although, curiously enough, also he stressed the importance of the Empiric Method by insisting in observation, measurements, and the value of analogy (also emphasized by Paracelsus); something which could be considered a precondition to the inductive method.

Van Helmont busied himself with obtaining the 'spirits' of many substances, but in the process discovered some that could not be subsequently condensed and he called 'gases', rightly pointing to their natures. Yet, as in the case of other vitalist thinkers, he also gave a numinous interpretation to his discoveries and thought these gases were the souls of the substances from where they were extracted.

In Ontology he, like Thales and the Milesians before, came to consider water as the original and most important element, after performing a curious experiment which appeared to prove the thesis. He planted a bush in a pot with a weighted amount of earth and watered it regularly for several years. He then weighted it again together with the pot. The bush did become much heavier (about one hundred pounds more) but the earth was the same. From these results Van Helmont concluded that, inasmuch as he only added water to the pot, then the extra weight of the bush resulted solely from the water; a very logical empiric assumption based in the aggregated knowledge of the age[2]. In Medicine Van Helmont maintained ideas identical to Paracelsus, in the sense that each disease was a true independent entity that when invading the organism (becoming an 'unknown guest') came to reside in an organ. Obviously, therefore, treatments, did have to be a 'specific' Medicine directed to evict from the body the given malady. (See also Chapter V)

The rejection of a mechanistic explanation for natural phenomena, the idea of life as a chemical factory and disease as a dis-balance caused by the intrusion of an unknown 'spirit' in the fabric of the body, are by far the most practical aspects of Iatrochemistry, from where grew a chemical tradition which direct ascertainable consequence was the enormous proliferation of therapeutic recipes; constituting in essence the backbone of medical pharmacopeia until the recent past.

The idea of 'vital spirits' as explanation for chemical reactions in general, and of life in particular, continued to dominate Centro-European scientific development and in the XVIII Century flourished into a robust dynamic theory which found staunch supporters and followers throughout Europe, including the bulwarks of mechanistic philosophy: France and England. This theory, advanced by Georg Ernst Stahl as an explanation for some phenomena related to combustion proposed the existence of an intangible chemical substance, labeled by them 'phlogiston', capable of explaining the odd transformations taking place both in the combustible body and the surrounding 'air'. Because I believe that the historical vicissitudes of this theory is revealing as to the manner the human mind understands and relate to its environment, it will be briefly sketch in its general characteristics.

The British chemists of the XVII Century had compared, by a

process of analogy akin to the Paracelsian method, combustion with the physiology of respiration. Following the lead of Robert Boyle, who had made the observation that an animal as well as the flame of a candle would both 'die' when placed in a closed air-tight container, Robert Hooke and Richard Lower found that dark blood did become bright red when exposed to air and, likewise, that in a suffocated animal, it was dark red but not so when aired with bellows. Following close on their heels their countryman John Mayow proposed that the combustion principle in air was a kind of particle (he and other mechanistic philosophers subscribed to the atomic theory of matter), which he called nitroso-air particles. Hooke had discovered a few years previously that saltpeter and gun powder burned in the absence of air and concluded that they carried within themselves the principle of combustion (they called it nitrogen), considered to be bound somehow to the air particles.

The postulation of the hypothesis of these 'piggy-bag' particles led British early chemical inquires into a blind alley. Nobody had ever 'seen', even less measure in any way, these invisible entities and, because the prevalence of the empiricist view point in England, soon the upholders of such theories were the subject of derision. On the other hand, and perhaps only naturally, such atomistic and mechanistic views of combustion could not appeal the German and Centro European spirit which, after a languishing period in the XVII, erupted anew in activity during the XVIII Century with the 'Phlogiston' Theory. This theory was entirely in keeping with the premises and ideas of the Iatrochemists and earlier alchemists and mystics who assumed that all substances and objects were made up of matter and a soul or spirit (Phlogiston) representing, in this context, the essential component which separated during combustion, and was therefore the combustible principle in all substances capable of undergoing such process.

But the phlogiston theoreticians did not stop in the formulation of a presumptive explanation for the phenomena of combustion. They proceeded also to measure the changes in weight resulting from this combustion, that is, they measured the bodies before and after it and in so doing found a perplexing loss of weight during the process. But intriguingly, in some cases, as in the calcination of metals (also considered by Stahl and rightly so a form of combustion) exactly the opposite took place: The metals actually gained weight. The results appeared in all respects contradictory and the inconsistency obviously should have, in ordinary circumstances, deterred against a blind endorsement of their hypothesis; but surprisingly enough that did not happened. A totally absurd explanation was found to salvage phlogiston: It was assumed that in some cases this principle had negative weight or positive lightness (something similar to water buoyancy) and so to account for the presumptive discrepancy!

The theory of phlogiston, despite such basic weaknesses, became very popular and found staunch supporters in Joseph Black, Henry Cavendish and Joseph Priestley. Black and his student, Daniel Rutherford, collected a gas evolved in the calcination of magnesium carbonate (which also lost weight in the reaction) and found that identical loss of weight and formation of gas took place upon treatment of the carbonate by an acid. Furthermore, these investigators also found that this gas had the same properties of what Boyle called 'factitious air', which they renamed 'fixed air' (and we today know as CO_2). This 'air', they further found out, did not support combustion or life when isolated and was assumed to be phlogiston itself.

The next experiment consisted in placing a lighted candle and mice inside sealed containers and, again, after a while they died. The gas left behind in the flasks appeared to have the same properties as the 'fixed air' obtained after the calcination of magnesium carbonate. The hypothesis advanced by them to explain the experimental results was that, as the candle burned or the mice breathe, there was a constant release of phlogiston which eventually did saturate the container. At this point no more phlogiston was allowed to leave the candle's flame or the mice breath and both, the fire and the life process, came to an abrupt end.

Shortly thereafter into the scene stepped Priestly who, upon heating mercury with a magnifying glass and the sun rays (then in vogue), discovered the formation on top of the metal of a reddish colored pellicle that, after been separated and further heated, gave rise to two 'vapors': One which upon condensation was found to be the same mercury and another which will not condense no matter how much he tried. He also discovered that this new gas did have some very interesting and peculiar properties. For instance, a flame will glow in it with unusual brightness and the combustion was more lively and easier. Likewise a mice placed in it did move faster and appeared much more active than in plain ordinary air. He himself breathed the 'gas' and found it very easy to breathe indeed.

Intriguingly, the gas Priestly isolated appeared to have properties in exact contraposition to the 'phlogisticated' air of Black and Rutherford. As a matter of fact it could not be anything other than 'dephlogisticated air' (still air was assumed to be a single element).To him the explanation of what had happened was as follows: The mercury, upon heating and 'rusting', first lost phlogiston and became more 'avid' for it. Upon further isolation and heating then phlogiston returned to the mercury so completely during the formation of the 'vapors' that what remained lost all its phlogiston. The apparent discrepancy of the gaining of weight in some cases upon combustion and rusting, and its loss in others was then 'explained' thus: Upon heating, the metals first lost phlogiston and because of its positive 'lightness' the flask and its contents did gain some weight. Subsequently, upon further heating, they absorbed phlogiston again and therefore lost weight. In this way the theory was vindicated and neatly explained both combustion and calcination. The ancient notion that fire was one of the primitive elements together with air, water and earth, hold its ground and remained a valid 'explanation'. Phlogiston was the 'substratum' and indispensable constituent of this fire.

Now, there was a young chemist in France named Antoine Laurent Lavoisier who disliked, in fact strongly disagreed, with the idea of such a principle as 'phlogiston'. Above all he could not conceive of any truly material substance which could have negative weight. That, he thought, would contradict all other available evidence. It did have to be a unique example of 'levitation' for which there was no precedent or paragon; actually such hypothesis would have challenge the universality and applicability of Newton's laws of gravitation, thus negating one of the cornerstones of the new Physics. Lavoisier was a meticulous man and commenced by repeating the experiments of his predecessors, which he thought gave rise to discrepancies and inconsistencies. (Ibid. P. 307)

Lavoisier, who had already disproved the contention of Van Helmont that, upon boiling, water was partially converted to earth (he showed that the formed sediment was material from the glass), began by repeating the experiment of Boyle with the calcination of tin. As in the case of his predecessor he corroborated the fact of an increase in weight. He then repeated again the experiment heating the tin, but now with the flask sealed. Intriguingly, the flask and its contents did not change weight. If the tin increase in weight, but the entire closed system did not, the air in the flask did have to weigh less than before, that is, a partial vacuum must have formed. This line of reasoning he then proceeded to prove by opening the flask and observing air rushing in; the attendant increase in weight now was equal to that of the piece of tin.

Lavoisier therefore had proved his point about a change in the air as the tin calcinated but many questions remained unanswered, above all, why only part of the air was bound to the tin. Upon repetition of the experiment, again only part of the air was used in the reaction and what was left had the properties of Boyle 'fixed air'. Perhaps the used up portion was the elusive phlogiston which then needed to have a positive rather than a negative weight.

In the year 1774 Priestly visited Paris and communicated to Lavoisier his isolation of 'dephlogisticated' air, which had been obtained shortly before by Scheele also. Lavoisier did not lose anytime in repeating the experiment, corroborating the results. He then proceeded to calcinate the tin in this new gas and confirmed that it was completely consumed in the process. Air, he found out, was not a pure element; on the contrary, it was a mixture of this element of combustion (which he named 'oxygen'-Greek sourness producing) and an inert component: 'nitrogen'. (At first he had thought oxygen was 'pure air', the remaining been 'impurities', but was convinced otherwise by Scheele).

Lavoisier became so infatuated with the idea of oxygen that he promoted this element to the category of a paramount explanatory principle. To many, however, oxygen appeared nothing else but phlogiston in reverse. Then, there were other inconsistencies. Respiration, since the times of Hooke and Mayow, was assumed to be a form of combustion. Lavoisier measured the amount of oxygen breathed in and collected the 'fixed air' coming out (carbon anhydrate), finding a discrepancy. If matter was not created or destroyed during a chemical transformation, as Lavoisier claimed, where then part of the oxygen went?

New developments in Britain were now to prove of momentous importance. Both Priestly and Cavendish had isolated a very light gas by the action of a diluted acid in metals. This gas was very flammable, almost explosively so, and Cavendish thought it was phlogiston itself. If that was the case, on combining with oxygen (considered to be 'dephlogisticated air') it would have produced normal or 'fixed air' according to the proportional amounts of each. When both, he and Priestly, carried out the experiment to their surprise they detected a liquid in the condensation chamber...it was water!

When Lavoisier repeated the experiment he discovered that two volumes of the new gas (hydrogen) did combined with one of 'oxygen' and concluded that water was NOT an element, as the ancients had believed, but a compound of these two gases; namely the oxide of hydrogen. The reason why a metal upon been treated with a diluted acid released hydrogen (Cavendish phlogiston) while its calx equally treated did not was, according to his conclusions, because the pure metal would combine with the oxygen of the water first and subsequently with the acid, releasing the hydrogen of the water, while the calx upon being acted by the acid would directly associate with it producing water in the reaction without any escape of gas. He also then was able to 'explain' why, in the act of respiration, he could not account for all the inhaled oxygen by the volume of fixed air exhaled; some was transformed into the water that damped the apparatus and was thought before to be a pure element unrelated to oxygen.

Lavoisier then proceeded to solemnly inaugurate a new epoch in chemistry. Madame Lavoisier committed the books of Stahl and other Iatrochemists to the pyre, in the same symbolic fashion of Paracelsus when he threw the works of Galen and Avicenna into the student's bonfire. No longer, she claimed, was there any more need to postulate the existence of a 'combustion principle'. Fire was not an 'element', as the Greeks believed, but a dynamic entity, the result of a chemical change or rather the 'perceptual' component of that process with a giving off of light, heat and smoke. No occult or hidden 'material reality' was behind the phenomena, and there was no need to postulate any other possibility when what was already known could be easily explained by the existence of the recently discovered gases. Lavoisier postulates appeared more solid and unassailable than ever. Phlogiston, the famous esoteric substance that meant different things for different people at different times, became a useless and dispensable notion not needed to 'explain' nature and although Priestly, as well as Cavendish, defended it at all costs to the end of their lives the theory lost support, became unpopular and finally died away.

Lavoisier greatest contribution to Science, before his head was eventually severed by the merciless workings of the guillotine, was his emphasis in a scrupulous method. He refused to believe in the promulgated vagaries of the phlogiston theory and endorsed a vigorous approach which can only be defined as modern. He demonstrated that simple, accurate measurements were sufficient to unsettle old beliefs. His unswerving materialism and intolerance for the inconsistencies inherent in the Phlogiston Theory can be considered a manifestation of the Enlightment 'Spirit'. Perhaps Lavoisier was also instrumental in the final break of the last link between science and religion, which had been surreptitiously embodied in this theory. Man was to replace the numinous content of Nature with a 'realistic view'.

Once an objectively verifiable hypothesis was at hand (The Principle of Conservation of Mass) permitting to 'explain' and account for all the phenomena related to combustion, it was possible for Lavoisier to use 'Ockham razor' and solemnly dispense with superfluous ideas and theories. Yet, and interestingly enough, the British chemists were those who performed all the investigative works that doomed the Phlogiston Theory by displaying its flaws, despite of not being able to draw the proper conclusions from their experiments and instead clinging to the old beliefs until the end of their lives. It is only ironic that Lavoisier, the man to whom we owed the birth of modern chemistry because of his ability to 'keep his head on' during the important formative period of this science, ended up by losing it to the French Revolution.

The history of phlogiston, I believe, is revealing as to the form and mode that scientific enterprises are conducted and achieved, in general representing a dramatic example of what constitute real progress in such endeavors. Natural phenomena are recorded and a rational hypothesis to account for and clarify them is advanced, preferably if it possesses predictive value. Phlogiston, although capable to do so for combustion, was confronted with the inconsistency in the weight of the reactants which was subsequently, upon repetition of the experiments in a closed system, shown to be due to changes in the composition of air (then discovered not to be an element) resulting from the transformation of a combustible substance mediated by 'oxygen' into 'fixed air'(carbon dioxide) and water; which was also discovered not to be an element.

Now, two preconditions had been necessary before the acceptance of the conclusions of Lavoisier: Firstly, the tacit acquiescence with the scientific postulates of objectivity and verifiability, that is to say, conclusions in Science could only come about and be 'accepted' by careful observation and measurements of physical phenomena, as Bacon did advocate. Secondly, the validity of the assumption that what we believe are meaningful events should be concatenated or interfaced in such a manner as to allow the application of the Inductive Method in Science, in other words, the formulation of general laws extrapolated from the observation of particular instances of a given 'happening'. In addition the experimental facts before being accepted need CORROBORATION, that is, repetition of the experiments by independent researchers

Lavoisier vehement defense of the premise that 'matter is neither created or destroyed but only transforms itself' was a crucial formulation. Perhaps he intuitively sensed that this notion was pivotal to the further development of Chemistry, because it permitted the acceptance of the investigative works being conducted at the time. Were it not because of this acceptance Chemistry would have face formidable obstacles to its development, and although we now know Lavoisier premises were only valid at OUR COSMIC LEVEL OF EXISTENCE (a fact that should alert us as to the limitations of the scientific method and the danger of extrapolating conclusion to different universal realms), this 'conservation law' served the purpose of clarifying this important issue in the development of Chemistry.

Yet, as we will now see, in following years some ancient beliefs were going to be resuscitated and eventually dominated the theory and practice of Chemistry and Physics even up to the present time. The next chapter of its history is, in my opinion, even more revealing. It commenced, we might say, where the 'Phlogiston Chapter' ended, fittingly with the ostentatious burning by Madame Lavoisier of the books of Stahl and the Iatrochemists. I believe it arbitrarily closed with a faithful gathering of prominent chemists at Karlsruhe, where a 'rape' of a sort took place.

In 1811 Amadeus Avogadro professor of Physics at Turin, made an interesting and surprising claim: Identical volumes of any gas at same conditions of pressures and temperatures should have AN EQUAL NUMBER OF ATOMS (at that time it was assumed that 'molecules' were made of single 'atoms'). This famous hypothesis was appealing because it would have finally permitted to 'elucidate' the actual molecular structures and the true elemental weights of all atoms. Ampere in 1814 made identical suggestion and some investigators began drawing tables of 'atomic weights'.

Some complications of theoretical and practical nature, however, impeded the wide acceptance of Avogadro's hypothesis. In the first place, such an authority as Dalton flatly denied it. For him one of the most important inherent qualities of chemical substances was, precisely, that the number of atoms per unit of volume depended on their size and weight. On the other hand, it was observed that when identical volumes of chlorine gas and hydrogen combined to produce hydrochloric acid the volume of the compound was not half of the sum of the reactant volumes, as Avogadro would have predicted, but equal to that sum. If the hypothesis was correct the only possible alternative was that chlorine and hydrogen natural states were di-atomic molecules which, according to Dalton, were an impossibility inasmuch as atoms of same kind should repel each other.

For the next fifty years chemistry remained in a state of confusion. Equivalent weights served a useful practical purpose but in the nascent field of Organic Chemistry the investigators were unable to 'visualize' the molecular constitutions and structures of chemical compounds. In 1860 August Kekule, a notable German chemist best known for his 'clarification' of the atomic structure of the Benzene nuclei, convoked a conference in Karlsruhe to interchange ideas in an attempt to dissipate the perplexity then prevalent. During the conference the Italian representative, expounded vigorously the Avogadro's hypothesis which had been rejected 50 years before. He reminded his audience about the need for 'clarifying' the atomic weights of all known chemical element so the mysteries and vagaries of molecular architectures and composition could be permanently dissipated. To this effect it was mandatory the acceptance of his compatriot ideas as to the constancies of atomic (or molecular) number in identical volumes of different gases, under same conditions of pressure and temperature.

The molecular weight of a gaseous compound, he claimed, could be determined by comparing its vapor density to that of hydrogen as a unit which, because he considered the hydrogen diatomic, should then be multiply by two. By choosing the smallest weight of a given element entering into the composition of its different compounds the atomic weight could then be determined.

It has been claimed that many of the scientists gathered in Karlsruhe remained unconvinced but in the following years the cherished Avogadro's hypothesis became quietly and generally accepted. For one thing, it represented the 'only' way of determining the atomic weight and molecular constitutions of chemical compounds. Nobody ever did or could possibly count, even less compared, the number of molecules in a given volume of gases at identical conditions of pressures and temperatures, but the need to compromise was too great to refuse the acceptance of the 'Avogadro's number'.

Chemists, like other scientists, had always thought and still think, that 'visualizing' molecular structures is very important. That allows them, the claim goes, to 'understand' better the nature of chemical reactions, to 'envisage' what is going on and, even more important from the practical stand point, to 'predict' what products, and in what proportions, would be formed when two reactants come together in a chemical reaction[3]

In the late 1860's Meyer, from Germany and Mendeleev, from Russia, both proposed a periodic law of variation in the properties of elements according to their atomic weights. Furthermore, Mendeleev described the properties of three of these presumptive elements years in advance of their eventual discovery. This, of course, was a resounding success which, in the eyes of all, ratified the correctness of the 'atomic theory' of matter. In fact such beliefs had not been seriously questioned, or challenged, in the hundred years elapsed since its acceptance by the scientific community. Because, at least, four generations of humanity have grown taking them for granted almost as a 'second nature', it becomes enormously difficult to analyze the situation with complete impartiality. Yet, it is important that we do so if we are going to really understand the purpose and method of science in the light of the internal organization and function of the perceiving organ 'per excellence': The Human Brain.

Man, we have to emphasize is a VISUAL ANIMAL. He understands his environment and relates to it visually. Our vocabulary is filled with words and expressions symbolizing this bias. We have to 'see in order to belief', goes the biblical expression of doubting Thomas and, literally, of human skepticism in general. We 'imagine' things (which come from the noun 'image'). A person, we say, does not 'picture', when he or she is incapable to understand something. It is a curious and baffling fact that nobody, as far as I know, whether scientist or layman, had ever, for instance, been preoccupied or concerned with the 'sound', 'taste' or 'feel' of an atom; we are only interested in how 'it looks'.

Let me clarify that I am not suggesting that the atomic theory NECESSARILY has to be wrong. What I am claiming is that its uncontested endorsement by modern physics and chemistry as the only true reality, is a presupposition resulting from a cognitive bias of man based, at least partially, in the fundamentalist approach of the Greeks, that passion to reduce phenomena to their minimal expression in order to facilitate comprehension, and also in man strange addiction to visual models as to 'how things work'. In the light of these considerations CHEMICAL FORMULAS MIGHT REPRESENT NOTHING MORE THAN SHORTHAND NOTATIONS EMBODYING THE MULTIPLE POSSIBLE CHEMICAL PROPERTIES OF A GIVEN SUBSTANCE, INCLUDING THE INFORMATION NEEDED TO PREDICT WHAT THE OUTCOME OF CHEMICAL REACTIONS WILL BE IN ANY SPECIFIC CASE. The formulas are compromises arrived at after an elaborated process of selection of the best possible 'code'; they condense and summarize the existing knowledge about a 'compound' and serve a useful, practical purpose. ANY ABBREVIATION SYSTEM WITH INCLUSION OF EVERY POSSIBLE PROPERTY OF A SUBSTANCE WOULD HAVE SERVED IDENTICAL PURPOSE AS THE 'ATOMIC THEORY'. Even the predictions of Mendeleev would have been possible by relating equivalent weights to chemical properties of the 'elements'. The gaps in the periodic table would have been found anyway.

If scientific theorizing is the result of man strive to 'see' the unseen by creating familiar models borrowed from his immediate experience and from societal organizational patterns, there are other instances when the problem has been, ironically enough, the opposite; in other words, true understanding has been impeded by man refusal to open his eyes and look around, as well as, his reluctance to accept facts and instead stubbornly cling to old dogmatic beliefs. The history of the discovery of blood circulation provides a beautiful case in point.

The Aristotelian theories embodied in Galenic conceptions, converted to Medieval dogma by Late Antiquity, had it that there was a triadic hierarchy of humors in the human body (we had seen that triads of all kinds abounded in religious beliefs at that time) to match three 'functional categories'. The dark blood was related to vegetative functions and centered its anatomical location in the liver. The red blood related to motions and animal kinetics, centering in the heart. Finally, the nervous fluids, controlling nervous irritability and sensitivity centered in the brain. All these 'humors' were totally independent and unconnected in any way.

Now, it seems to me that, somebody during the near 1 1/2 millennium lapsing from Galen to Servetus should have, at least, 'thought' about the possibility of a 'circulation' of the blood. The idea, however, was taboo, since medieval dogma had incorporated the Aristotelian views ascribing circular motions only to celestial, therefore divine, bodies. Mental barriers of this order seemed to have 'blinded' people and impeded any real physiological progress.

It was only by the time of the Renaissance, when a new intolerance to existing beliefs began to manifest itself in some quarters, that man began to open their eyes to nature in an inquiring fashion. The first outburst of dissent was, of course, the Copernican revolution with its heliocentric world view and the demotion of circular trajectories from its divine throne; further establishing that imperfect material bodies, like the 'Evil Earth', also followed circular paths in its celestial wanderings. Once this theory with all its implications and consequences was accepted it certainly led the door opened to search for additional 'circularities'. Michael Servetus, Professor of Medicine at the Sorbonne, was the first to challenge Galenic ideas. He expressed vocally the opinion that the blood 'circulates' from the right chambers of the heart thru the lungs and back to the heart, but to its left chambers.

Such a hypothesis, it has to be understood, completely contradicted Galen's teachings inasmuch as it pointed to a UNITARAN view of the bloody fluids. But unfortunately Servetus also was a Unitarian in other more 'dangerous' matters. He, for instance, adamantly opposed the belief in that pillar of Christian Church' principles' explicitly expressed and accepted in the First Ecumenical Council at Nicaea: God's Trinity. Instead he endorsed the 'heretical' Arian concept that the Son could not be co-eternal with the Father, and further considered that the Holy Ghost was only an intangible exhalation: 'The breath of God' as he defined it; a 'pneuma' of the World. Man therefore in the act of respiration infuses himself with the Holy Spirit.

Servetus did make also two important shrewd physiological observations which seemed to support his basic assumptions. On the one hand he pointed out that the caliber of the pulmonary artery was larger than expected if the blood going to the lungs had only a nourishing function (as it was held at the time), and on the other he called attention upon the fact that the blood in the pulmonary veins was 'ruddy', rather than 'dark' as in the artery. The difference, he concluded, was the result of the 'purification' it underwent by the pneuma in the lungs, which became the abode of continuous 'covenant' with the Holy Ghost. As a matter of fact he went even beyond, to claim that the blood itself was the soul of man, a conviction which engendered one of the charges brought against him by Calvin; who thought that such a notion implied the finitude of the soul (because the blood did 'die' with the body) and that was a heresy.

Servetus paid with his life for those daring 'outrageous' religious ideas and in the pyre where he burned also were placed most of his books. Yet, the challenge he posed to established dogma was not lost. Andrea Vesalius, his pupil, who subsequently established the impossibility that the blood could traverse the cardiac septum (as Galen had maintained), brought Servetus theories with him to Padua, destined to become an 'avant guard' center for medical studies in the years to follow.

Paralleled to the notion of the circular motion of the blood which Servetus, perhaps not totally disentangled from Aristotelian influences, was close to call 'divine', there was also a promotion of the heart to the prominence of most important organ of the body ("The first to live, the source of heat in the middle of the body"-he commented). If the Sun was the center of circular motion to the planets, by extension the heart became in a sense the center of the blood 'revolution'. The comparison with the 'king of planets' was not far off. Cesalpino, who is credited with the first complete enunciation of the circulation theory of the blood, (also Bruno made reference to it) and William Harvey explicitly stated such comparison.[4]

The idea of the equivalence of Man and Nature having its roots in ancient agrarian societies had been a never dying subterranean current in humanity, finding an explicit representation in the conceptions of Harvey. Not surprisingly he was a disciple of Fabricus, a prominent Paduan himself and disciple of Columbus (a colleague of Vesalius) who came to hold beliefs very similar to Servetus (probably influenced by him and so closing the 'line of continuity' to Harvey). Fabricus had discovered the venous valves, but Harvey was the first to attribute the right function to these appendages, that is, to assure the irreversible progression of blood toward the heart which, supported by the 'one way distribution' of their cardiac counterparts, provided an anatomical substratum for the circulatory theory. Harvey dissected extensively the arterial and venous trees and, although he was unable to discover the microscopic capillary network links, concluded 'rationally' the need for their existence because, he argued, otherwise the blood would need continuously to form and destroy itself, something unconceivable, particularly after it was demonstrated that the amount of blood passing thru the heart in one hour exceeded the weight of a man.

Harvey, perhaps unavoidably considering the social and cultural 'climate' of his times, shrouded his works with quasi-religious ideas akin, in many respects, to Servetus 'promulgations'. He held, for instance, that the heart produced 'vital spirits' and shared the latter opinion that 'the soul of man is the blood'. Nevertheless, his extensive investigations in more than 40 different animal species convinced him that the heart was a hollowed muscle with the specific function of propelling the passing blood, in other words, a sort of bellows.

Harvey toward the end of his life enjoyed a deserved fame and a comfortable economic position. Although unable to discover 'the ultimate link' (the blood capillaries) demanded by his circulation theory, his works extant as a typical example of inferential conclusions based in collected information by means of observations, that is to say, of scientific empiricism. They represent a 'Baconian' feat (oddly enough, although contemporaries, these two men never seem to have met each other) supported firstly by a perceived analogy, perhaps better definable as 'mystical' and ancestral to humanity, of similarities between the 'constitution' of man and the Universe, an harmonious correspondence of structural and functional components between both dimensions, and secondly, in a commonsensical (that characteristically British notion) belief in the necessary existence of 'channels' of communication between arteries and veins, after a refusal to accept the alternate hypothesis of continuous formation at the venous and destruction at the arterial end of the vascular system.

Harvey's empiric conclusions were reasonable but by no means represented, as many historians of Medicine wanted us to believe, a 'final prove' of circulation; inasmuch as he could not conclusively prove the existence of the blood channels of communication between the arterial and venous compartments. Such ultimate prove was only provided by the works of Malpighi, who discovered by direct visualization thru the microscope the 'existence' of the putative ultramicroscopic 'avenues of communication', and by Anthony van Leeuwenhoek who observed the passing of blood thru the capillaries in the tail of a tadpole and in the foot of a frog. (See also Chapter V)

The history of blood circulation provides a revealing example as to the nature, scope and limits of the empiric inductive scientific method. Harvey's conclusions that a means of conveyance, a bridge between the venous and arterial systems, did exist was an extension, or extrapolation, to the particular case of blood motion of notions based in everyday common place experience in man's immediate environment, in other words, that a way of communication needed to 'exist' in order to transport something from one place to another, because blood could not have formed at the venous end and destroyed at the arterial terminus of the vascular system AT A RATE comparable to its intravascular velocity; another inference based in experiences drawn from man's immediate environment AND JUSTIFIED BY THEIR ULTIMATE ACCESSIBILITY TO DIRECT VISUAL CORROBORATION.

In this specific case the use of the Empiric Method proved a resounding success. The 'speed' of blood's motion was a clue as to the reality of the unseen channels between the arteries and veins providing for a doubly 'closed' circular system. Yet, it cannot be emphasized enough, it is a misconception to consider that Harvey provided the ultimate 'prove'. As it was said before THAT was only assured with the discoveries of the microscopic channels by Malpighi and the actual 'transit' of blood thru these channels by Leeuwenhoek.

Man's discovery of blood circulation was a deliberate search into a process, an inquire made possible by a radical change of attitude in society from blind acceptance of revered dogma to an empiric method which lent credibility to sensual perception as the true, and for many ONLY possible source of knowledge. This 'open eye' mood permitted the Copernican revolution against Hellenistic beliefs weaved into the fabric of Christian fundamental creed and served as a preamble, perhaps necessary, to Harvey's Theory.

A new freedom from intellectual constrains, anew intolerance and rebelliousness against established dogma was a kind of underlining mood that appropriated the powerful 'new' (perhaps it should better be considered rediscovered) empiric method, allowing suddenly to unveil a novel series of 'circularities' in Nature, which curiously enough, appeared to have been 'suppressed' by human bigotry till then. It hardly needs to be emphasized that all types of scientific 'advances' require identical type of unconformity against established dogmas.

The ultimate prove the human intellect demand, and accepts, is the DIRECT CONFIRMATION OF WHATEVER IS BEEN INVESTIGATED, in the sense that Malpighi and Leeuwenhoek 'saw' the passage of blood thru the capillaries (or else a verified recording from a measuring apparatus of experimental facts). These are the only kind of true 'discoveries' and the only true type of demonstrations acceptable as knowledge in the physical sciences. But when man searches into universal dimensions forbidden to his direct ascertainment, theorizing, the creation of explanatory models, becomes progressively more and more difficult the farther removed from our immediate surrounding we explore, in fact becoming in some cases a hindrance to knowledge, as we will soon see. Its validity is limited and useful at our cosmic level of existence, but increasingly questionable the farther we search in our quests.

Man can also be deceived by his senses or emotions even in something conceivably as simple as these recordings of 'observational' facts. The fallacy that science is an objective, emotionally detached, intellectual activity carried out by cool dispassionate devotees could be easily dispelled by mentioning a single revealing instance which historic evolution, in many respects, represent a parody of the process of 'scientific discovery' in general.

At the turn of the XX Century the scene in the field of Physics was in ferment. Wilhelm Roentgen had just discovered the X-rays, which energetic power miraculously penetrated many objects opaque to conventional 'light', and Madame Curie had serendipitously also 'stumbled over' radioactivity. After 1895 the much decorated prestigious professor Rene Blondlot, of the University of Nancy in France, became heavily involved in X-rays research. He was particularly interested in clarifying the 'nature' of such fascinating 'disturbances', in other words, in the 'elucidation' of whether the rays in question represented 'particles' or, as Foucault had 'shown' for light, electromagnetic 'waves'. Knowing that particles from an electrical source, carrying an electrical charge, will be deflected in an electrified field while waves will only be polarized, he aligned an stop-gap detector with different orientations in the presumptive trajectory of the generated rays, hoping that an increase in brightness from the spark of the detector would appear in certain orientation indicating the polarization in such position of the radiation, therefore an incontrovertible evidence of the wave nature of the rays (at that time the postulated dual nature, wave-particle, of microcosmic phenomena had not been yet enunciated and these events were either viewed as one or the other with the exclusion of the opposite modality).

To his delight Blondlot discovered an increase in the spark brightness for certain specific positions of the stop-gap detector, but subsequently he realized with dismay that the radiation in question could be deflected by a quartz prism; something impossible for X-rays. There was then, of course, the possibility that what the stop-gap was detecting as increased brightness might had been some contaminant 'light' from the source.

To investigate, and possible to rule out, this possibility he then proceeded to enclose the detector in a cardboard box known to be opaque to 'ordinary' light and then repeated the experiment. Again to make the setup as 'objective' as possible he included under the detector a photographic film covered by a ground glass screen to magnify the presumptive sensitization of the latter. To his delight Blondlot detected increased impressions upon the photographic film corresponding to the intervals of radiation generation by the source. Now, if the radiation penetrated thru card board opaque to ordinary light, but on the other hand was also deflected by quartz prisms, something that X-rays did not do, it was obvious, he concluded, that it represented the effect of a 'new' type of radiation, a kind of hybrid between conventional light and X-rays; undoubtedly a revolutionary discovery of far reaching consequences.

In the months and years following Blondlot 'discovery' at Nancy numerous investigators in France and outside its frontiers, attested to the veracity of his findings by repeating successfully his experiments. Unquestionably science was bearing witness to yet another earth-shaking revelation of Nature, one of his jealously hidden secrets. The N-rays, as they were called, proved to possess strange and intriguing qualities indeed. As a matter of fact they were opaque to those substances transparent to ordinary light, like water and rock salt, and on the other hand transparent to those substances opaque to such light, like wood, paper, sheets of iron and other metals, even including gold.

Likewise the rays were found to be emitted by innumerable sources including, not only heated pieces of silver, sheath of iron and some popular lamps used at the turn of the XX Century, but also astral objects like the sun and even the human body! This last point was, perhaps not too surprisingly, discovered by one of Blondlot colleagues at Nancy: Professor Agustin Charpentier from the faculty of Medical Physics.

Again, and quite predictably, in the months after the publication of Blondlot findings many other scientists claimed priority in the 'discoveries', adducing that they had been the first to 'investigate' such remarkable radiations; but all were summarily and 'officially' dismissed by the prestigious French Academy of Sciences, which then proceeded ceremoniously to bestowed upon Blondlot, in 1904, the Grand Prix Leconte, including an award of 50000 francs. Although the prize, pointedly, was awarded on the basis of 'the whole of his works' it appeared at the time, according to popular belief circulating in France, that the discovery of the N-rays certainly had been the most important factor in the decision to laureate Blondlot with such honor; which constituted a most welcome stimulus for the continuation of research in that field.

To give an idea of the degree of encouragement resulting from the bestowal of the Prix Leconte in the year to follow Blondlot's prize, the number of publications related to N-rays grew astronomically from four papers to a total of 54, coming to a sudden halt following, pointedly enough, criticisms leveled to the researches by the American physicist R.W. Wood, who visited France and Blondlot laboratories about that time. (See the 'N-ray story' by Irving M. Klutz Scientific American, May 1978, P. 168)

This curious episode, I believe, is revealing to something fundamental in the scientific method: Knowledge of facts needs CORROBORATION, in other words, before it is established conclusively that something is the case it is mandatory that the results obtained by an experimenter be consistently reproduced by INDEPENDENT OBSERVERS. (See the Conclusion). Consensus therefore is a primordial necessity, a precondition to the acceptance of experimental evidence. Subscription to a postulate of 'objectivity' at all costs eventually was what alienated the scientific community from the trust and belief in N-rays and Blondlot claims. But then, somebody might ask, what were the retinue of eminent scientist who claimed to have repeated successfully Blondlot's experiments looking at? Could the episode have represented a case of collective mass delusion?

When analyzed impartially the events can scarcely be conceived in any other way, which means that scientific activity can hardly be understood as the cool detached endeavor most of us believe it is. The authority and prestige of a known and respected scientist could produce in others a 'state of trance' or emotional predisposition to believe whatever is proposed, and this belief strongly influences and bias experimental conditions and results. In this particular case of N-rays it took the diligence of a scientist from another land far removed from the 'sphere of influence' of Blondlot and his French colleagues, to ultimately dispel a fabricated myth stubbornly shared by them. Perhaps the atmosphere of sectarian patriotism prevailing in the early part of the XX Century helped to finally expose the biases, errors and pitfalls plaguing the fiasco. One can only wonder what would had happened if Wood would have never gone to Nancy, or otherwise not being interested in the subject at all. How many more articles would have been written and prizes awarded for this 'brilliant contribution to knowledge' is only anybody's guess. I strongly think they would have not been insignificant.

The need to serve science with models to 'explain' reality came to a convulsive epitome when physics began to explore universal realms far removed from the vicinity of mankind universal neighborhood. In 1838 at a village in Moravia born a man of rare genius, one who although forgotten and in a sense discredited today, truly was instrumental in the revolution of scientific thought which was to take place in the next 100 years. Ernst Mach was a veritable pioneer of the mind, a brave soul who charged valiantly against the established dogma of the age and fearlessly pointed out its weaknesses and pitfalls. Mach brought a fresh interest about the Cosmo because, as Einstein once said, "He looked into the World with the curious eyes of a child"

Now this 'child', as many path-setters in history, suffered strong rejections and bitter lack of understanding from those who took direct care of him during his formative years; including his own father who attempted to be his teacher for a while when the good Benedictine priest who schooled the boy during his early education found young Ernst "Very much lacking in ability", and recommended his progenitor to teach him some 'trade' and forget about 'higher' education.

Grown in contact with Nature in the farm of his parents, Mach developed an early respect for manual labor, which he undertook for a while when learning the trade of cabinet maker. He was not a man to be deterred by the opinion of others and soon re-entered school at a Moravia Gymnasium where he finished secondary education, with some aversion for religious duties, before proceeded to the University. Mach 'distasteful' childhood experiences, I think, probably influenced in no small way the genesis of his ulterior scientific formation. It has been suggested that his determined denials of the validity of absolute time, as well as his anti-causality and anti-atomistic bias, had its roots in a father-hate Edipo complex aberration leading him to oppose, emotionally and intellectually, any claims to preferential status. Perhaps Mach himself contributed in a degree to these wild speculations about his psychological motivations by his frequent recounting of childhood experiences and dreams (like the occasion when he first observed in a wind-mill how the cogs of the axle engaged the cogs driving the mill-stones; an incident subsequently construed as an expression of his anti-causality and anti-privilege attitudes). Undoubtedly young Ernst was a rather withdrawal, taciturn, self-centered and at the same time self-denying lad whose anti-materialism, ironically enough, reflected in a radical empiricist approach to Nature, at times reaching the proportions of authentic solipsism.

Important also in understanding Mach's scientific lineage is the cultural and social milieu, as well as the historic background, of the period when he grew. (We had seen that scientific theories are influenced by these factors). Mach's childhood elapsed during the convulsive times of the so-called 1848 revolution and his youth during the aftermath of profound disenchantment that followed. We cannot forget either that the geographic place where he matured as a scientist was the cultural locus of the great Centro-European mystic tradition. As Mach himself once said," The great contribution of the physical sciences is going to be in making man disappear in the All, in annihilating him so to speak..." (Popular Scientific Lectures P. 88). The physicist Erwin Schrodinger once commented: "The idea of Mach comes as near to the orthodox doctrines of the Upanishads as it could possibly do without stating it Expressis verbes".

Whatever the 'reasons' we can adduce and fabricate for Mach's thoughts his radical empiricist method placed him squarely in the uncompromising tradition of that greatest of British anti-materialist: David Hume. Mach's definition of the World as a 'coherent mass of sensations' clearly resembles the Humean definition of 'things' as 'bundles of sensations'. Mach greatest contribution to modern physical laws is today, for many, not the known postulate about physical laws been economic devices to better remember 'knowledge', but rather that he was the first to clearly enunciate the 'relative' point of view about natural phenomena. (See 'Physical thought from the Pre-Socratics to Quantum Physicists'. Edited by Shmuel Sambursky. Pica Press. 1975, P. 465.)

The generic empiricism of Mach inaugurated, in a way, a phenomenological approach to Nature, a search without preconceptions where NO PRIVILAGED FRAME OF REFERENCE WAS ALLOWED. Such radical attitude, which forcefully rejected 'a priori' images of the World, became for a brief period 'the fashion' in Central Europe, and represented the formative milieu where Relativity was engendered and rendered its most precious fruits. That much Einstein himself, in his late years, admitted.

Although he once commented that 'Mach premises are essentially untenable', he also conceded the great influence he had in the late XIX and early XX centuries generation of scientists. As he once claimed: "Even Mach opponents hardly know how much they have sucked of the Machian approach with their mother's milk". [5]

Mach remains a pivotal figure in scientific thought at the turn of the XX Century, a destroyer of dogmas and preconceived notions whose 'child-like' curiosity prompted him to DISPENSE WITH IMAGES OF REALITY. Emotionally Mach represented a scientific version of the MYSTIC ICONOCLAST who hold so important role in the evolution of abstract religions, mostly in the Orient. Historically he belongs to the great Centro-European animistic cultural stream although methodologically subscribing to the empiricist tradition. To such pioneer of thought rallied a number of the young intellectuals early in the XX Century. The 'Olympian circle', to which Einstein himself belonged during the early years, was one of those groups of enthusiastic young rebellious adepts who endorsed Mach ideas.

Physical iconoclasticism being a rare commodity indeed, after 'sparking' some general departures from traditional molds of thought, died away shortly after the great physicist Edwin Boltzman, an unrepented atomist and founder of Statistical Thermodynamics, committed suicide in 1906; allegedly depressed by the criticisms and verbal attacks leveled against him by radical Machian scientific partisans. Max Plank, the discoverer of the physical constant that today bears his name and one of the 'founding fathers' of Quantum Mechanics, took upon his shoulders the task of restoring atomism to its lost pedestal (and what a restoration it was!). Under his leadership 'particles' became, not only the most cherished property of matter, but energy itself became 'traded' in discrete 'quantitized' form. The great Boltzman himself seems to have suggested to Plank the 'right' path when, upon analyzing his research, commented that it was impossible to arrive at a truly adequate theory of the statistical thermodynamics of radiation without introducing an element of discontinuity still unknown.

The famous and well know experiments of Plank with black body radiation and his discovery of the 'constant' of energetic quantum around which hinges the development of the entire field of Quantum Mechanics, is too well known to require detailed narration. Contrary to predictions for the Wave Theory of Light (first enunciated by Lord Raleigh in 1900), Plank found an answer as to how black bodies emitted radiation when they were progressively heated to higher temperatures (glowing first with red light and subsequently, as it was raised, becoming successively orange, yellow, white and finally blue). This experimental fact implied selective emission of radiation (in this case light) at certain specific wavelengths according to the temperature; something contrary to the principle of equipartition of energy which predicted higher radiation always in the short wavelengths (simply because there was more of this kind than of longer types).

Plank pointed out that if the radiation was given out in discontinuous quanta in such a manner that the energy of the quantum was proportional to the wavelength, the emission towards the red end of the spectrum will be favored at lower temperatures(less energetic radiation) and vise versa. Energy therefore was emitted and interchanged in small discrete amounts, which in identical experimental circumstances was always the same. This, of course, amounted to the belief that energy is distributed in 'capsules' or particles, in the case of light reviving the forgotten notion of the 'photon'.

About this time in history the theory advanced by Helmholtz, based on his electrolytic experiments (that electricity consisted also of particles named 'electrons'), was gaining favor with the discovery of 'cathodic' rays and the realization that this negatively charged radiation possessed significant momentum. Thompson had opportunely shown that these electric 'particles' were ubiquitous in all matter and thought that they represented the fundamental building blocks of it. With the discovery of radioactivity a further complication was introduced, and Rutherford then observed that alpha 'particles' were deflected by matter. Wandering about the nature of the occasional marked deflection of these particles (he calculated one in 2000 suffered such deflection) Rutherford had a 'brilliant' intuition, a vision that converted him in the Copernicus of this microcosm and immediately captured the imagination of physicists around the world: Matter, he concluded, was concentrated at certain points in the elemental atoms. These 'condensations' obviously were separated by vast empty spaces, as suggested by the result of the experiment, and also were of equal charges than the alpha particles. The mass centers could be compared to the sun. The atom, he contended, was nothing more or less than A MINIATURE SOLAR SYSTEM, 'complete' with a central sun (the nucleus) and its 'corona' of planets (the electrons). The Universe was a fractal manifold!

There was however one persistent and in a sense formidable problem. According to Classic Electrodynamics the electrons would follow in their orbits spiral trajectories and promptly collapse into the nucleus. Something, it was concluded, had to keep the electrons in their orbits if the beauty of the 'atomic model' was to be kept 'alive'. Into the scene jumped then the well known Danish physicist Niels Bohr who had another genial idea. He, in a sense, reverted the terms and advanced the hypothesis that nothing was necessary to keep the electrons in their orbits. There was no expenditure of energy in that situation, as would in a macrocosmic system. In fact, he added, the energy is spent or acquired only when the electron 'change' orbits. Furthermore, he contended, the amount of energy exchanged would be in all occasions discrete and always the same for a given orbital level. These discrete energetic 'quantum's' were multiples of certain irreducible amount and a function of 'Plank's constant!

Clarified also appeared the mysterious spectroscopic emission or absorption lines of the different elements: They were nothing else but the specific pattern of photonic quanta exchanged when the electrons 'jumped' orbits within the atoms themselves. Being the atomic structure 'constant' for a given element that also 'explained' why the spectral lines were always the same in each case. Spectrophotometry became a powerful tool in the field of 'analytical' physics, and gave a tremendous impulse to the branch of Astrophysics.

Why, we may ask, did the scientific community accepted so eagerly, and with so little disturbance or resistance, the 'Solar System' model of the atom? Why, in reality, were physicists so moved in preserving this notion apparently 'at all costs'? Was any memory of the recent Machian iconoclasticism still alive? Many would not even acknowledge the validity of these questions and will dismiss them lightly by claiming that the 'truth is self-evident'. The fact of the matter, however, is that there was not one iota of evidential prove as to the correctness of the Solar System Model of the atom, not a single one of the subsequent earthshaking accomplishments of atomic physics needed such an hypothesis. A number of other schemes would have been possible. No need for adoption of a nucleocentric 'atomic' form was demanded by the experimental facts.

Perhaps a 'sense' of universal symmetry prompted man to embrace enthusiastically the 'solar system' paradigm of the atom, a belief that the infinitely small replicates exactly the infinitely large (a notion similar to the one that envisages within every seed a miniature tree or within every egg a miniature animal). Be it as it may, the wonderful world of atomic physics became opened again when it was 'realized' that 'atoms' were not the solid irreducible units thought by the previous generations, but immensely complex structures, raising the exciting prospect of new and far reaching discoveries waiting to be 'captured' by the experimenter's mind. Physical iconoclasticism was at a 'visual' dead end and the refreshing new 'vistas' lurking beyond the microcosmic horizon were alluring the mind and curiosity of a new generation.

It is interesting to notice how crucial scientific controversies died out, not necessarily because a 'solution' is found 'objectively' acceptable to all, but simply because they loss its 'appeal' to new generations. Significant in this regard, I believe, are the words of Plank, who engaged Mach in a controversy after the suicide of Boltzmann. According to Plank Mach's ideas were utterly sterile because they lacked a 'guiding picture' concerning the 'nature' of the World. How then did he explain the popularity of Mach with the generation of 1900? Plainly, he answered caustically, the reason could be reduced to one word: 'Disenchantment', 'a reaction against the proud expectations of previous generations associated with special mechanical phenomena following the discovery of the energy principle'. (' A survey of physics: A collection of lectures and assays'. Trans. R. Jones and D.H. Williams. London 1925, P. 35-38).

Plank proceeded in ever more personal attacks to accuse Mach of being a 'false prophet'. He claimed that the way of 'reason' was not to abandon world 'pictures' but to try to construct one capable of encompassing the entire 'physical reality'. Mach answered him by stating that the embracing of 'unproved' hypothesis was alien to the spirit of Science and that Physics was in the way of becoming a Church. The detailed recount of this long forgotten controversy is beyond the intent or scope of this assay but it seems to me worth to comment on the main arguments advanced from both sides because they are revealing as to the inner 'mechanism' of scientific enterprises in general and the 'mode of workings' of the human 'mind' in particular. The words of Plank have an eternal ring and address something very fundamental regarding our scientific method and the dynamics of Western thought: Mach ideas were 'sterile' because the way to 'reason' was not to abandon 'world pictures'.

Man, being a 'visual animal', there is always an urge to express himself in images which have a heuristic power for human thought and action. Iconoclastic views, Mach should have realized, had no more appeal in Science than they possess in Religion. In general THEY LACK EMOTIONAL APPEAL and driving force capable of firing the imagination or catalyzing human action. Only with the achievement of a mature phase in its evolution Science might, like Religion before, escape the binding spells of physical 'images' [6]

In the first few decades of the XX Century the new exciting 'discoveries' in Atomic Physics recruited the efforts, talents and initiative of a new generation of humans enlisted eagerly in the titanic efforts to unravel the 'secrets' of the infinitely small. The greatest 'actor' in the drama that followed was Niels Bohr. We have already seen his endorsement, with some modifications, of Rutherford's atomic model (in whose laboratory he was then working). His preoccupation with the electrodynamic contradictions posed by the conceptions under development by his associate brought Bohr to postulate his memorable formula, which reconciled classic physics with the new quantum 'dimension' explored and introduced before by Plank. The heuristicity of the beautiful solar 'image' had to be preserved at all costs!

Now, Bohr upbringing had been a solid one and he was not so naive as to entertain, even in his most optimistic mood, the belief and hope that he had truly unraveled the ultimate 'secrets' of nature. During his formative years Bohr was influenced by the great Danish philosopher Harald Hoffding, a personal friend of his father with whom he met often in Bohr's house to discuss philosophical themes; and who subsequently became his teacher at the university. Hoffding was an admirer of the American pragmatic William James, who he met in 1904 in a visit he made to the U.S. and was otherwise, and not unexpectedly, also influenced by the contemporary ideas of the great Danish existentialist Soren Kierkegaard.

Hoffding greatest emphasis, however, was in the themes of the discontinuities in natural phenomena and ultimate in individual factors; not only in what refers to personal life but also in matters of Science. This, of course, is a thoroughly existentialistic standpoint, again with a long tradition in Centro-European mystic vitalism; except that Kierkegaard stopped short of extending it into scientific endeavors claiming that in research 'the personality was effaced', while Hoffding held the opposite opinion because, as he contended, scientific work 'never stop being a work of personality'. Otherwise, however, Hoffding was completely imbued with a Kierkegaardian spirit, being mainly instrumental in the popularization of the teachings of the great philosopher among the Danish 'generation of the 1900'.

Kierkegaard, as a reaction to the tyranny of Hegelian dialectics with its absolutist all encompassing flavor, had inaugurated what he called 'qualitative dialectic', emphasizing the irreconcilable nature of different forms of existence and life; their 'separateness' stemming from the irreducibility of boundaries which therefore demanded the existential choice, his unavoidable 'Either-Or'. Existence in general, he repeated again and again, led the individual to cross-roads proceeding forward by 'jumps and jolts'.

These Kierkegaardian conceptions Hoffding extended to the realm of Science. After all, that Nature at times 'progresses' by jolts was proved evident, at least in the biological field, by the Dutch Hugo de Vries who thought that causality, as we know it, was a superfluous postulate. Echoing Kierkegaard he was of the opinion that a complete all-inclusive system of Nature was impossible, a deception of the human mind, an unreachable hope.

But Kierkegaard had gone even further along this line of inquire. Existence, he asserted, is afflicted by an OBJECTIVE UNCERTAINTY in direct relation to the contradictory character of its content. The idea of 'truth in itself' should be rejected; all we could hope to achieve was a psychological 'insight' into Reality. TRUTH WAS A SUBJECTIVE NOTION AND HENCE COULD BE GRASPED ONLY 'SUBJECTIVELY'. The similarity to the mystic epistemological position is evident; it allures visions of an Indian 'ascetic of the forest' achieving 'enlightenment' after closing his eyes to the 'world of the senses' and opening the 'inner eye' of consciousness.[7]

Hoffding, in his lectures, had reiterated many times that 'absolute' systematizations of knowledge was not possible and echoing James insisted that systems only serve a 'pragmatic' use or intent. Invariably, he claimed, when there is an attempt to 'extend an analogy ' based on a part of existence to the 'whole', no verification is possible. For him the fundamental philosophical questions were essentially 'insoluble'. When a selected 'point of view', or 'analogy', was applied to the whole this led to 'anthropomorphism', that is, an 'image' that claims to be more than that.

A considerable doses of iconoclasticism is evident in these philosophical speculations, that is, in the denial that a wholly comprehensive world picture is reachable. In reality most of what Hoffding was saying was what Mach had said before but with different words. It is apparent that they belonged to the same tradition in Western thought, traceable perhaps to the oriental fable of the three wise blind Indians who wanted to 'know' how an elephant truly was like by extrapolating from their own personal experiences. One said that the elephant was like a tree, after embracing a leg with his open arms. Another claimed it was like a snake when feeling his trump, while the third insisted it was like a bird after touching his ears.

The parable, obviously, epitomized the central theme of these great thinkers which are manifestations of the mystic vitalism of Centro-European thought. VIEWS OR MODELS OF THE WHOLE BASED IN EXTRAPOLATIONS FROM LIMITED HUMAN PERSPECTIVES WERE INVALID ASSUMPTIONS. The inductive method, they claimed, has its limits.

XIX Century Phenomenology, with its insistence in the rejection of all preconceptions and dispensation with all structural models of 'reality', constitutes in science a plead for a regression to a pre- empiricist point of view, akin to that of the Oriental Philosophies, but where the senses remained the 'avenues of knowledge', albeit of a fragmented limited kind, sufficient however to allow the formulation of laws of relational terms between phenomena. That is why Mystic Vitalism, as expressed thru phenomenological notions, cannot avoid a touch of Empiricism. THE 'SENSES' FOR BOTH ARE THE ONLY ACCEPTABLE AVENUE OF INQUIRE ABOUT THE PHYSICAL WORLD. [8]

Regarding the Kierkegaardian conception of discontinuities in life, his notion of psychological 'evolution' by leaps and jolts, the conviction that the 'world' could only be grasped in its meaning subjectively and the view that no all-inclusive model could be constructed, it certainly is intriguing that many quantum mechanical notions do partake in the realm of quantum physics of what Kierkegaard considered properties of the 'psychological'.

For all that has been said it is quite apparent that Bohr was instilled in no small measure, and by way of Hoffding, with a Kierkegaardian spirit which cultural roots, we have already suggested, had to be found in Centro-European metaphysical conceptions with their individualistic anti-causality outlook, graphically expressed in Leibnitz's 'windowless monads'. Yet, it could not be denied that Bohr's major accomplishments in the field of physics was in trying to preserve the validity of the 'solar system model' of the atom, the 'genial' insight of his predecessor Rutherford.

It behooved another great Centro-European scientist the dubious glory of establishing conclusively the limitations of visual models as tools to search and probe into the microcosm and, therefore, of their capacity to unravel its secrets. With him finally XX Century physics found its most stubborn iconoclast, a man with strong aversions to 'images'. The anti-materialistic bias of Werner Heisenberg, even in his early formative years, was very clearly manifested in his revulsion towards 'pictorial' blue-prints of microcosmic realities. (See 'Einstein and the Generation of Science'. L. S. Feuer. Basics Books Inc. 1974, P. 163).

It will be futile any attempt to find psychological 'explanations' for the behavior and emotional affiliations of such a prominent physicist as Heisenberg, and for that matter of anybody. The 'science' of psychology has not advanced yet to the point where 'causal links' can be established in this regard and it is questionable whether it would ever be. All that can be done is to speculate as to the possible reasons for certain behavioral traits by searching into environmental and biological presumptive influences, without the hope of ever reaching a definitive conclusion. Heisenberg 'Principle of Indeterminacy', which represents a formidable insurmountable barrier to our capacity to 'visualize' the subatomic structure of matter, has been traced by Feuer to the indeterminacies and unpredictability of the historic times (the immediate aftermath of the First World War period in Germany) during his formative years. (Ibid, P. 167).

In a convulsed, disorderly and unpredictable historic period, however, we can make the reasonable claim that the 'natural tendency' of a human is to seek solace, repose and spiritual refuge in eternal unperturbed realms; like the diverse religious manifestations which are nothing but longings of the human spirit for stability of values, capable of providing 'consolation' to the embattled soul from the vicissitudes and anguish of life uncertainties. It would not be far fetch, therefore, to consider that young Werner assuaged uncertainties about a crumbling world in his assiduous reading of Plato's works; whose 'eternal forms' provided the safe-buoy allowing him to coast the storms where the world of his elders had been wrecked.

But Heisenberg actually felt an strong and profound aversion for images, to the point of being 'disquieted' by the thought of the possibility of ever being invented a microscope powerful enough to 'see' those hated atoms of his high school textbooks. On the other hand, it also can be asserted, young Werner was not a rebel against his elders; neither in thought nor in action. As a matter of fact, his early struggles were directed precisely to the preservation of their society against the hated atheist Bolsheviks, who taking advantage of the ruin and shame of Germany had meddle in the chaos and temporarily conquered the heart of Bavaria. In reality, if anything, Werner was a TRADITIONALIST who, by his own admission, almost 'suffered physically' because of the collapse of the old order. His youthful mind was full of questions as to the 'why' things were happening in the way they were. (Ibid P. 166).

On the light of the evidence at hand it can be cogently argued that Heisenberg life efforts were an anxious search in a shattered world for a new 'order' to restitute the sense of 'equilibrium' lost in the maelstrom of the First World War. Admittedly, the old 'eternal' Platonic Forms were antiquated 'formulas', but new ones could be found. The ancient Platonic-Aristotelian insight that the microcosm was accessible to mathematical descriptions was to be preserved, although not necessarily the deterministic notion that events are forever pre-established; that was a 'fatalistic streak' foreign to the German soul. Now, it is one thing to doubt on 'empirical basis' an unseen interpretational hypothesis and another to intensely desire such hypothesis to be false; as it is very obvious, and by his own admission, in the case of Heisenberg. This clearly indicates a profoundly felt visceral reaction 'against' the acceptance of pictorial representations. The lad was a modern iconoclast in the great Centro-European tradition, a worthy heir to Ernst Mach and scientific vitalism.

The works of Heisenberg, like those of any other great scientist, could not be understood without reference to the cultural tradition and the social milieu where they were 'concocted'. These cultural traditions are usually not shallow historic perspectives but deeply rooted emotional undercurrents spanning many centuries and even millennia. Heisenberg revulsion, expressed in his resentment for 'atomic models', was against the deterministic, rationalistic, bourgeoisie-merchant Western philosophical heritage, the way of thinking subscribed by Descartes, Newton and Spinoza; the mechanistic paradigm which gave birth to evolutionary theory and modern atomism. It could be reasonably argued that his emotional lineage was with the 'mystic', vitalistic philosophical movement, with those who extolled an anti-causal and anti-materialistic 'view' of the Cosmo, with men like Boehme, Leibnitz, Goethe and the Nature-Philosophers; those who abhorred the rigidities and formalities where 'Reason' had casted Western thought and who ultimately embraced the scientific phenomenological movement which aroused in Europe after the First World War. Heisenberg principle of indeterminacy implied the impossibility to ascertain SIMULTANEOUSY the position and momentum of an electron. The unpredictable fluctuations that we encounter, the 'frothiness' prevailing at these unimaginably small magnitudes frustrated all efforts. Objectivity lost its old meaning with his postulate. Even our comfortable conception of space-time was difficult to reconcile with experimental results.

Quantum mechanics postulate of incertitude poses a true limit to the predictability and comprehension of microcosmic events. Does it represent a faithful frontier to the search by the human intellect or a mere 'bankruptcy' or exhaustion of a 'point of view'? Are we victims or prisoners of our own cognitive apparatus? Why do we insist in interpretations based in terms and categories borrowed from our cosmic level of existence to unseen and unfathomable realms? Do we truly need such hypothesis and models? Many will answer positively but bias and presuppositions in our lines of enquire are real hindrances and could lead us astray. As Heisenberg declared in 1945 ' understanding of the atomic world in that primary sensuous fashion....is impossible'.

The fact of the matter is that it becomes enormously difficult for the human intellect to transcend his cognitive barriers, those resulting from the marvelous coupling of the nervous system to the immediate environment of man. To overcome the attachment of the mind to its sensorial apparatus becomes for many a distasteful and even unprofitable undertaking (a 'sterile' lack of imagination, as Plank once said). Yet, to embrace enthusiastically scientific 'model building', despite of the obvious appeal and glamorous promises which it holds for many, could be a wasteful and unnecessary enterprise, a drain of energy and resources with no ultimate explicit or implicit purpose.

No modern theory of science illustrates this point more vividly than the Atomic Theory. As Heisenberg commented, microcosmic events can only be related by a series of partial differential equations that afford ALL possible predictions into 'atomic' phenomena. To give those phenomena a 'sensuous' translation is a futile and useless effort of the mind, only adding confusion to the comprehension of such inapprehensible realities so far removed from the immediate experience of Man.

Atomism, that mechanistic 'dream' of commercial maritime societies, has eventually prevail upon a minority of disgruntled opponents and today is a solidly established and entrenched physical dogma; in fact it actually represents THE most popular scientific belief of the XX Century[9]. Today no serious scientist will question its validity, notwithstanding conflicting results of experimental nature at times seeming to support the 'particle' quality of microcosmic events and in others the 'wave' character of them. This should have been sufficient warning to investigators but that was not the case; the search for the solidity and tangibility of 'nice little billiard balls' not only continues unabated but has influenced the allocations of large sums of money to an insane quest for the 'fundamental building blocks' (the universal material substratum)[10] despite disquieting suggestions that, in effect, the search is a useless chasing after phantoms. Abstract microcosmic conceptions are distasteful and abhorrent to human understanding. Man is much more comfortable with the support provided by 'material' solid bodies rather than with the ethereal evanescent quality of 'elusive events', or, even worse, with the cool, detach and 'sterile' descriptions provided by mathematical equations.(See Appendix IV)

—————— CHAPTER III ——————

Central to any inquire into the way that man understand and relates to his environment is, precisely, 'knowledge' of the organ we utilized in the process, that is, the Nervous System: Our relational apparatus, the source of the 'intellect' which complexity is epitomized in the intricate organization of the Brain.

Although the general characteristics of Neuro-anatomy and Neuro-physiology are well known for more than a century, and ever since Broca and other investigators established the existence of functional specializations by means of clinical-pathological correlations (although much need to be understood about the workings of this perplexing organ), enough had been accomplish, particularly since the middle of the XX Century, to permit some basic conclusions.

The basic architecture of the system consist of complex networks of interconnected neurons (by way of contact points or synapses), related to each other by means of prolongations of their bodies referred to as dendrites and axons. The meaning of these interconnections, firstly identified and described with silver impregnation techniques by Ramon y Cajal and Golgi at the turn of the XX Century, had also been sufficiently elucidated. Some neurons bring in sensory information from diverse sites of the animal body while others, the effectors, transmit messages to other neurons and to the organs of locomotion and visceral systems.

In the simple 'reflex arch' the sensory information brought in is directly converted into commands without any appreciable further elaboration. That is the case with the so-called 'spinal reflexes' in vertebrates, as well as, with many of the nervous 'activities' in more primitive animals. As a matter of fact, in some simple organisms as sea anemones, there are instances of neuronal circuits where a single cell acts as 'sensory' and 'motor' units simultaneously. The obvious characteristics of these elemental system is this: A sensory perception will 'necessarily' and 'fatally' give rise to a command of some sort which will be 'decoded' in the 'target' organ into some invariant activity, whether it be muscular contraction, glandular secretion, etc.

In some more elaborated and complex cases the sensory information carried by the 'afferent' neurons will be further elaborated in an 'intermediate' array of other neurons before giving rise to commands by the 'effector' neurons. This intermediate array could be extremely complex; in fact the entire brain of vertebrates, that is to say, the portion of the neuronal apparatus lying between the sensory and motor neurons (in humans amounting to more than 100 billion cells, or as many neurons as there are stars in our galaxy) are, by definition, this type of intermediate array. It is not difficult to understand the enormous proliferation of potential commands that could emerge from such a labyrinthine web.

The trajectory of a nerve impulse thru that complex network frequently is impossible to be followed, and even less predicted; but the reason for this 'incertitude' is not only the structural complexities. The neurons themselves are very sophisticated units animated with the property of nerve 'conductivity', and the impulses traversing their bodies are essentially a wave of electrical charges produced at the cell membrane level by changes in permeability to sodium and potassium ions controlled and mediated by selective channeled proteins 'gated' to changes in electrical potentials or to specific chemical transmitters. The latter kind abounds in the post-synaptic zone because the 'impulses' are propagated from neuron to neuron, and to other end organs, by means of chemical mediators (acetyl-choline, serotonin etc.), whereas the former predominate at the axon level and are primarily entrusted with conveying impulses thru the cell bodies to the pre-synaptic terminals.

Now, as far as has been determined all nerve impulses in a given neuron generate 'waves' of identical amplitude but of variable frequencies according to the 'intensities' of the originating stimulus. How qualitative differences are transmitted and identified from quantitative parameters is still a matter of active investigation. Recent research had determined the vital role of transient rises in voltage (spikes) in intercellular communication. The coordinated timing of arrival of such signals in a neuron is what frequently elicits the firing by that neuron to other regions of the neuronal apparatus. It has been determined that signals which are not temporarily grouped in general had less influence in triggering a neuronal response. Usually the higher the synchronized firing rate the strongest the response. In what refers to higher association centers (the visual field for instance), fewer cells in the visual cortex receiving inputs from lower areas (like the Thalamus) need to fire to represent an object in our conscience. Even single spiny stellate neurons seemed to have a preferred visual stimulus that triggers a high firing rate.(Terry Sejnowski & Tobi Delbruck. Scientific American Vol. 307, Number 4, Oct. 2012)

Because further detailed neurophysiologic descriptions are beyond the purpose and scope of this analysis, it should suffice to add that of the hundreds and thousands of 'connections' that many vertebrate neurons establish with neighbors and distant counterparts some are 'excitatory', but others are 'inhibitory' of the impulses, that is to say, some will transmit stimulus while others suppress them; being their direction and the type of function (excitatory or inhibitory), as far as can be tell, always the same at each individual 'contact' or synapse.

From these facts it follows that a given nerve impulse, when it reaches the axonic portion of the neuron body, is essentially a SUMMATION of diverse excitatory and inhibitory action potentials (in fact some brain neurons even have the capacity to fire back at other neurons from where a given stimulus is received). In this diversity precisely resides the incertitude of neuronal activity in animals. The more intricate the association patterns among the clusters of neurons participating in a response to a given stimulus, the more unpredictable it is.

Even more intriguing is the capacity of neurons to learn and remember. Experiments had demonstrated that this potentiality is not necessarily exclusive patrimony of the higher vertebrate brains, but that in fact is already present, although obviously in a more rudimentary form, in the nerve systems of primitive invertebrates. Eric R. Kandel working with sea snails (Scientific American 'Small systems of neurons' Sept. 1979, P. 67) discovered that the gill retraction reflex following stimulation of the siphon area was capable of being reinforced, or inhibited, when preceded in time by an injurious or neutral stimulus.

These facilitations and/or inhibitions could be short lived or last for long periods of time depending on the way that the stimulation takes place, and in essence represents a type of memory and learning in a small nerve ganglia of a primitive invertebrate. The neurobiological mechanism of this 'memory' appears to be a remarkable capacity for increasing or decreasing, in facilitation and inhibition respectively, of the neuronal membrane permeability at the axonal end to Calcium ions, which in turn produce an augmentation or diminution, respectively, of the secretion of acetylcholine (the substance mediating the transmission of nerve impulses at the synaptic junction)[1].

How is this variable permeability to Calcium mediated is still unknown but the apparent purpose is clear; it helps the animal to 'guard against' injurious stimuli (enhancement of facilitation), or not to 'pay attention' (inhibition or retardation) to those which are irrelevant and not dangerous. Such modulations of nerve activity are of great significance in the relational life of an animal and actually represent a type of CONDITIONING; a forerunner, we might call it, of the more elaborated conditioned reflexes firstly described by Pavlov in higher vertebrates.

Learning and memory in their simplest expression, at least in primitive neuronal systems, ARE therefore forms of neuronal conditioning which together with the existence of wiring diagrams (apparently invariable characteristics of a given species according to evidence also accruing from neuroanatomical studies in simple animal forms, that is, stereotyped blueprints of a sort) are the most notorious and revealing features of the relational apparatus, the marvelous machine we have inherited from our ancestors and serve as substratum to all 'knowledge'.

Conductivity, therefore, is the property that, together with the associational patterns of the nervous system, permits the transmission and translation of relevant sensory information into animal 'actions'; thus forming the basis of more or less complex types of behavior ranging from the most elemental 'reflexes' to the more elaborate constructions (such as stereotyped instinctual rituals, and for the apparently 'flexible' responses of higher vertebrates as well as the seemingly infinite potentiality of the human intellect). We also have seen, however, that another functional elemental property regulates nerve responses and ultimately behavior: Modulation or conditioning (reinforcement and facilitation, or on the other hand, inhibitions in the propagation of stimuli) regulates the capabilities of neuronal systems allowing for the process of learning, that is to say, the modification of behavioral patterns according to changing environmental situations and the needs of an organism.

This conditioning, by expanding the animal 'action options', opens new alternatives and so creates the possibility of 'improving' his adaptation to the environment; in essence permitting the spatio-temporal interplaying of sensory stimuli which de facto represents an elemental form of pre-reflective induction. When an original indifferent stimuli is frequently enough repeated in sequence to another pleasurable or injurious one it results in an animal response to it, AS IF, in effect, the first gives rise to the second. Now, such association truly implies a sort of trust in a CAUSAL PRECEDENCE; in a way a generalization, whereby it is 'taken for granted' that if two events (the percepts and the sequential stimuli) have been always associated in the past (in this case during the period of conditioning), they also will be equally associated in the future.

Conductibility and modulation, however, do not exhaust the list of important functional neuronal peculiarities. Another of paramount importance is ABSTRACTION, the capacity to modify the nature of the nerve stimuli to fit certain specific responses to the reception of sensory impulses. Significant progress in this regard has been accomplished in recent years. (See David H. Hubel and Torsten N. Wiesel 'Brain mechanisms of vision', Scientific American, Sept. 1979 P. 150)

What seems to distill from these experiments is, in the first place, the fact that the Visual Cortex integrates contrasting patterns of luminosities, appearing to be important for perception of forms, shapes and profiles. Although 'knowledge' of neurophysiology is still extremely rudimentary, I believe that another conclusion which could be drawn from the experiments is that sensory information is processed by progressive ABSTRACTION of the perceptual material thru a process of selection ; implicating necessarily a discarding of certain portions of the original stimuli and preservation of others that will form the ultimate 'percepts'. When analyzed thoroughly, however, this neuronal property is no different, and in fact is a type of modulation which joins conductivity as basic neuronal properties determining the way we perceive and relate to our environment.

The next question we need to touch on in our brief overview of neuronal organization and function is that of the discriminatory capacity of the Nervous System, that is, what is the lower limit or threshold of awareness for perceiving as separate two independent events. These limits are of two kinds: Spatial and temporal. It will be very difficult to detect a spatial neuronal limit, in view of its dependence on size, position and luminosity of the given events. Although this limit of detectability ultimately relates to the number of retinal cells sensitized by a given stimuli, no studies to my knowledge, had yet produced this 'magic' number, notwithstanding the fact that its existence is an incontrovertible reality exemplified by the visualization and discovery of 'microscopic objects' only identified with the help of certain optical devices.

In fact, the so-called 'two point discrimination', whether tactile of visual, appears to change from area to area of a given sensorial field. For instance, it is more developed, say at the tip of the fingers (where it is a matter of millimeters) than at the level of the thoracic skin; or in the case of the Retina, it is better at the level of the central zone of the visual field than at the periphery. This peculiar variability seems to depend primarily in the richness of the neuronal web supplying the different sensorial zones, in other words, the number of neurons encoding sensorial information for equal area surfaces is larger in the zones of greater discriminatory capacity.

Be it as it may, the existence of a discriminatory LIMIT is apparent for anatomical and structural reasons. Events closer in space than a given threshold, would appear to consciousness as a single one beyond certain limit, depending of the size, distance, position and strength of the stimulus and the place of the sensorial field where the given stimuli converge.

What about the 'temporal' discriminatory capacity? As with its spatial counterpart there is no doubt about the existence of a limit. Light scintillations, for instance, flickering at certain speed could give the impression of a luminous 'point' and, according with their intensity and position in the visual field, could create the impression of tridimensional luminous spheres; even 'bouncing' and 'colliding' among themselves (Bela Julesz 'Texture of visual perception' Scientific American, Feb. 1965).

Such perceptual properties, no doubt, do have an underlining functional substratum, in other words, by necessity depend in general biological peculiarities of the nervous system as a whole, and of the neurons in particular. In the case of vision we talk about a mysterious 'persistence of the images in the Retina', which is difficult to refer to any part of the sensorial system or perceptive mechanism. We however know that in neurons, after each action potential go thru, there is a period (measured as a fraction of a second) of refractoriness. If another stimulus is applied then, no nerve impulse will be generated during this short interval. Obviously only those events succeeding each other in a time sequence longer than this refractory lapse will generate another nerve impulse.

If, as it is clear from the above described experiments, the Nervous System represents a progressively more complex integration of neurons with the site of consciousness finally gathering all the collected diverse information, and if the neuron, or neurons, representing this consciousness also possess refractory periods similar to the primary neurons and necessarily in synchrony with them, it will be logical to assume that their capacity to perceive as separate successive temporal events should also be limited by this interval.

What all this means is that the existence of refractory lapses of time in higher association centers places a limit to the temporal discriminatory capacity of human consciousness. Sufficiently temporal proximity of events of same kind, which also are adequately close in space, will be perceived AS MOTION OF SAME SPATIO-TEMPORAL 'OBJECTS'. Now, it follows from these considerations that during the periods of refractoriness no incoming stimulus could sensitize the neurons and therefore translate as impulse. When another similar impulse is generated immediately after the cessation of this period it will not be conceived as something different, but rather as an slight spatial displacement (if they are sufficiently closed in space) OF THE SAME THING; the successive events will be 'bridged' by consciousness, as could be clearly demonstrated with the frames of the cinematographic strip (to be perceived as different 'things' will require longer intervals between the given stimuli than this minimal discriminatory threshold).

Human consciousness, however, will be totally unaware of these physical gaps, or blanks, as much as it is unaware of the blind spot in the Retina, and will be incapable of resolving them into what they are. Consciousness itself will also be incapable of detecting ITS OWN discontinuity inasmuch as it would be 'suspended' during the neuronal refractory period and, therefore, would conceive itself as a continuous stream without detectable interruptions.

In summary, there are three peculiar characteristics of the nervous system, three inherent qualities that determine the way we perceive and understand. They are: conductivity, conditioning or modulation (also allowing the elaboration or 'data processing' referred to as 'abstraction'), and finally refractoriness; a period during which stimuli will be incapable of eliciting a nerve impulse and relate to the power of discrimination of our consciousness. Such peculiarities necessarily influence and determine the manner we cognize and relate to our environment. As we will see, all scientific activity is 'per force' determined by the internal 'architecture' and performance characteristics of this relational apparatus: The Human Brain. How neuronal properties and organization corresponds to Man's intellectual faculties will preoccupy us in the next chapter.

CHAPTER IV

Pervading all scientific thought ever since the early Ionians, and certainly implicit in Aristotle and Bacon, there is the notion of 'causality', referring as such the capacity of some phenomena to 'bring about', 'produce' or influence other phenomena.(See Chapter I). Our vocabulary is full of words corresponding to this conception, as the above cited verb and also many others which are intimately associated or dependent on it clearly points out. Take the term 'force'. We seem to be unable to understand motion of 'bodies' without the postulation of a 'mover', or cause, mediated by something; a type of effector. When we talk of causes in this sense we refer to 'reasons to be'. Some authorities feel that such conceptions as causality and induction are anthropomorphic and arrived at by analogy to man's world. We 'cause' things to happen, we employ forces in attempts to modify and induce events.

As a matter of fact, Science has rarely overcome, or gone beyond, Baconian and Aristotelian epistemological principles and still, for lack of need, endorses naive causality (causality as explanation and final causes), induction and classificatory schemes as 'knowledge' itself; or as a precondition in the elaboration of hypothesis as to 'how things work'.

As we have seen, a basic pillar or prelude to scientific pursues is the conviction, expressed by many scientists, that the elaboration of explanations as to the 'why' the World of phenomena is the way it is, represents a mandatory or absolute necessity if any kind of advance or 'progress' is going to be realized. According to these authorities Science without elaboration of hypothesis becomes an empty tabulation of facts, a recording of phenomena and a measurement of parameters; an activity that by itself will be conducive to no fruitful end. Hypothesis and theories are, they claim, the 'glue' that articulate the disparate scientific facts.

Scientists since the 'Age or Reason', better known as the 'Enlightment', had turned their backs on philosophy and resolutely ignored the predication of those who had denied the possibility of knowledge of 'outside' reality. Such abhorred position, incompatible with any scientific endeavor, was to be looked upon, at least, with suspiciousness and contempt. After all, the 'existence' of an outside world was a precondition to any science.

Perhaps because of this attitude scientists were unable, in their great majority, to hear the voice of somebody we already know: David Hume, the man who reputedly awoke Kant from his 'dogmatic slumber', but otherwise did not make any great impact with his theories (except among a reduced circle of philosophical inclined friends). Adducing the impossibility of perceiving between two consecutive events nothing else but a time sequence or 'invariable precedence', he challenged one of the most solid pillars of the scientific method: The naive 'common sense' where we take refuge in times of tribulation.

Hume used the famous Cartesian example of the synchronized clocks programmed to toll their bells one immediately following the other to make his point clear. The time sequence of these events do not mean, he claimed, the existence of any 'influence' of one upon the other or of a demonstrable relationship among them; their temporal 'contiguity' was ALL that can be ascertain. Any other opinion or theory was simply a superfluous inference from the observable phenomena.

Now, this was a frontal assault on the basic tenants of our beloved 'common sense'. Causality (as efficient cause) for him was then neither necessary nor sufficient; it merely represented an UNTESTABLE HYPOTHESIS. Yet, if the knowability of the external World is accepted in principle, what determines the mysterious association of events allowing the effectiveness of the induction principle?

Kant, as we saw, has an original opinion in this regard. His fertile imagination touched in a potential answer when insisting that 'the mind' categorizes events. Substance and causality were two of his most important categories of understanding. Phenomena, he thought, in order to be identified needed also to be imbued with an underlining substantiality, a solidity 'coupled with' reality least they are confused with the ethereal qualities of imagination, the stuff from where dreams, hallucinations and memories arise. Likewise, he insisted, the mind utilizes the criteria of causality as a necessary link between events contiguous in time. Man's comprehension of the World rested precisely in this support without which phenomena would appear to consciousness as a chaotic disarray. (See Chapter I)

Kant also did have to provide with a frame for events that permit their orderliness and correlations to be manifested and revealed. Space and time, he claimed, were 'forms of intuition' allowing such assortment and the intelligibility of the Cosmo; what instilled meaning to our lives.

Not many philosophers, and certainly, no scientist today would agree that space and time (or as it is the fashion today 'space-time') are 'forms' of the human mind, that is to say, something merely subjective and devoid of true external validity. After all, if that is the case, why then would they serve as the support of all predictive physical laws? If they were arbitrary, would they have helped us in the way and to the extent they have? These are pertinent questions and, assuming the existence of an 'external reality', it is worthy to study and analyze the fundamental tenants of human understanding. The answer to the question as to how much can we hope to know of that external World, and to what extent can we expect to discern and eventually to control this assumed reality, will depend of up to what measure the attributes of putative 'Nature' are true parts of perceived phenomena, or else, properties of the cognitive apparatus.

If Hume attacked the principle of causality demonstrating the impossibility of any final prove of it, Hume himself and others (Karl Popper for instance), had criticized induction; again pointing out that merely because some events have been always observed in the past to be associated in a given way does not necessarily implies a similar correspondence in the future. Even if all known ravens are black this does not necessarily means that the next one we see could not necessarily display a different color, or that just because all donkeys we have ever seen possess four legs the next one we encounter couldn't display five or three.

These remarks are very relevant. Induction and Causality cannot be 'demonstrated' to represent real entities or parts of an outside world, in other words, attributes of the physical environment despite their success as predictors of events in all fields of Science and their tacit endorsement everywhere by all denominations of humanity since early man walked the Earth. The fact remains, however, that phenomena are frequently associated in our immediate environment in such a way as to allow us to manipulate causality and induction in our analysis of Nature.

Actually such premises of 'understanding' are automatically assumed in everyday life, not only by the human species but also by all living creatures. Consider, for instance, the case of a group of gazelles stampeding at the sight, or even at the smell, of a lion. A type of pre-reflective categorization, or classificatory activity, did by necessity have had to take place in the brains of the gazelles. The shape, color, body structure, roar, body smells etc., needed to be grouped and arranged in 'their minds' in a manner capable of triggering a rudimentary, probably pre-conscious, ordering; a precondition to ALL kinds of identification processes (See also Chapter I). Furthermore, there had also to be an assumption by the gazelle, based on previous experience, as to a possible association of the presence of the lion with an attack, even if not all the characteristics of a previous association (the sight of the animal for instance) are perceived now all at once.

For the gazelle to flee implies a pre-reflective endorsement of causality and induction, that is, the belief that the lion was THE CAUSE of the death of other gazelles, and also that if those events (the lion and the death) were associated in the past, there was all reason to suppose they also would be similarly associated in the future. As a matter of fact, animal behavior indicates that these two most basic tenants of the scientific method are deeply ingrained in the function and anatomy of the nervous system. Even more, the most elemental structural units of this system are arranged to that effect. It could be convincingly argued that the reflex arch (fundamental in the already studied physiologic property of conductivity) IMPLIES CAUSALITY, and that the more elaborated concatenation of reflexes (facilitated by the neuronal property of modulation) in conditioned animal behavior DOES THE SAME THING FOR INDUCTION.

Let us take a simple case: A medullary reflex in a decorticated frog. A leg contraction 'produced' by the application of an injurious stimulus to the extremity is precisely a defense against assumed damage or destruction of such anatomical appendage, in other words, the animal Nervous System, even at its most elemental functional level, is arranged in such a way as to suggest that the agent applied to the leg of the frog (an electrical current or a flame) WILL INVARIABLY PRODUCE, OR CAUSE, a potential serious injury to it. The conclusion of these experiments with simple medullary reflexes in frogs (necessitating no more than two neurons, one sensory and another motor) seems inescapable: CAUSALITY IS DEEPLY ROOTED IN THE INTERNAL ORGANIZATION OF THE NERVOUS SYSTEM.

Likewise, a conditioned reflex implies induction. We do not have to look beyond the classical experiments of Pavlov. This investigator was capable, consistently, of eliciting gastric secretion in gastrostomized dogs (dogs with their stomachs surgically opened to permit direct visualization of the gastric mucosa) by the mere tolling of a bell, when such artificial stimulus was previously frequently associated (conditioned) to the administration of food. Obviously here the Nervous System 'reacts' as IF previous associations of phenomena will produce, with all probability, similar associations in the future. If bell tolling and offering of food came together in the past they likely will also come together again in future.

The facts are, I think, incontrovertible and illuminating at the same time: CAUSALITY AND INDUCTION, THE SOLID PILLARDS OF WHAT WE DEFINE AND VIEW AS THE SCIENTIFIC METHOD, ARE DEEPLY ROOTED IN THE INTERNAL ORGANIZATION OF THE NERVOUS SYSTEM, in its elemental anatomic and functional unit: The reflex arch and in the mechanisms allowing and facilitating the further integration of such arches in more complex circuit patterns. This means that CAUSALITY AND INDUCTION ARE INTEGRATED INTO THE WIRING OF THE NEURONAL APPARATUS. From this standpoint Kant appears to be right; causality is a category of human understanding. Here, consequently, resides the need for Science and scientists to formulate explanatory theories. This behavioral pattern is supported and facilitated by the architecture of the Human Brain, the wiring of the relational apparatus.

Let us now proceed to consider the case of another of Kant categories: that of Substance. Underlining the entire realm of physical phenomena is the notion of a 'substratum'. Events 'happen' to things and it just does not make sense to think that they could have any independent 'physical' existence. How else could it be? If there is a fire, again, 'something' has to burn. Every possible 'activity' that can be conceived is, by necessity, related to an 'object' of some kind or another; something partaking of 'substantiality'. Even if I think, the act of 'thinking 'is necessarily related to something located in space and time (the Cartesian cogito). All our vocabulary hinges and revolves about 'facts' which our common sense assumes relates to our surrounding external reality. How could it be then that substance or 'materiality' represents a category of our intellect rather than obvious 'fact'? Anybody with a healthy dose of 'common sense' will resolutely reject such idea. Yet, the more man advances his inquires into Nature, the more he search into the microcosm, the more elusive, incorporeal, vague and fuzzy the 'objects' of scientific scrutiny become. Matter and energy (an imponderable 'substance', in the traditional sense), we discover, are interchangeable physical notions. Naive conception of 'forces' (one of the putative sources of causality) becomes a qualified notion, gravitation corresponding to the curvature of space-time associated with centers of 'mass' (See the Conclusion). Subatomic 'particles' partake of a wave phenomenon and, although we persist in talking about 'material particles', they have transformed into ghostly intangible objects; something far removed from our sensory understanding. In fact, as modern physics has demonstrated, the term 'particles' could easily be replaced, in quantum mechanics, by that of 'events' and nothing will change or suffer; in actuality, the term 'particle', in the traditional sense, becomes a dispensable notion. The 'world' we know and share might be basically constituted by a succession of vanishing, imponderable, fleeting and ghostly phenomena .

Now, if the Universe we know consist of an aggregate of evanescent microcosmic events which we could conceive as their building blocks, then, it follows, that what we 'see' and 'feel' could not be more tangible and factual than its formative components; matter might be nothing but a form of perceived collective phenomena in an space- time manifold. However, if we conceive these events as 'discrete' entities with a 'point like' location in this space-time, a 'particle' (an identifiable object with an extended existence thru a given lapse in that space and time) may only be A SUMMATION OF A SUCESSION OF DISCERNIBLE EVENTS.

If that is the case, how then could it be possible that we do 'conceive' this succession of phenomena as forming an space-time continuum, a toto which we identify as a given object?, could there be any 'explanation' for this presumptive cognitive failure? I believe there is and, again, the possible explanation depends of a functional characteristic of the Nervous System: ITS INCAPACITY TO DISCRIMINATE BETWEEN SUCCESSIVE PHENOMENA BEYOND CERTAIN IRREDUCIBLE TEMPORAL LIMIT; THEREFORE A CONSEQUENCE OF THE NEURONAL PROPERTY OF REFRACTORINESS (See Chapter III).

A typical example of such happening is the so-called 'neuronal persistence' we referred to above; a peculiarity permitting our enjoyment of the cinemascope, among other things. According to the speed we project the cinematographic strip we 'see' either individual frames or 'action' at different tempo, from slow to fast. On the other hand, we have the capacity to 'abstract' from lower levels of neuronal associations meaningful sensorial data to be integrated further. This property of abstraction allows a given collection of percepts to transform into 'objects' of cognition.

These peculiarities of the nervous system justifies the formulation of the following hypothesis: The appearance of continuity we obtain from the surrounding world might be, in actuality, an illusion depending of the RHYTHM OF ACTUALIZATION OF OUR CONSCIOUSNESS, related irrevocably to functional characteristics of our relational apparatus. Causality, Induction and Substantiality might, therefore, be TRUE categories of our understanding accounting for our apparent need to search for 'mechanisms' and explanations in our interpretation of a putative 'external world'.

Now, if the cognitive system of man 'understand' the world causally, inductively and substantially (corresponding to the neuronal properties of conductivity, modulation and neuronal persistence based in refractoriness), does that means such 'categories' are arbitrary arrangement of events or, on the contrary, do they relate to something 'real'?

No answer to this question can we expect from the epistemological standpoint because, as we have seen, Philosophy has not been able to find a solution to this quandary. Yet, if we accept the a priori scientific axiom that this reality exist, then it is reasonable and commonsensical to assume that the way we perceive and cognize should keep some relationship to 'something out there' in Nature. This, of course, does not mean these categories reflect or are 'copies' of worldly events; at least not NECESSARILY SO. Sufficient is to postulate an organizational pattern, a peculiar ordering of phenomena at our cosmic level of existence allowing predictions to be made using the means at the disposal of our cognitive apparatus and that we construe as Causality, Induction and Substantiality; because our brains are already organized in such a way as to imply these categories, in other words they are already ingrained in our nervous system BECAUSE THEY ARE ESSENTIAL TO OUR SURVIVAL. This, however, doesn't means that at other dimensions of reality far removed from ours these categories are valid and capable of affording any useful value to man's enquiring mind.

In fact, the limitations in the discriminatory capacity among closely arranged phenomena (as exemplified by this illusion of an smooth continuity between the frames of a cinematographic strip), could lead us in principle to the acceptance of the possibility of an infinitude of potential universes, of which we are unaware because literally our consciousness evolves its activity OUT OF TUNE with these presumptive realities.

A thought experiment might help to clarify this point. Assume that there is an intermittent white light which we are looking at. Now also assume that on every occasion the light is on our eyes are opened, and likewise that each time when the light is off our eyes are closed. We only will be aware of the white light. On the other hand, if our eyes are opened when the light is always off we will be unaware of its existence. Now assume that instead of being no light at all when our eyes are closed there is a red light on. If we are 'tuned on' to the white light, we obviously will never see the red light and vise versa. In fact, somebody else in tune with the red light will have not the slightest inkling about the existence of the white light.

But let us consider that when our eyes are opened our consciousness is on, and off when they are closed. Let us also postulate that space-time is real and, again, synchronized with our consciousness and the light in such a way that it is on exclusively when consciousness is on. Because of the impossibility of ascertaining how many space-time frames INDEPENDENT of our consciousness truly exist the presumptive number of unknown or unknowable worlds is potentially infinite. In fact, finiteness will ONLY BE POSSIBLE IF THERE IS AN ABSOLUTE

SPACE-TIME FRAME OF REFERENCE. It is clear that for the mind 'in tune' with the blinking red light reality will appear entirely different to the mind in tune with the blinking white light, and both 'images' will be far removed from true 'reality' which will be an aggregation of both.

A Universe composed solely of discontinuous but highly structured events BRIDGED by human consciousness and understanding is therefore a theoretical possibility. Even naive conceptions of Space and Time might not be true ultimate dimensions of such a Cosmo although they would refer to something 'real' for us.

To understand how this is possible consider, for example, the case of a television receptor screen. According to the specific SEQUENCE of reception the electromagnetic waves are assigned a place in the screen, which integration forms the image. Clearly, this amounts to a TRANSLATION OF TIME INTO SPACE. Conversely, the filming camera realizes the opposite operation; that is, translates space into time.

Now, the assignment of a place in a frame could be effected as long as there is an established CODE. Theoretically, therefore, our space-time could represent a transcription of sensorial information based on the peculiar way the Brain has of processing incoming 'information'. It should be emphasized that this encoding do not classifies arbitrarily chaotic stimuli; on the contrary, it should correspond to highly structure sensory data in order for the transcription to be meaningful.

There are numerous experiments proving the ability of the mind, or at least of our cognitive apparatus, to 'create' its own conventional space as well as to establish the conversion of successive discontinuous events into 'an object'. The mind can elaborate out of discrete light events a reality 'in sync ' with consciousness (See Chapter III). There is, therefore, no reason why to assume that similar processing peculiarities of perceptual stimuli do not account for our conceptions of the physical world and the way we view and relate to this putative existence. This seemingly inferential obfuscation is behind all claims as to the need for causal explanations in Science and the assertion that dispensing with speculation will reduce Science to an 'sterile recording of data'.

Now, causality, substantiality and induction had served us well; after all, the morphology and function of the nervous system is, as we saw, arranged to respond AS IF these conceptions were true existing constituents of our World. Something completely different, however, happens when we try to carry them with us in our exploration of other cosmic dimensions. It is here, in an strange environment, where those categories rather than serving an heuristic role and facilitate the postulation of association laws (as we had said the ultimate aim of any scientific endeavor is to allow prediction and 'control' phenomena) in effect constitute a hindrance to this effort, a failure resulting from our stubborn insistence in the application of said notions (causality, induction and substantiality) to a world far removed from our sensory reach and therefore INACCESSIBLE to human 'commonsensical' understanding.

The well known typical instance of such a situation is, of course, the already mentioned case of the emphasis, in Physics, of 'viewing' the microcosm as 'particles' and 'waves'. Some prominent physicists, like Max Born, trying to preserve the reality of microcosmic particles conceived the waves only as a statistical probabilistic contraption indicating the space-time domain where ' the particles' could be found. [1]

By insisting in keeping notions of our intellect, based in our immediate direct experience when searching into a far removed and alien world, we introduce in our inquires unnecessary difficulties which, I believe, ultimate could result in a slowing of further progress . Clearly the cognitive categories of our understanding are here rendering us a disservice, playing 'a trick' with our minds, expressed dramatically in our incapacity to determine, simultaneously, the 'position' and 'momentum' of infra-atomic particles; something demanding, of course, the 'a priori' acceptance of such borrowed unelaborated conceptions to apply in a radically different unperceived expanse of physical reality.

As a matter of fact, there is also strong evidence to suggest that our 'taken for granted' rules of classic 'Logic' do not 'work' in here. In 1964 John S. Bell discovered a discrepancy in the predicted relations of the values for spins recorded in three chosen spatial axis from singlet proton pairs between the results anticipated by commonsensical scientific logic and those postulated by quantum mechanics. When the experiments were carried out ('Quantum theory and Reality' by Bernard d'Pagnat on Scientific American, Nov. 1979, P. 158) the results, in most instances, were in agreement with the predictions of quantum mechanics and against those of our conventional understanding.

Now, we can conceived the possibility of a Cosmo constituted by mysteriously entangled 'discrete' discontinuous events, framed in a space-time manifold and arranged in an orderly structured pattern allowing predictions to be made and laws to be formulated. This World picture, DEVOID of the common categories of cognitive reasoning (and therefore without causality, motion, matter and energy or force) could be AS REAL AS THE CONVENTIONAL ONE AND ESSENTIALLY CANNOT BE DISPROVED in view of the fact that what we consider as 'real' could be the PARTICULAR WAY of how we perceive that Universe; something, as was said before, in itself grounded in the way we interpret a putative 'reality', which depends in the organization of our Nervous System (another complex of events defined by the mind and as such in synchrony with the cosmic level where we conduct our lives), that is, in the wiring of our information retrieval apparatus: In Neuroanatomy and Neurophysiology. Consciousness when 'bridging' the discrete and discontinuous events could, as we pointed out, produce the illusion of CONTINUITY or temporal and spatial extension.

In the light of these 'neural' facts it is not difficult to understand the reluctance of scientists to part with our cherished common-sensical categories of reality (causality, induction and substantiality), as well as, the insistence that the 'business' of Science is to provide for 'explanations' supported by these categories. It is reasonable to assume that this attitude is possible because of a correspondence of events in our immediate environment with the complex of events forming 'The Self'. If this is correct there would be an artificiality of what we conceive as 'outside' and 'inside'; terms which might be meaningless and to be replaced by a GELSTAD of all universal phenomena.

But how, somebody might ask, can we overcome a bias rooted in the morphology and physiology of the nervous system? The human brain has a very remarkable capacity: That of being capable of studying its own activity and structure, in other words, of auto-examination and self-analysis. This peculiarity is tantamount of the potentiality to apprehend oneself as an 'object' of knowledge; the observer becomes the observed and identifies with it. This self-analytic capacity requires as a pre- condition A REFLECTING ACT, the assumption of a differentiated I, the 'I' of the Descartes cogito who was able to surmise his own separate existence by the awareness of his thinking activity. Such reflective quality implies the possibility to 'transcend' our immediate experience and environment.

Transcendence, in this particular context, represents a conscious rejection by the high neuronal centers precisely of the very premises of our understanding which we have just postulated to be engrained in the fabric of our neuronal apparatus (causality, induction and substantiality) which had served us so well in the adaptation to our immediate environment.

But how could this be possible if our claim that these categories are based in neuronal properties (conductivity, association and refractoriness) is true? How could we be able to overcome our neurophysiologic constrains in an ever expanding quest for knowledge and control in strange and ever farther removed cosmic scenarios?

Many of our concepts and symbols, furthermore, are generalizations arrived at (velocity, weight, density) often after a process of formal learning implying the free use of induction. Now, abstraction and induction, we have seen, are cognitive attributes that follow from the neuronal property of modulation or conditioning; therefore in themselves also rooted in neurophysiologic determinants. This way of conceptualizing by means of ever more complex abstractions could reach a point when notions far removed from our ordinary perceptual everyday experience are created and integrated in our cognitive symbols, although incapable of being translated into 'images' because they are only reached by way of logico-mathematical manipulations, elicited thru experimental maneuvers precisely design to reveal them to our consciousness.

The acceptance of these new symbols, however, will force us to discard or reject old conventions, something entirely possible by the modulating capacity of neurons; an activity akin to the complicated elaborations of visual percepts in the cognitive centers of our Visual Cortex. (See Chapter III). Naive causality, the causality of nervous conductivity and reflex arches, could be replaced by that of 'invariable precedence', in a similar manner that light sensations are integrated into recognizable images; the difference only being that the former will requires a deliberate or conscious intellectual effort while the latter proceeds thru a pre-programmed and pre-conscious developmental pattern of integrated neuronal circuits.

But if the human mind implies causality and induction, as we have seen it also possess the capacity to abstract, to transcend the frame of references we take for granted. The laws of Nature are only applicable to our immediate neighborhood from where we borrow images and models we feel had universal validity. That provokes perplexity and confusion when we try to carry them to far removed dimensions. Nothing is more typical of this obfuscation that the already mentioned attempt to convey to the microcosm our concepts of 'particles' and 'waves' which for us carry the notion of 'distinct entities', only to find that events there often partake of both 'qualities'. If we ask equivocal question to nature could we expect unequivocal answers? Is the impossibility to determine in these microcosmic 'particles' simultaneously 'position and momentum' resulting from our stubborn persistence of carrying categories from our immediate environment to far removed world realities? Is the microcosmic 'frothiness' beyond the so-called 'Planck dimension' the result of conceptual difficulties stemming from our desire to frame reality in inapplicable conventions? Is the phenomenon of microcosmic 'entanglement' indication that traditional notions of space and time are comfortable conceptions not applicable to far removed horizons?

Early in the XX Century Kurt Godel published his two incompleteness theorems establishing that any recursive consistent axiomatic system referable to the natural numbers will fail to prove some true propositions based in its axioms. This is tantamount to affirm that any axiomatic system is insufficient, in other words, that there are within the system truths that are not demonstrable according to its own established rules. Are those limitations due to the incompleteness of the system we have created or do they obey to a deeper constrain in Nature? If the first possibility is the case, could it be that far removed physical realities are inaccessible to apprehension with the current corpus of mathematical knowledge? Do we need a new mathematics and/or do we need the formulation of novel conceptual systems applicable to remote physical realities? Could it be possible that in this regard we are reduced to perpetual impotence?

The capacity of the human mind to transcend its limitations, the fetters that restrict our sensorium is dramatically demonstrated in the 'invention' of the already mentioned non-Euclidian geometries (See Chapter I). The rejection by the mind of the taken for granted belief that space has to be flat was a leap to the unknown which proved reach in consequences. In fact Relativity and many concepts of modern physics would not have been possible without the formulations of Riemannian Geometries. A new vista was necessary for the revolutionary leap of the new physics.

If the physical laws we accept as universals are only approximations of an ultimate reality, could we ever be able to reach it? Is the assumption that these mathematical postulates are universally applicable to other cosmic levels of reality valid? Could the perplexities we find, for instance, in Quantum Theory obey to our insistence to apply 'the wrong tools or categories' for the intending job?

This, of course, is impossible to decide given our present stage of knowledge, but it is not unreasonable to speculate that as it happened with Geometry we might need new conceptual forms in several or many branches of mathematics to be able to plow ahead in our search for the ultimate universal 'truth'. I believe that the abstracting capacity of our relational apparatus, the human brain, is marvelously capable to face the challenge...or maybe computers unencumbered by the biological machine Nature has serve us with eventually will bridge the gap.

In conclusion, I think we can be hopeful that what today is considered the basic tenets of the scientific enterprise, the entrenched premises of our 'Reason' (the principles of causality, induction and substantiality) which had served us so well in our cosmic quests, lack universal and paramount validity but could be TRANSCENDED by the immense plasticity and potentiality of the human relational apparatus: The Brain.

The neuronal properties which explain the acceptance of these, once assumed by Kant to be categorical imperatives of our cognition, also, ironically enough, could account for our capacity to transcend and overcome them and their intellectual limitations. The vast expanse of our complex cognition system has the power (by conscious modulation and abstraction) of creating symbols and concepts devoid of immediate perceptual meaning, and to replace with them all those (like the alluded substitution of 'force of gravity' by curved space-time) grounded in our common everyday experience. The relational apparatus of human beings possess unlimited capacities to elaborate new symbols and notions no matter how far removed from our direct sensorial capacity they reside.

The insistence that science has to provide for 'causes' and 'explanations' capable of been understood at the level of our present day sensual frame of reference, is an invalid assumption, an emotional 'hang over' easy to explain but lacking scientific and philosophical support. 'Common sense' is a dispensable ingredient of our Reason, a term which should be redefined after freeing it from its present cultural connotation.

The frontier of microphysics, in conclusion, provides information which, not only place in dubious and ambiguous position all the traditional categories of our understanding, but also points out to an intimate interdependence of reality and consciousness, of phenomena and the 'knowing act'; a merging and fusion of Ontology and Epistemology. Existence without a 'perceiving' mind becomes a useless and dispensable hypothesis devoid of any relevance.

I have hoped in the preceding pages to persuade the reader to the fact that our cognitive activities and in general the process of learning, including scientific pursues, had been based in the tacit acceptance of certain premises of our intellect (causality, induction and substantiality) which, I have suggested, are expressions of the structural characteristics of the nervous system IN TUNE WITH EVENTS AT OUR COSMIC LEVEL OF ACTIVITY, and forming the supporting frame of our cognition and for the mistaken insistence that science has to provide 'explanations'. Such obfuscation, I believe, could eventually result in a retardation in the progress or development of scientific thought (similar to that caused by the prolonged clout of Aristotelian dogma in Western Thought) but, nevertheless, might be overcome by another important and fundamental characteristic of the nervous system: THE CAPACITY FOR TRANSCENDANCE, which could allow the emancipation of our intellect from these extraneous constrains.

These considerations are not sterile platitudes. The informational explosion we are witnessing need to be channeled and selected to produce relevant results and avoid becoming lost in a labyrinthine web of meaningless data or useless theorizing catalyzed by archaic neurobiological operational blueprints.

It is not beyond reason to conceive that in the not too distant future many of the intellectual faculties of humans will be reproduced by ever more sophisticated computers. Now, although there is a lot yet to be learn about the structure and performance characteristics of the Brain and Nervous system, in general it is not too far fetch to conclude that there are vast differences between the latter and the electronic gadgets to which we are becoming so addicted. True, both are in essence data processing devices utilizing electrical impulses, as well as, integrations of basic relay units associated and interrelated in sequences allowing the apparatus, at least in principle, to achieve an end or result. But, at least at the present, here all similarities end.

The brain has the capacity of being self programmable, to be influenced by emotions and instinctual drives besides the inputs from external sources. More important for our purpose is the fact that our neurobiological machine is an old one, as a matter of fact as old as animal life on Earth; a machine therefore that has undergone numerous modifications to improve its performance and to adjust its multifarious functions to the continuous environmental changes experienced by the World thru the ages.

Now, one of the characteristics of many biological systems is the superposition of new structural changes upon older configurations. This process, in the Nervous System, has given rise to a progressive stratified integration of neuronal groups; something often referred by neurophysiologists as 'corticalization' of functions. The brain cortex has become supreme in the higher vertebrates, a place where most sensorial inputs are processed and integrated, enormously increasing the behavioral options of the living organisms and so freeing them from the stereotyped rigidities of the lower association centers.

What all this amounts to is that relay posts in the brain (the neurons) ARE ARRANGED IN A HIERARCHICAL FASHION and although they have the capacity of abstraction and therefore of transcending the sensorial fretters to which by the necessity of biological evolution we are permanently bound, nonetheless they impose upon our consciousness an strong pressure to accept as universally valid the traditional terms of our understanding; like causality, substantiality etc.

Computers and artificial intelligence machines, on the other hand, are not subjected to these biological constrains. Such machines are capable of carrying out operations upon abstract information fed directly into them without the need to 'visualize' phenomena or to 'explain', by way of our traditional mode of thought, the cosmic events. Computers are not restricted by archaic remnants of a previous era; new programs are not bogged down by the vestiges of outmoded wiring schemes.

What all this amounts to is that computers, and their relatives mechanical robots, will only be limited by the adequacy and reliability of their software. Although their problem solving capacity is much larger than the human brain, it would only be optimally utilized if the programmer aims at relating meaningful parameters with a practical intent and avoid the temptation of requesting answers rooted in sensorial interpretations to questions based in preconceived notions of the 'real World'. Their optimal utilization will require in the programmer a renunciation of human perceptual constrains and cognitive conventional forms. The orchestration of abstract configuration patterns of thought will be the only valid intent. The flickering Promethean light should be replaced by a laser beam!

CONCLUSION

Western science has thru the ages developed solidly supported in a conception of knowledge partaking of both, the empiric and rationalistic attires that Greek thought had dressed it with. In scientific matters we affirm to deal with the FACTS, in other words, with the data we collect by means of our perceptive apparatus, and with THE INTERPRETATION, implying with this a further elaboration of a given data so 'sense could be made', or 'understanding', of what is 'meant'. Ordinarily this last 'mental activity' involves an attempt to 'explain' the facts, a search for 'causes' and 'mechanisms'.

We usually rest satisfied if a plausible 'model', capable of accounting for the gathered data, is found. The search, we then will conclude, 'had been fruitful' and barring evidence to the contrary it would lead us, by a process of induction, to formulation of a 'general theory' encompassing all similar instances. INTERPRETATIONS THEN BECOME FACTS THEMSELVES.

Several typical examples of this peculiar way the Western mind 'function' had already been pointed out. One case is that paradigm of Modern Science: The Darwinian theory of evolution. The 'facts', in this peculiar case, are the convincing fossil record, the discovery of extinguished animal and vegetable forms displaying physical characteristics appearing to indicate a gradual development of a scale of creatures with frequent transitional stages. The 'interpretation', on the other hand, is in this case the teleological conception that this evolution was the result of natural selection by way of the 'survival of the fittest'. It is important to realize this difference of factual and speculative aspects of Western theories. Undoubtedly the postulated ' mechanism' could account for the facts of evolution, but as we have seen, other possibilities could, and were not, ruled out. In actuality the acceptance of such 'point of view' by no means signified an EXHAUSTIVE proof of its validity.

Another quite characteristic example also is the Theory of Universal Gravitation. Newton in order to 'explain' the facts represented by the actual motion of the celestial bodies, postulated the existence of a UNIVERSAL FORCE, (the 'cause'), which given certain specifications, could satisfy by means of his famous formulas every possible instance of celestial motion. Now, a 'force' is something totally 'invisible'; nobody had ever 'seen' one, although we claim to actually 'feel' them under certain conditions or to witness the consequences of their 'actions'.

As a matter of fact, this notion of 'force' is essentially intuitive, derived from our own bodily sensations, originally experienced when we try to move inert bodies around or when we 'act' against other states of motions such as, for example, swimming against a current or raising a heavy object above our heads. It was 'logical' to assume that this 'something' which 'acts' or 'causes' a change in the state of motion, could similarly, when extrapolated to a cosmic scale, by induction 'explain' universal orchestrated kinematics.

The force of gravity 'causes' celestial motions as the 'survival of the fittest', 'acting' in random mutations, 'caused' evolution. Ultimately, therefore, to 'explain' something is to postulate a discernible 'cause'. We need to 'single out' or identify a presumed 'reason' for the phenomena we observe in our surroundings; be it in our neighbor backyard or in an extragalactic dimension. Western Man, in order to 'understand' universal events at any level, has to 'visualize' in his own mind 'how things come about'; something entailing, as it was said before, the elaboration of models accessible to his intellect precisely by their being drawn from his immediate experience. The 'survival of the fittest' was a view deeply ingrained in the protestant ethic of bourgeoisie English society. In like manner it was easy to construct a model whereby a deflection by a 'force' of a body's trajectory would produce a circular motion. All you have to do, our high school teacher told us, was to tie a stone at the end of a string and 'swing it around'.

The 'orderliness' and predictability of Newtonian mechanics was well suited to the deistic creed that stormed the Western World during the XVII Century, a predictable, regimented universe which subsequently crystallized with the Enlightment; an harmonious, comforting world view with enormous appeal to the rising bourgeoisie. Eventually, however, as experimental systems became more refined, there were 'facts' which could not be explained by established theories or its laws. The result of the experiment of Michelson-Morley was hard to reconcile, for instance, with classic Newtonian mechanics UNLESS there was a 'contraction' of the body in motion in the direction of such motion. It took the sublime simplicity of a mind unencumbered by what Poincare called 'the history of space and time theories', in essence free from the drag of 'sedimented' knowledge, to come up with the disarmingly naive, perhaps even child-like hypothesis, of 'A SHORTENING' OF SPACE ITSELF in the direction of motion in reference to an observer outside the system.

Now, Einstein revolutionary idea represented a radical departure from traditional modes of thought rooted in the human mind since most remote times. Space was for people either totally filled, and then a plenum as Parmenides thought, or mostly empty, as the atomists maintained: A CONTAINER, that is, a tridimensional 'vault' were ' things' unfolded their existence. The objects 'within it' could change their shape without altering the dimensional specifications of the vault. Space, and also time, were absolute and immutable; two independent frames where everything that existed took its place.

The Special Theory of Relativity, with its dependence of space-time dimensional values in the 'state of motion' of the observed phenomena in relation to the observer's system, was an unprecedented rejection of 'commonsensical' evidence provided by our perceptual apparatus (or at least of the way how man had come to interpret this evidence). We all have seen 'objects' or bodies capable of changes in dimensions, but that the dimensions of the measuring frame themselves would depend on the relative motion of the observed system-frame in relation to that of the observer was a postulate far removed from our everyday experience because the effect, according to the theory, was negligible at the very low 'relative' velocities of our immediate surroundings.

The universal kinematics ultimately evolving from these fateful conceptions, as we all know, also dispensed entirely with the comfortable and reassuring traditional notion of 'force of gravity'; replacing it with the idea of a 'warping' of space-time itself taking place around 'centers' of mass [1]. Strange as these conceptions might be, still they are based in 'facts' (the experimental and observational evidence), and still provide with a 'cause' for 'explanation' and formulation of the necessary mathematical relational equations (for the curvature of space -time instead of the traditional Newtonian mechanics). Likewise, they also still provided 'a model' which could be understandable to our intellect (we all had seen a curved railway track and experienced a 'pull', due to 'inertia', when a train at high speed takes a turn). Newtonian 'Universal Gravitation' became a special case of the more general Theory of Relativity only applicable, as the theory goes, at the 'low' speeds we encounter in our cosmic surroundings.

Undoubtedly the idea that the 'curved thing' IS space itself was a 'weird' one, something difficult to 'conceive', but by analogy, at least, we are capable of 'imagining', or 'visualizing', the possibility of such a happening. By the same talking, the relativity of space, time and mass upon 'state of motions', although strange to us, was entirely conceivable because, as had been pointed out before, we all have seen objects shortening in size and clocks 'slowing down' (admittedly for different reasons) but nevertheless we are able to 'imagine' those things happening.

One point needs to be emphasized: Any scientific theory no matter how beautiful, to be 'useful' NEEED TO HAVE PREDICTIVE VALUE, otherwise it will be no better than a colorful dress. The possession of this predictive capacity, however, does not indicate it is necessarily UNIVERSALLY TRUE, as we have seen in the example of Newtonian mechanics. Many other examples could be found. Copernican Heliocentrically Theory did have more predictive value than Ptolemy conception of a central position for the Earth with his proposals of 'hemicycles', and despite of vigorous resistance by the powers to be it was finally accepted. For similar reasons Relativity debunked the theory of a 'luminiferous ether', but it then was unable to account for quantum effects. The 'ultimate truth' encompassing all possible universal scenarios is an elusive concept, incapable of being reach by scientific means. ALL WE CAN HOPE ARE APPROXIMATIONS BY A PROCESS OF PROGRESSIVE ACCRETION (each theory having better predictive value than it's immediate predecessor).

Western Man not satisfied with the discovery of useful relations among clusters of events had embarked in the unprecedented and monumental task of 'explaining' WHY these events are so grouped, in other words, to search for an ulterior REASON; something which betrays a belief in a purposeful unfolding of nature, the EXISTENCE of final causes capable of instilling meaning and content to our lives, in essence a quasi-religious quest.

After divesting themselves from the numinous conception of Nature our forebears were to discover with their Promethean fire the 'truth' behind appearances. A mathematical 'demonstration', as it was already pointed out, is not more than a 'revelation' of hidden associations between assumed logical parameters ultimately representing CONCEPTIONS OF THE HUMAN MIND, but which, nevertheless, keep a CLOSE RESEMBLANCE to physical categories at our cosmic 'level of existence'.

It is precisely the early Greek 'confusion' between the MEASURING DEVICES AND WHAT IS MEASURED that underlines much argument and epistemological perplexity in our culture which had lasted, amazingly enough, up to our own 'gloriously advanced' present day technological civilization. It already appeared clearly defined in the Pythagorean belief that 'everything are numbers' and was subsequently embodied in Plato's theory of knowledge, where he distinctly formulates the thesis that ultimate truth resides in the mind. Later on it ran undisturbed in the blood and soul of the scholastics and Renaissance Rationalists, from whom in time it was borrowed, without questions or hesitations, by all branches of our distinguished and advanced 'exact' sciences.

Relational laws applicable to the physical world are only elaborations resulting from a peculiar, perhaps even 'mysterious', concatenation of phenomena at our cosmic level of reality which our brains are marvelously equipped to group or relate, but which are not necessarily valid at different universal horizons; something that becomes more and more obvious the farther removed from our vicinity we choose to apply our assumptions. Our categories of cognition serve us well when related to phenomena in our immediate physical neighborhood, BUT LACK absolute universal validity applicable to all dimensions. The conviction, when we organize our perceptions according to associative laws of our making, that we had 'understood' the phenomena 'explained' by them is a mistaken illusion based in an old epistemological obfuscation probably arising in the religion-substitutive nature of Greek Science.

This profound Western bias, which I believe originated in the atheism of the Ionian mind and, strangely enough, influenced the dogmas of post-Hellenistic religion, is behind our compulsive need for 'models' ever since the dawn of Greek Civilization and has prospered unencumbered until our 'amazing' XXI Century. The anxious search for the 'primordial' had no parallel in any other world culture, the enquire into Nature has never reached such apotheosic magnitude anywhere; it is a futile search for 'primeval truth'.

Do we need to 'explain' evolution of organic life in order to advance biological science, or merely to ACCEPT IT? Do we need a 'model' of infracosmic phenomena to UNDERSTAND them, or would had we 'progressed ' in this field equally satisfactorily by recording the facts and manipulating them for our convenience? Did we need to 'extrapolate' images from our cosmic level into infraphysics in order to, for instance, construct the 'atomic bomb', or would have been enough a rigorous integration of observable facts without further elaborations of preconceived notions upon the structure of 'matter'? Do we need 'models' in order to device appropriate experimental designs, or would be enough to base them in gathered information in the given subject?

The problem in providing adequate answers to these questions is that more than 3000 years of cultural accretions had conditioned our minds to take for granted the imperious need for such models. If the history of science is closely reviewed, 'explanations' by these means of 'how things happens' are A POSTERIORI speculations which in themselves DO NOT ADD ANYTHING PRACTICAL to the given observational facts or experimental results (besides being not necessarily 'true' in the conventional sense) and, as a matter of fact might, in some cases, have the detrimental effect of diverting or detracting investigators from further experimentation along some profitable lines of inquire. Nature, like a dumb teacher, only 'answers' us in the same terms of the questions we formulate. Has the experimental evidence, for example, completely ruled out all possible evolutionary hypothesis other than 'natural selection'? Of course not, but this hypothesis has become a handed down unassailable dogma of our 'conventional wisdom'. I can 'conceive', for instance, of mutations not being 'random', but rather the final event in a reversed process of translation and transcription 'triggered' by environmental factors. Have any experimental design ever been setup to specifically disprove that possibility? If not, why investigators stubbornly denied any environmental INFLUENCE in mutations by simply adducing that 'there is no evidence to the contrary'? Isn't strange, for example, that literally from millions of structural possibilities the immune cells, by random chance, undergo THE mutations which allows them to 'produce' a specific antibody? How long will take a chimp to write a poem by random clicking in the keyboard of a typewriter machine? [2]

Something very similar to 'dogmatic blindness' also took place in Physics, where Classic Mechanical postulates never went challenged for more than 300 years. Were not for the 'strange' curiosity of Michelson, who developed the 'useless' desire to measure the 'ether wind', we would have lack the experimental incentive for the assault on classic concepts crystallizing in Relativity. It is not difficult to imagine the retardation that this deprivation would have meant to modern physics not, as ordinarily we are 'accustomed' to think, because of the attendant 'lack in understanding' that would have result from it, but because of the incapacity to 'predict' more accurately a whole array of cosmic events which we are now better equipped to conduct. The fact of the matter is that no theory 'invented' by the human mind can ever hope to afford a complete 'explanation' of natural phenomena and the farther removed from our immediate environment we probe the less that we can base our relational formulas to something tangible capable of being 'visualized' by the human mind; in fact such reductionist approach will led us astray and actually retard progress.

We can pointed out to many other deeply settled scientific beliefs that still today are held dogmatically and as much charged with emotions as those of antiquity. It will be a modern sacrilege for instance, to question, the 'Big Bang' theory. It allures notions of a biblical churning 'Chaos' deeply rooted in the Christian mind and the violent powers of Nature we have unleashed with this 'Nuclear Age'. But what is the convincing evidence? Could the facts, like the 'red shift', the homogeneity of the cosmic background radiation, or the recently discovered 'primordial gravitational waves', have any other explanation than universal 'expansion'? Other possibilities have not been seriously explored and soon theory crystallized as a 'fact' itself. The generating power of article 'THE' will seal its fate. THE Big Bang is here to stay. Never mind the existence of a mysterious 'inflationary period' (which it is assumed to be 'documented' now by the discovery of these putative 'primordial gravitational waves') postulated to erase some discrepancies in the rate of expansion of the early Universe, or the apparent acceleration of this expansion by a putative 'dark energy' that acts as reverse gravitation. This entrenched dogmatic view of the Cosmo will be held until some new incontrovertible evident comes along.

The eschatological version of the disappearance of dinosaurs at the end of the Cretaceous is another case. Never mind that we do not have a clear definition of what a dinosaur was, or that nobody had a clear reason why other living forms, like many birds and mammals survived this putative disaster. This theory is held heroically and passionately, becoming another entrenched dogma of the age. Other possibilities are flatly denied. We can also mention as another example the passion surrounding the theory of man-made climatic change. Different explanations for the change are flippantly dismissed despite of the fact that long term climatic fluctuations had not been well understood or recorded. Let me clarify that I believe human pollution should be controlled for reasons related to health and environmental hazards, but long term reasons for temperature fluctuation are multi-factorial and not well understood.

What counts, as it was said before and can hardly be overemphasized, ARE RESULTS FOLLOWED BY CORROBORATION OF FINDINGS BY INDEPENDING INVESTIGATORS. (A typical example of this need is the already alluded case of the N-Rays affair. See Chapter II).Theories as to why and how can be dispensed with, particularly when it is realized that all explanations proposed by man necessarily are incomplete views of reality conceived by our imperfect relational apparatus, a marvelously complex machine but nevertheless, as it was said before, adapted solely to processing and utilizing information from our immediate cosmic neighborhood; yet progressively less capable of affording practical help the farther remove we proceed in our quest of universal horizons. Research, at the present, frequently is an expensive business enterprise enlisting large groups of investigators and special equipment, making materially and practically impossible to carry the investigations in the ideal conditions by making very difficult the most important and critical step of all: CORROBORATION. Also frequently the institutions conducting the experiments do possess hidden agendas which distort and trivialize the results with the attendant waste and, even more, the danger of wrong conclusions.

Yet, it should be emphasized again, the PREDICTIVE POWER of corroborated findings is the main value of any scientific endeavor and its ultimate justification. The affirmation of a superfluous world view based in equivocal ontological premises rooted in cognitive categories dependent, in the last analysis, in notions based on dispensable properties of our relational apparatus, can only lead to a confused epistemology more evident and dramatic the farther we inquire into the vast scenarios of the Cosmo, and the more removed from everyday experience the search proceeds. But our neurological machine (The Human Brain) also possess, as we had proposed, the biological capacity to TRANSCEND ITS OWN COGNITIVE FRAME OF REFERENCES and obtain, not 'understanding', but practical advantage in the exploration of far removed cosmic horizons. (See Chapter IV)

———————— CHAPTER V ————————

It is perhaps in the field of Medicine where the inconsistencies of the Western epistemological position become more blatant and manifested. Traditionally an harmonious blend of an original 'healing art' indigenous to all primitive societies and Greek Science, Western Medicine has developed into a highly refined technical oriented enterprise which, for all its widely publicized spectacular achievements, parades more prominently than any other science the consequences of the misguided and peculiarly distorted views of Greek theory of knowledge.

Maybe no other scientific discipline in modern times partakes more notoriously from the original Western obsession with 'explanations' and 'mechanisms'. Diseases, we affirm, have to be understood in order to 'rationally' tackle the problem of therapy. To proceed otherwise, we contend disdainfully, is to be 'empiric' (a term semantically bastardized to mean arbitrariness). Knowledge of causes and pathogenesis, we adamantly emphasize, is the only 'logical' way to advance the possibility of controlling, curing and avoiding the ravages of diseases upon the human community. Yet, and paradoxically, it is precisely in the history of the 'maiden science' where we can witness more vividly exemplified the excesses that subscription to rational Western epistemological values can bring upon a human activity.

The pitfalls plaguing medical epistemology thru the ages are complex; although they have, perhaps not unexpectedly, being as a whole poorly understood when not completely unrecognized or unaccepted. It is a peculiarity of our profession, stemming from its very nature, to be subdivided in practical and academic endeavors. The first imparted treatment and render service to the public, while the second is assumed to investigate the 'nature' and 'mechanisms' of disease, to search for new therapeutic avenues and to occupy themselves with teaching duties.

Modern technology has become the great despot of Science which, as far as Medicine is concern, has provoked a situation whereby experimentation has turned progressively more expensive and, in many instances, ever more removed from the comprehension of the practicing physician; who is increasingly less capable of analyzing critically the excellence of the conclusions which he is demanded to accept as unquestionable truths.

As a result of this prevailing situation the medical profession has come to resemble strangely a religious congregation. It has its hierarchy of ordained ecclesiastics: The egregious academician. Its infatuated body of devotee followers: The common physician. Its own liturgy: The meeting and workshops where the high priests impart the dogma received with submissive owe by the believers, who at the conclusion are rewarded with a general dispensation of alms and blessings: The continuous medical education credits. Finally Medicine also has its sacramental mystery: The ceremonial and official assignment of special names to sundry symptomatic complexes which, henceforth, 'materialize' out of nowhere into specific, and hitherto unrecognized, 'nosological entities'. The miraculous power of words renders tangibility and cast away all doubts, explaining something until then baffling and obscure. Naming something is in fact to 'know' what that something is; a granting of existence.

The situation is neither new not surprising. Ever since the times of Aristotle there has been a pernicious tendency to equate classification with knowledge (perhaps it is not a coincidence that so many physicians of the past had been botanists or vise versa). The origin of this misconceived approach in what concerns medical sciences will be explored subsequently more in detail but, suffice is to mention the excesses and distortions of the so-called 'Natural History School' of Schonlein, Fuchs and Constatt based upon their 'Fundamentum Divisionis'.

The impressive edifice of Medicine, perhaps because of its dual character as science and art, since time immemorial has been extremely vulnerable to assaults by all kinds of quacks, charlatans, mountebanks and other assortments of colorful personalities. Maybe more dangerous and deleterious, however, has been the tendency to revert frequently to unchallenged dogma and sophistical analysis disguised as 'good science'; which, I believe, has indulge in unnecessary wastage of time and efforts, resulting in a monumental growth of a meaningless literature, already envisaged by Garrison in the first quarter of the XX Century when protesting that 'never have medical authors been so verbose and to so little purpose!'('History of Medicine'. Saunders Co. 1929, P. 679).

The reductionist approach of Western intellect, the search for fundamentals as a base for 'knowing' and controlling the environment, nowhere confronts more formidable obstacles than in what concerns biological phenomena and, among the latter, there hardly could be found any more elusive and difficult to comprehend, and apprehend, than the 'deranged states of health' commonly known as 'diseases'; a notion, as we will see later on, which, thanks to the diligence of physicians thru the ages conveys such a variety of meaning and connotation as to serve more to confuse than to help in the understanding of those 'derangements'.

The reason, as we commence to realize, is that 'diseases' are multi-factorial arrays of interpenetrated biological processes unfolding over time and which complexities frequently defy a clear understanding by the human mind. To be sure, some facts, or factors, in disease could be identified and even isolated for everybody to see. Microorganisms, which we assume 'produce' sickness, can be isolated and manipulated to experimentally elicit an illness similar to that suffered by the patient from whom they were originally recovered. But we all know today that it takes more than a colonization of a given kind of pathogenic microorganism to 'provoke' a given disease. An infectious process represents a complex interrelation of environmental and host factors, of deleterious and immunologic events still very incompletely understood in our present day marvelous technological age.

This peculiar dichotomy of Medicine, based in the eminently dual origin of the profession is, I believe, in itself a weakness not shared to the same extent by any other branch of modern science. That is why from being defined in its inception as an 'art' Medicine is today considered also by most as a 'science'. The modern physician is then by the nature of his activities, as Castiglione said, a 'demiurge', a duality of investigator and practitioner. Few if any, however, can held successfully in modern times to both banners. The breath and expansion of knowledge and techniques is such that requires the organization of specialties and subspecialties within the large domains of research and practice.

The demands that have brought about this proclivity have given rise to an ever growing division. No longer is it possible for a man with a stethoscope or a microscope to singlehanded make significant contributions in his field of expertise. The necessity for ever expanding and complex paraphernalia of sophisticated instrumentation, and of field trials and collaborative projects, have increasingly divorce research from practice. The former, by natural gravitation, has become the providence of academic centers and research institutes, which are the only capable of mustering the resources necessary for investigative work in modern scale.

Research, because of its complexity, has become a group enterprise with self imposed aims and a burgeoning bureaucracy ever farther removed from the needs and realities of the medical practitioner, and, even more, from his level of understanding of basic disciplines and/ or statistical methodology utilized in analyzing results and evaluate conclusions intelligently.

Because of the increasing needs to compete for a limited supply of funds, whether from government grants or other donating organizations (always tied-in with the capacity to 'produce' specific results in a rigid and demanding time frame), there arises in the academic centers an understandable pressure to publish which has eventuate in the exuberant proliferation and growth of medical literature, with a concomitant decrease in quality; a wasteful drain in time, resources and effort. Productivity 'at all costs' has become the battle cry and main goal of modern research and Medicine is no exception.

The situation in the last quarter of the XX Century had already reached the proportions of a true deluge, and there is around not even the semblance of a Noah's Arch! The exuberant prose coupled with little originality and worth, intriguingly, resembles the economic inflation-recession that is threatening the fabric of Western Society.

There is high time to pause momentarily the insane race and ponder upon the origin and nature of medical and biological knowledge, and also the validity of its premises and purposes. In order to understand the epistemological problems germane to this science it is, however, necessary to place them in an historic perspective. We will then commence our inquires with a synoptic attempt which, hopefully, will help us to better comprehend the origin and evolution of the problems plaguing today our profession.

The staff of Asclepius is a most important riddle confronted in any careful search for the historical origin of Western Medicine. Its meaning is deeply buried in the mist of the legendary past. Our first clue is the curling and twisting serpent threatening, in many of the pictorial and architectonic depictions of the venerable God, to crawl up his arm. Man among other things, is a symbolizing creature and here, in the realm of allegoric expressivity, is where we should seek the hidden meaning of such mythological renditions.

The serpent, the mysterious reptile devoid of motile appendages, the animal who periodically changes its skin and frequently surfaces to the ground from deep crevices and orifices seemingly spurting from the entrails of Mother Earth was, since early times, identified by primitive man with chthonian forces, and so venerated among ancient Neolithic agricultural societies as a God in its own right, the principle controlling the rhythmic and periodic unfolding patterns of Nature: Like the seasons, the moon phases, the growth of crops and, most revealingly, the menstrual cycle. (See Joseph Campbell 'The Mask of the Gods. Occidental Mythology' . The Viking Press. 1972, P. 9)

The serpent, therefore, was a symbolic representation of the chthonian powers and knew of the mysteries of cyclic rebirth in Nature, of which the periodic waning of its skin was a typical example, clearly reminiscent of that other great biologic rhythm: The menstruation. Its allegoric force as embodiment of the secret of THE FEMENINE is then easily understood. Human fertility cycles were naturally tied-in, among primitive agricultural societies, with the grand fertility cycles of 'mother earth'; as the impressive archeological evidence in the Mediterranean basin, India, and China in the form of numerous statuilles of female figures frequently displaying oversized genitals, (probably representing fertility goddesses or votive charms) sufficiently substantiates.

But the serpent, also in its capacity as the 'up-keeper' of rhythmic balances and seasonal universal changes from which bronze-age agricultural societies depended so much for their livelihood was, by analogy and extension, viewed as a god of healing, in other words, as repository of a power capable of restituting health (diseases being conceived by ancient Levantine people as a 'disruption' in an inner organic equilibrium). In this capacity (as a healing deity) she was even worshiped in ancient Babylon and Esmun, where a Semitic god strangely reminiscent of Asclepius was depicted with a couple of twisted serpents in his rod. Legend tells us also that Asclepius was taught the healing arts by the centaur Chiron (himself an incarnation of the wild spirits of the forests) and apparently its cult originated in Thessaly; although this point has not been sufficiently proved. Subsequently, according to Pindar, he was struck by Zeus thunderbolt because the latter was jealous of his powers.

Now, Zeus we know, was the highest deity in the Olympian Pantheon, a conglomerate of divinities which, according to the mythological record, appears to have superseded an ancient group of divinities (See Appendix II) and probably represented originally an Indo-European tutelary god. Ultimately Asclepius, the story goes, is finally admitted to Olympus with full status, indeed as a son of Apollo, himself a prototype of the new divinities whom made their abode in the mythical mountain.

This legend clearly suggest that Asclepius, the possessor of the wisdom of the serpent and so imbued with the mysterious power of healing, was originally a bronze-age deity, one of a class displaced when the Indo-European invasions conquered the primitive Aegean races, and who was eventually restituted to his ancient importance when a process of transculturation between the older populations and the invaders took place.

By then, of course, his ritual cures were dispensed in sanctuaries erected throughout the land, and a priestly class was in charge of the elaborated ceremonies of the cult. This exegesis of mythological evidence is also consistent with anthropological and archeological evidences, suggesting a very early development of the healing arts associated with ancient religious practices among primitive peoples around the world, aimed at conjuring the powers of Nature in the restitution of the 'loss balance' of health, set asunder, according to belief, by demonic forces.

The scientific spirit, and Medicine was one of its manifestations, was firstly kindled in the West among the Ionians descendents of the Aegean races displaced by the Indo-European invasions, and who casted away the numinous in the search for 'truth'. From among the Pythagoreans emerged some of the earliest true Greek medical theoreticians, like Alcmaeon of Croton and Philolaus of Tarentum, who championed the thesis of the harmony and identification of the Cosmo with Man, and who apparently first expounded the concept of the 'central fire', 'the heat of the seed', as the source of life. Their theoretical conceptions explained the act of respiration as a cooling mechanism of the body acting thru the four humors: blood, phlegm, black and yellow bile. Some of their biological ideas, such as these concepts of the four humors and the central position of the liver in human physiology (originally tied-in with divination practices), as well as the importance of respiration (one of the basic tenants of Egyptian Medicine), apparently originated in the Fertile Crescent. These beliefs subsequently found their way into the Hippocratic Corpus, which also availed itself of ideas of 'critical days', again of Pythagorean origin and rooted in astrological conceptions common at the time among agricultural societies in this geographical locus. As a matter of fact, those speculative notions, together with the Empedoclean theory of man as a microcosm (also, as we have seen, an old Levantine belief) composed of the same four elements (earth, water, air and fire) as the Cosmo itself, in essence summarize the basic concepts of that Corpus as far as biological theories is concern.

Indeed, and to the horror of those medical purists who romantically trace the ancestry of Modern Medicine to Hippocrates, there is little originality, as far as basic ideas are concern, in the extant compilations of his writings. On the other hand, scanty credit is given by modern medical scholars to the true forefathers of theoretical medical principles, while no eulogy is spare, or appears quite sufficient, in extolling the purported methodological excellence of the saga of Cos, who, we are told, based his conclusions in 'observation and experience tempered by reason'. Examples of this idolatry are so frequent and common place as to seem almost pointless to mention some.

Garrison in his massive and ponderous history tells us: "Hippocrates was not acquainted with experiment BUT NO PHYSICIAN EVER PROFITED MORE BY EXPERIENCE" ('History of Medicine' Saunders Co. 1929, P. 94. Italics are mine).

The blatant contradiction between these renditions and the basic tenants of the first aphorism is immediately obvious. According to the immortal locution "Life is short and the art long, the occasion fleeting, experience fallacious and judgment difficult".

Now, this can hardly be a statement referable to the same source as that which our distinguish historian alluded above and which we have held to epitomize the cannons of Hippocratic Medicine. It can hardly be ascribed to the man who had been venerated with a quasi-religious fervor for over 2500 years. Yet, we will have to admit, the reference is absolutely in keeping, and totally congruent, with the mainstream of Classic Greek thought and philosophical conceptions ever since the pre-Socratics. Appearances are deceptive and not to be trusted, perceptions are elusive and 'the truth' lies deeply hidden beyond the world of sensory data, only to be grasped by 'Reason'. It is a theme sounded above all by the Eleatics and subsequently integrated in the epistemology of Plato; becoming, as we have seen, a subject of heated controversy in philosophy among Rationalist and Empiricists up to the XVIII Century.

Why then, do we in the medical profession adamantly and unequivocally, without even the semblance of a doubt as far as I know, affirm that Hippocrates was the champion of the empiric method? It will be ludicrous to suppose that these illustrious and enormously learned authors have not read, or somehow forgotten, the continuously quoted first aphorism. Have not they sensed the contradiction? How could anybody who questions the validity of sense experience base his method JUST IN THAT?

To those acquainted with the Corpus the reasons are clear: Because, surprisingly enough, such a warning or similar commentaries are notoriously absent from the remainder of the Hippocratic works, which endorse, without further elaboration or assumptions, the method of 'bedside' observation as the basis for prognosis and treatment, upholding it as the most important functions and task of Medicine; indeed constituting that 'practical approach' which has brought fame to this most ancient body of medical writings.

"It is necessary to study all that can be seen, feel and hear everything that one can recognize and use" is explicitly stated in 'The diagnosis'. Medicine was truly AN ART in need to avail itself of sensory data for its works; as much as sculpture, painting, or any other practical craft does. It could hardly have been otherwise.

The answer then to the contradictions within the fabric of the Hippocratic Corpus is, of course, that they represent A COPILATION of works of diverse origin incorporating, according to modern view, not only the ethical and practical canons of the Coan School, but also some Cnidian contributions and, as mentioned before, speculative theorizing of Empedoclean and Pythagorean sources. This main body of thought and practice (perhaps first organized during the Alexandrian period by the command of the Egyptian diadochi to be collected for the library of Alexandria) has kept alluring us because of its ethical supremacy and individualized approach to patient care which, with the schizophrenic tendency characteristic of modern times, we assiduously emphasize in our rhetoric, despite of becoming ever more remote and meaningless to our spirit in this detached technological and impersonalized age.

Hippocrates, we have reluctantly to admit, is A SYMBOL, a synthetic ideal (in the Platonic sense) of the qualities we prize the most in a physician, an emotional hangover from a remote past with very little relevance to modern medical practice, when the health sciences had become an industry and the profession an incorporated business enterprise. Yet, very revealingly, we continue to worship with idolatry that ideal.

Now, this is not a disclaim as to the existence of the historical Hippocrates, but rather a remainder of the fact that, as with so many of the early philosophers, his historical personality have been so much altered by legend, plagiarism and distortions of all sorts, as to render impossible a clear assessment of what is original in their works and what is not. It is beyond the scope of this work to delve in detail into the authenticity of the Hippocratic Canon, but we should mention that according to Emerson Crosby Kelly the only treatises which are reasonably assumed today to be genuine are: The Prognosis, On Airs etc., On Regimen in Acute Diseases, seven of the books of aphorisms, Epidemics I and III, On the Articulations, On Fractures, On the Instruments of Reductions and the Oath.('The Genuine Works of Hippocrates'. Francis Adams. 1972, Introduction vii) [1]

For all we know, as it is the case with many ancient works, the question of authenticity is largely controversial and very likely never would be conclusively settled, but this fact should not unduly concern us here. Regardless of whether 'the father of Western Medicine' was a man or an ideal it seems pretty obvious that, at the time of the Greek Golden Age, there was already in existence a class (sects should be better called) of skillful practitioners whose bedside methods, personalized approach and high ethical standards had served as examples and inspiration to countless generations of physicians since the XVIII Century (in some cases even as early as the Renaissance), not counting its more vital and immediate influence in the Ancient World, particularly in the Alexandrian School.

Hippocratic Medicine is eminently observational, then empiric, as had been pointed out by Burnet; perhaps one of the earliest sciences so approached in the ancient world. It emphasizes, above all, prognosis and prophylaxis as well as reject 'idle' theorizing. Its practical character transpires in words that reach us thru the ages. The endorsement of verifiability as a basis for scientific method, the insistence that 'from things above and below nothing could be referred to in order to discover the truth', represents an explicit plead for the observational method in Science, almost in complete contraposition to the speculative features in some of the treatises integrated into the Hippocratic Corpus (even including the 'On the Nature of Man' where the theory of the humors is developed with its characteristic Pythagorean and Empedoklean flavor; but, it should be pointed out, is not considered by some a part of the genuine writings) [2] (Ibid. P. 1-2)

What transpire, therefore, from those tracts of the Hippocratic writings considered as genuine, is an eminently empiric and practical approach to Medicine, explaining the un-hesitant ordering of such activities among the arts. Healing facilitated by proper medication was the ultimate goal of the sect of dedicated physicians and, as a matter of fact, the most important if not the only justification for its existence.

After divesting itself of its original numinous content this mistress of the sciences, primarily and for good reasons considered an art deeply rooted in nature, was more than any other discipline to champion the principle of observation as the basis of all knowledge, against the inroads of 'Greek Reason' and also of oriental mysticism, which questioned the validity of sensory information (maya, the world illusion of the Dravidian 'ascetic of the forest') and came to believe that 'truth' could only be ascertained by meditation upon the nature of the Cosmo, in other words, by an introverted search.

Medicine, originally and above all, was a practical discipline, a true craft, an eminently 'down to earth' occupation which, after rejecting the original prevalent notion that disease was the result of the 'activity' of an spiritual agent needing somehow to be exorcised, came during the dawn of Greek thought and philosophy to be viewed as an in-balance, that is, a disruption in a state of equilibrium which 'restitution' by way of diet and medication was the 'business' of Medicine to attempt. Revealingly enough, the goal of all treatment was to 'help Nature'. The method, by necessity, needed to be empiric, observational, divested of any 'empty hypothesis' or of nothing which could not be referred to 'in order to discover the truth'. The success of a medication, or of any other form of treatment, was measured by its ability to restitute health; a pure observational fact.

If incantations and purifications were not able to 'drive away afflictions' they also would not be able to 'induce' them; so 'that the cause was no longer divine but human'. This simple and clear point of view indicates that if Man could meddle in health matters, as in any other universal phenomena, he will be in control of the Cosmo, which was absurd. A great dose of respect and awe for Nature and its workings is betrayed in these passages of Hippocratic writings. The numinous had commenced to dissipate from Man's horizons.

At no time, it is apparent, were the Early Greek Physicians thinking that, in attempting by means of their diets and medications a restitution of health, they were in any sense 'opposing' Nature grand designs or struggling against Fate, but rather helping it to fulfill its purpose; a teleological ultimate end. Medical activities, instead, were more akin to a 'propitiation' but without rituals or invocations; an activity devoid of magic content. In health matters God has been removed from the immediate experience and accessibility of Man. Greek rationalism, despite of the suggestions of the first aphorism, had, not yet, infiltrated and distorted the fabric of ancient Medicine.

Paralleled to the Coan School there emerged in Cnidus another school of medical thought that, although little of their writings and even less of their medical theories have survived, ironically enough appears to have exerted a more permanent, actually an everlasting influence in the medical profession. By all indications it was this school the one which firstly expounded the view of disease as an 'entity', therefore inaugurating the nomenclatural deluge which still today plague modern Medicine. In the inimitable words of Garrison:

"Cnidian Medicine, the Medicine of library classifiers, of the pathological specimen of Broussais 'disease served on a plate', is largely the Medicine of our own period of ultra-refined diagnosis and highly specialized therapy" ('History of Medicine'. Saunders Co. 1929, P. 99)

According to Galen, for the Cnidians symptoms represented diseases in their own right, and they described seven types of bile, four of consumptions and twelve of the urinary bladder. Classificatory obsession had an early start in the history of Medicine stemming, it appears clearly, in a profound unremitting and early confusion about what a 'disease' really was. Revealingly, the classificatory efforts and theoretical preoccupations of the Cnidians were not translated into more efficacious therapeutic regimes. As a matter of fact, their medications consisted of simple traditional methods of purgation, dieting, hygiene etc.

During the Golden Age of Greek civilization, besides Hippocrates and the Cnidian School, it took also place the extensive biological studies of Aristotle and Theophrastus; but the next period of importance from the standpoint of the evolution of medical thinking was, without doubt, the Ptolemaic Empire during the Hellenistic Period. Here, under the auspices of sympathetic rulers who graciously helped to foster the scientific spirit, worked and toil men of the stature of Euclid and Ptolemy (among others), whose contributions to geometry and astronomy are well known to require any comments. Also in Alexandria there was an exuberant proliferation of medical sects. Among them the more notorious were: The Dogmatic, Empiricist, Methodist, Pneumatics and the Eclectics. In fact, the terms 'dogmatic' and 'empiricist' were perhaps firstly applied in the field of Medicine. This fact, more than any other, underscores the dual roots of medical thought, the ambivalence, and perhaps identity crisis of its practitioners who, even from the beginning, could not make up their minds as to whether they were 'craftsmen' of 'scientists-philosophers'.

The Dogmatics displayed in Medicine an unmistakable rationalistic approach and searched for the 'hidden causes' behind appearances, making abundant use of a highly speculative 'rational' enquire; while the empiricists maintained the view that the invisible could not be known and therefore the uselessness and irrelevancy of speculative thought. For them all that mattered were results unencumbered by inferential logic or 'idle theorizing'.

It was in the field of Medicine where the confrontation between theory and practice, between intellectual inquire into the nature of things and the application of techniques and procedures for the explicit purpose of obtaining 'results', was more clearly manifested. No better ground that the human body could be found to test the capacity of the different schools of thought to prove their value. The restitution and maintenance of health has been thru the ages one, if not the most, cherished desire of the human soul. Among the Medical Empiricists the great skeptic movement, which swept Hellenistic Greece after the crumbling and fragmentation of Alexander Empire, found its most vigorous and constructive expression as well as its most influential manifestation.

The urge to discover the 'hidden truth' behind the veil of appearance found its greatest expression in the anatomists of Alexandria during the Hellenistic Period, whom apparently had no difficulties in obtaining corpses for their studies. A curious and contradictory fact was that the physical penetration into the human body was considered by many Dogmatics necessary to unravel the mystery of disease.

It is beyond the purpose of our inquire to delve in the detailed achievements of the great Anatomists, although their studies certainly helped to promote a 'mechanistic' view of man. For Erasistratus the process of 'digestion' was not a 'concoction', as Aristotle had postulated before, but rather a 'grinding' of food; which subsequently was transformed into 'chyle' and literally squeeze into the lymphatic system. The bile and urine were also, according to him, produced by a mechanical process involving a separation from the blood thru a complex system of vessels of differing relative sizes.

This emphasis in mechanical explanations of bodily functions probably stemmed from the inexistence, at that time, of chemical 'knowledge'; here the need, therefore, to provide 'explanations' based in familiar 'mechanisms". Erasistratus, for instance, perhaps based in vivisections (at least in animals, but very possible also in humans according to comments from Celsus), conceived of the heart as a pump, although its mission was to 'blow' air from the lungs into the arterial system which, in ordinary circumstances, was only filled with 'pneuma '(the all-pervading principle of the Stoics which in the hands of Athenaeus of Cilicia became, in the First Century, the principle for the Pneumatic School). The blood rushed into the arteries from the veins, after percolating thru pores or 'anastomosis', by the action of the 'horror vacui'(a notion first postulated by Strato and of which he made abundant use in explaining the distribution of body fluids into the different anatomical compartments). [3]

It follows naturally, from the conception of the human body as a machine, that disease was a 'breaking down' and that the 'job' of the doctor was that of 'fixing' or repairing whatever was broken. It would have then been obvious to expect a 'flourishing' of surgery during the immediate post-Alexandrian Period and this was true to a certain extent, but for obscure reasons the art of dissection declined; maybe because of later difficulties in obtaining cadavers, as Rufus and Galen suggest in some of their writings. Yet, nothing conclusive could be categorically stated in this regard. Ironically, the practice of Medicine and the prescription of medications were as 'empiric' with the Dogmatics as with any of the other contemporary Alexandrian sects. Neither the characteristic Greek preoccupation with fundamentals and mechanisms, nor the classificatory obsession so early manifested in Western Medicine were of any help in healing the sick. Medical theories were superfluous embellishments of the 'maiden of science'.

With Galen finally crystallized a mixing of ancient Greek Cosmology and Biology with early medical theories and practices, giving rise to a well balance coherent body of knowledge acceptable to Christianity, and which tyrannized Western medical views for over 1500 years. It has been fashionable to attribute such durability to the surprising proportion of Galen's writings surviving to our own times (more than 83 treatises from a total number of about 500 had survived). On second thoughts, however, it is more likely that it was precisely BECAUSE of his popularity that so many of his original assays had endured for so long.

The works of Galen represent a final, all inclusive, synthesis of pre-Socratic and Platonic-Aristotelian theories with contemporary Stoic and vitalistic ideas. No questions remained unanswered, no curiosity unfulfilled. When no clear or obvious explanation of a bodily function was to be found, it was referred to an obscured 'dynamic faculty'. Teleology, as expressed in the concept of Aristotelian 'entelechia' (final causes), was deeply imbued in the fabric of Galenic Dogma, easily accounting for its gratuitous and enthusiastic endorsement by the proponents of the Christian faith.

Not, of course, that Galen lacked worth as a medical scientist. He has been acknowledged as a keen investigator and healer who acquired extensive first hand anatomical knowledge with his dissections and vivisections in animals, mostly in monkeys (he proved, among other things, that Erasistratus was wrong in assuming that the arteries contained air by legating off segments of them and demonstrating that they were filled with blood), but such accomplishments would have not suffice. It was to the extent that his avowed eclecticism effected the marriage of medical practice with a world view, in other words, of the microcosm of man with a universal order acceptable to the Church, that the works of Galen had successfully endure the embattles of time. This is the measure of his everlasting importance in the history of Medicine and human thought; here lay the revelations shone by the light of his works into the historic evolution of man cultural endeavors and intellectual life.

The man from Pergamum, needless to say, was a child of his age and thoroughly acquainted with Platonic-Aristotelian logico-methaphysical speculation; which he set to reconcile with bodily function and anatomic evidence. From Hippocrates and the Pres-Socratics he picked up the Empedoclean notion of the four basic primary elements (fire, air, water and earth) and the four primary qualities referable to them (hot, cold, wet and dry). Their combination explained the 'physics' of everything, although he realized the difficulties of objective definitions of these terms. From Hippocrates also he received, and accepted, the concept of the four humors (phlegm, blood, yellow and black bile) which dis-balances did explained illness; but he expanded the concept to encompass the different 'dispositions of character' or personalities traits(phlegmatic, sanguine, bilious or choleric and melancholic). His popularity, however, was mostly the result of his reconciliation of the Aristotelian 'qualities of the soul' with a specific anatomical locus in the human body for those 'entities'.

The rational (logistikon), spirited (thymoides), and appetitive (epithymetikon) faculties were centered by Galen in the Brain, Heart and Liver respectively. The vegetative or appetitive spirit received the absorbed chyle, after digestion in the intestines, and there it was transformed into the dark venous blood, before proceeding to the Heart by way of the vena cava. From the right side of the heart blood leaked partially thru 'pores' in the septum and in part went to the lungs. Once in the left chambers blood mixed with air, brought from the lungs, and separated off a 'vital spirit' (pneuma) giving rise to the bright arterial blood which was the vehicle of animal activities. On reaching the Brain by way of the 'rete mirable' the vital spirit then evolved from itself the 'psychical spirit', responsible for consciousness and the sensory-motor functions of the Nervous System. The wastage then went to the spleen where it was converted into the black bile.

Galen, therefore, borrowed from the Pneumatics, and consequently ultimately from the Stoics, the concept of the all pervading 'pneuma' and integrated it with the Aristotelian 'spirits' in his explanations of bodily functions referable to specific anatomic loci. Here resides the appeal of his theories and their final acceptance as a lasting dogma of amazing endurance and vitality, which monopolized and governed medical thought until the Renaissance.

To be sure Galen was an original and penetrating thinker, a man of vast culture. His synthesis of popular and respected philosophical ideas with the reality of human life and disease was imbued with a purpose and finality of quasi-religious flavor. Significantly, however, Galen's medical theories and speculations were not conducive to any therapeutic approach supported by them. He seems to have availed himself of every known modality, including surgery, blood-letting and purging, as well as, the more conservative courses recommended by Hippocrates; like diet, rest, hygiene etc. His medical recipes became world famous and some of them included more than seventy ingredients. Known as therics these true 'panaceas' were occasionally still being used up to the beginning of the XIX Century.

Actually then, even at the close of late antiquity, the difference between a quack or charlatan and a physician was a nebulous, and at the best a thin line. Because of the basic dichotomy originating with the Greeks, Medicine was considered by some a craft, an art of healing, an eminently practical discipline, and by others it was a 'philosophy' or 'science', in the sense of deductive logic and speculative theorizing about the composition and purpose of the human body; a microcosm with structural and functional similarities to the universal order, which so much impressed the early secular philosophers.

Precisely because of this duality of meanings is that the all-encompassing broad term of 'physician' could be applied originally to every person who attempted to cure or alleviate sickness or ill-health. Some wanted such eponym to be reserved only to those who administered treatment based in a 'rational approach' or a 'theory of disease', but, as we have seen, there was an ancient sect as 'legitimate' as any other medical sect (The Empiricists) who spurned any kind of theorizing as useless additions to the 'art of Medicine' and instead focused in 'practical results'. As a matter of fact, because of the perception of healing as an art, in Greece as much as in Rome, Medicine was often not considered as a deserving occupation for 'well born' or noble classes; which often viewed with contempt and disdain the ubiquitous physician itinerant who settled up shop in the market place, or close nearby, ministering drugs and cures for a fee to passer bys.

This is not to imply that medical studies were unpopular. As a matter of fact, the ideal curriculum of studies in Classic Greece included Medicine, besides Rhetoric, Philosophy and 'Science'; but the 'lovers' of knowledge for knowledge sake, following the main-stream of ancient Greco-Roman tradition, shunted the 'practice' of Medicine. Men of the stature of Aristotle, Theophrastus, Celsus and Pliny, wrote extensively about Medicine without actually becoming true dedicated professionals in this field. Pythagorean and Empedoclean beliefs formed the basis of the Hippocratic theoretical notions, and we have just seen the enormous eclectic efforts to which, more than anything else, Galen owed his everlasting fame.

We also should remember that theorizing and speculating as to the 'causes' and 'mechanisms' about the Universe, and the microcosm that was for them the human body and its 'diseases', was an early urge of the Cnidian Greek School, which was largely instrumental in allowing the unambiguous categorization of Medicine as an intellectual activity worthy of the status of a 'science'. The 'maiden of sciences' was forgetting its eminently empiric (practical) origin. Physicians were those practitioners who subscribed to popular and established dogma, or that because of the charisma and zest of their personalities lend credibility to their conceptions, ideas and hypothesis. Impostors, needless to say, were those who did not fall in this category, whether because 'strange' ideas, bizarre therapeutic methods, and/ or poor results, inspired mistrust and fear. Not that there were lack of attempts to regulate the practice of Medicine during this long period, especially in Rome. Yet it was not until the times of Severus Alexander (222-235 A.D.) that a workable system of training and certification was instituted in the Empire and a privately financed education was structured and supervised by a Collegium Archiatri.

With the decline of Greco-Roman civilization and the rise of Christianity, secular 'scientific' Medicine all but disappeared from Europe during the Dark Ages. Otherworldly and eschatological justifications for disease then became prevalent. But Nestorian Christian refugees, escaping persecution, migrated from Byzantium to Syria and later on to Persia, where the Sassanid kings offered them protection. Among the ancient texts which they translated into Syriac were some of the works of Aristotle, Hippocrates and Galen. These émigrés eventually founded in Gundishapur a great center of learning, which medical school kept the Greek tradition alive and transferred its seeds to the invading Arabs in the VII Century A.D.

During the remaining so-called Dark Ages Medicine, in the Western World, became eminently monastic, and secular hospitals were practically extinct. Christian dogma imposed a rigid ban in experimental activity of all kinds, and sickness was widely accepted as a curse or punishment for Man's sins. It followed that cures were only provided by the Grace of the Almighty, something totally out of human control, and that repentance and acts of attunement to propitiate the 'Creator' represented, like to primitive man many centuries before, the natural avenue opened when confronted with disease. It was possible perhaps to alleviate the suffering body, but healing was the prerogative of the Lord.

By the High Middle Ages, with the discouraging of monastic Medicine by Church authorities, there took place a revival of laic hospitals and practices of what can be called 'scientific Medicine'; perhaps propitiated by a cross insemination, in the geographic optimal locus of Southern Italy, of converging Arabian, Jewish, Latin and Greek influences. In this fertile soil grew the school of Salerno, followed soon by others at Montpellier,

Paris, and Oxford etc. It is important to note, however, that despite of the existence of these new centers which permitted the intercourse of the great minds of that time, Galenic and Hippocratic beliefs and practices continued to prevail unhindered and no significant new contributions were made.

Swine dissection provided for the practical anatomy of the Salernists who, however, continued to repeat without the slightest critical spirit the old Galenic mistakes. Even although human autopsies began to be practiced again (after being sanctioned by the popes), the errors continued to be parroted by the dissectors, perhaps at least, partially due to the costume of performing the actual procedure while the presiding 'authority' read pontifically to the students quoting from ancient texts. The resemblance to Christian liturgy was striking. By the Late Middle Ages medical teaching had acquired the trappings and pomposity of a religious ceremony.

Not that there was absence of some progress of a sort. The Arab world reached its cultural pinnacle about the year 1000 A.D. and was majorly instrumental in the development of Chemistry and Pharmacy as sciences. Procedures for sublimation, distillation etc., were developed and the preparation of drugs and medications became an elaborated art. Remarkably well organized hospital systems took form throughout the land at the centers of Damascus, Baghdad and especially Egypt, where in Cairo the Al-Mansur hospital was a model of organization and care for the patients. Physicians learned their trade in schools of unaffiliated hospitals, and after the X Century the Abbasid dynasty in Baghdad established regulations for the licensing of physicians. It was a happy coincidence that the Golden Age of Arabian Medicine occurred when Western Europe was emerging from the Dark Ages and the works of Avicenna, Avenzoar, Albucasis and Rhazes filtered into the West, particularly thru the Salernian melting pot. Essentially, however, the practice of Medicine during the Middle Ages remained eminently unregulated, and the theoretical basis was provided by the unchallenged and petrified Greek dogma, which, not satisfied with its overwhelming influence upon Roman culture, also, strangely enough, subdued alike Moslems and Christians.[4]

Despite of superficial differences the medieval practitioner differed from his counterpart of ancient times solely in the complexities and elaborations of his medical 'concoctions', and the perspective of his religious beliefs. Paradoxically, the foundation of the first universities and the formation of guilds of physicians only helped to perpetuate 'the teaching of the ancients' which, in accordance with the religious mood of this historic period, were requested to be trusted and accepted AS AN ARTICLE OF FAITH.

During this period too Medicine reached formally, and by way of the academic curriculum demanded to become 'a doctor', the status of a philosophy or science. The dichotomy already envisaged in the ancient world between those who speculated 'rationally' upon the causes of disease in order to effect a diagnosis and arrive at a prognosis leading perhaps to a 'logical' therapy, and those 'uncultured' practitioners who would lay their hands on a patient without resorting to any conventional or accepted theory with the hope of curing or alleviating the sick, became formalized and structured into the medical profession. The former became the true physician or 'doctor' graduated from a university, while the others (barber surgeons, mountebanks etc.) were inferior practitioners, looked down with contempt by their better instructed peers who considered them no more than mere 'charlatans'; coming to represent anyone who offered treatments or held theories not sanctioned by orthodox established beliefs elaborated in the high centers of learning. Medieval Dogma, by casting a rigid and stultifying mold into the profession, led no room for the empiricist point of view, which was looked upon with disdain and suspicion. Empiricism came to be synonymous with arbitrariness and unscientific speculation.

It followed from this peculiar trait in the historic development of Medicine (something that in many ways still today haunt and pervade the profession) that therapies in order to be 'scientific' needed to address themselves to the accepted theories of disease. The emphasis was, as in ancient times, in redressing the dis-balances of the humors with cathartics, emetics, diuretics and, if all failed, blood-letting (ordinarily prescribed but not performed by physicians).

A clear evidence of the rabid anti-empiricism of the epoch is the total lack of acknowledgment for the necessarily poor results of the therapeutic maneuvers then in vogue. The attitude of blind faith so typical of radical religious positions, that characteristic 'closing of the eyes' to physical reality, was never better exemplified than in the stubborn endorsement of Galenic and Hippocratic theories by the high priests of Medieval Medicine. The 'mistress of sciences' had acquired a pious attire.

With the rise in power of the bourgeoisie in the Early Renaissance the new humanistic 'outlook' searched into the past for the lost ancient Greek ideals as the foundation for the cultural rebirth. The imposing hierarchical-Aristotelian system had to be rejected if the new class was to have a dialectic justification for its new ascendancy in a radically change society, and received dogma had to be demolished if there was going to be any hope of success.

In Medicine there was consequently need to return to the mood of personal, original and unbiased observation of the human body in health and illness in order to, by way of first hand information, understand better the morbid stages, and hopefully then to institute 'rational' therapy. The 'breaking of the ice', not surprisingly, was led by the artists, those less unencumbered by sedimented prejudices and trained to look at nature with freshness and curiosity. Leonardo de Vinci was one of the first to plow in the new fertile soil, followed by the great anatomists Eustacchio, Fallopious, Colombo, and above all, Andrea Vesalius. These were still vacillating steps taken fearfully in the shadow of the inquisitionist, often justifying their new discoveries hesitantly and defensively against the still entrenched Galenic Dogma. But the universities of Northern Italy flourished, and, especially Padua for a while became a sort of medical Mecca enjoying great reputation.

The new technical advances, also the product of bourgeoisie ingenuity, propelled an intellectual ferment culminating with the astronomical feats of Copernicus and Kepler; followed later on by the development of the Newtonian synthesis. These resounding successes in the field of universal mechanics, were, likewise, thought to be a triumph of 'Reason'; the stolen Promethean light which Western man enthroned as a god in its own right. The fundamentalist-reductionist approach of the Greek mind was to be accepted and clearly enunciated in the Baconian inductive method. Nature's secrets were to be unraveled by means of 'ratiocinations' upon the 'elemental' facts of observation. Causes and explanations, once discovered, would then lead to better control and understanding of the Universe. Both Empiricism and Rationalism were to be embraced by the nascent science.

But man, the reasoning animal per-excellence, was part of Nature also, in fact being considered by many a true microcosm. If the mechanistic outlook proposed by Descartes in the XVII Century was to be wholly adequate, it would, of course, need to include man himself; and in that case all physical principles discovered and applicable to the totality would also be valid in studying him. Man was a biological 'machine' capable of being analyzed and explained by physical means. Perhaps this notion, together with the new 'circularities' found in nature, were, as we have seen, majorly instrumental in the discovery of blood circulation; more to the point, these ideas crystallized in the Iatrophysic School in Medicine. Diverse biological parameters were going to be carefully measured and quantified in health and disease to help to unravel the secrets of the human body, the hidden 'mechanism' of life, and maybe even provide for a 'rational' cure of many organic disturbances.

Needless to say, these early attempts in Medicine never met the success of their counterparts in celestial mechanics, if one makes exception for the already cited case of blood circulation. Even this discovery, although of momentous importance, hardly could be compared with the Copernican or Newtonian feats. As many authorities had admitted, the facts of blood circulation were staring at the face of man for more than 2000 years and it was only the power of ancient dogma, with its religious aversion for non-divine 'circular motions', what kept the truth concealed for so long.

Nevertheless, a beginning of a sort was accomplished with the objective quantification of biological phenomena by Sanctorius Sanctorius[5] in metabolism with his famous steel yard, and the works of Giovanni Borelli, who employed true mathematical methods in physiological processes such as locomotion, respiration etc, shortly after Harvey's studies.

But another very important trend in Western thought commenced also during the same period to influence medical and biological ideas, a trend which, we have seen, originated with orientalizing tendencies in Greek philosophy and proceeded by way of the Stoics and Neoplatonists to influence the Renaissance Reformation: The vitalistic, Centro-European mystical conceptions that, as we have seen, were expressed in science by the alchemical works of Paracelsus and also represented by Jean Baptiste Van Helmot of Brussels, a renegade capuchin friar who was one of the great promoters of the Iatrochemical school of Medicine, which in many ways translated the ideas of Leibnitz into biology.(See also Chapters I and II)

Paracelsus conception of disease as 'entities' stemmed from an application to Medicine of his vitalistic notion that 'all things' (including morbid processes) consisted of individual or autonomous beings possessing an specific vital nature or soul (Archeus), which fought with the archeus of the body, its success or failure producing the disease or not, as the case may be. The medications also contained an archeus opposing that of the disease. Because of the belief that man's body was a microcosm and a replica of the Universe as a whole, knowledge was to be obtained by mystical insights seeking for analogies between the two.

Like Paracelsus Van Helmont believed in the existence behind any biological process (which for him were all strictly chemical) of an Archeus, Anima or Blas, controlling the processes by means of ferments or 'gases' (he discovered 'gas Sylvester' or CO_2). Van Helmont acridly criticized Galenic Dogma and the notion that 'diseases' were unbalances of the humors; a concept held in Western thought at least since the times of Hippocrates, and probably even before. For him 'diseases' were true living entities (a point of view which, as we has seen, was one of the central tenures of the Cnidian School of ancient Greece) also with their own archeus or anima, generating the morbid process by way of activating 'ideas' included in 'seeds' thru which agency the disease itself unfolded its own pattern.

Van Helmont and his followers Francois de la Boe (Sylvius), Thomas Willis and others, are historically important not so much for their 'discoveries' in Medicine as for the light they shed upon the evolution of scientific thought. Together with the iatrophysics they represent irruptions into Medicine of philosophical positions (vitalistic) which, having their roots in ancient Bronze Age civilizations, stirred with new life after the Renaissance, when the mystics in the Germanic lands appropriated the ancient 'nature outlook' and applied it into the newly flourishing scientific disciplines. Ironically, these novel and wonderful conceptions coming to replace established dogmas, in their turn created passions and dogmatic views of their own contributing very little to advance the cause of the 'art of healing'.

A reaction of a sort, however, eventually took place against this renewed proclivity to 'idle theorizing' in the raising clamor of few 'sane' minds, who bade physicians to return to the bedside as the only sure way to help suffering mankind. The voices of Sydenham, Ramazzini and Glisson, among others, plead for a revival of the Hippocratic ideal, but frequently to no avail. The theoreticians continued their endless arguments and the practitioners serving their 'concoctions'. In fact, not even in surgery, despite of the great advances in Anatomy, was there a significant progress during this period. In many universities of Europe Galenic Medicine was still faithfully thought during the XVII Century although, in some quarters, the new Anatomy and physiology were freely detailed. As far as therapeutics, however, no significant progress was achieved. Institutionalized dogma, old and new, was as prevalent as ever.

But the technical advances of the age, particularly in optic, allowed excellent investigative work by few gifted individuals who, singlehanded and almost in isolation, achieved enormous true progress in selected areas of expertise, often, significantly enough, 'outside' of the academic environment. Rarely personalized work had accomplished more than in this happy age. Witness for instance the already alluded case of Antoni Van Leeuwenhoek, a draper from Delft, who never even attended a university or was acquainted with Greek and Latin. He, however, is reputed to be the first person to use systematically the microscope, and achieved an amazing degree of technical expertise in the manufacture and handling of the new portentous instrument. Among his remarkable feats were a fairly close estimate of the size of red cells, histological studies in the structure of teeth and blood vessels, the crystalline lens, and the discovery of many oral microorganisms.

The enviable tranquil existence of Leeuwenhoek was not disturbed by passionate controversy stemming from his highly individualistic and original initiative, as unquestionably would have been the case had he belonged to the scientific establishment of the day. Being an 'outsider', and economically independent, he was impervious to 'peer pressures' and free from the stultifying accretion of petrified dogma.

Not so lucky was his contemporary Malpighi, who found inveterate hostility within his profession, both at Bologna and Messina, reaching even the point of physical assault. Yet, eventually, and perhaps significantly, his merits were appreciated outside his native country when elected in 1669 to the Royal Society of London. [6]

Of course, it is not coincidence that much of the new discoveries were realized in the Netherlands and England. The geographic locus of the cultural revival which began in the Italic peninsula (also the civilized center of the ancient world before the demise of the Roman Empire) drifted north, to escape the gagging influence of the inquisition tribunals, into lands where a 'freer' cultural atmosphere permitted individual independent research to proceed unimpeded.

The rise of bourgeoisie power brought in its wake the enshrining of the conception of 'progress' and the perfectibility of man, leading, by the process of 'nature projection' already alluded, to the theories of evolution of biological beings. Living species in Nature, like Man in society, were undergoing a continuous transformation to ever more complex, refined and 'superior' forms, similar to the steady 'advances' and improvements of mankind, an ascent with no perceptible material or spiritual limitations, conditioned and catapulted by that marvelous Science and Technology nurtured and delivered by man intellect and fortitude.(See Appendix I)

About this time a unification of the craft and scholarly traditions in Medicine finally took hold in the West (exemplified by the incorporation of the barber-surgeons into Medicine and medical schools), and science progressively became the providence of 'expert' professionals, instead of all-embracing philosophers, who were left to exercise their skills on ethical and epistemological questions at the margin of religion, or in the socio-political sphere where much later on their theorizing had far reaching consequences with the raise of Marxist Doctrine.

What was properly to be considered 'knowledge', however, was to be decided within each scientific discipline by the 'expert', the only one with the necessary attributes and accreditations to talk with enough credibility and authority in his own field of 'specialization'; initiating a trend that today with the technological explosion of the last two centuries has reached, with the ramifications and sub-ramifications undergone by all scientific fields, an extreme degree of 'narrowness'. The original dichotomy between scholars and craft-man, when reconciled, brought into the different medical fields the early scholarly notion that 'true knowledge' was needed for 'explanations' of phenomena, in other words a ratification of the change of causality, of how things 'come about'. It was cogently and convincingly argued that only when 'causes' are identified can we, in addressing ourselves to them, 'rationally' attempt to manipulate circumstances and gain mastery over the world of events.

The notion of progress emerged as a typical XVIII Century bourgeoisie notion inextricably related to the urges and hopes of a raising new class. The new ferment permeated not only the social ambit but also the scientific field. There were system builders in philosophy (See Chapter I and Appendix I) as well as in science. Apparently the Kantian view point that the human mind, by way of its 'Reason', was capable of providing true 'knowledge' (his a priori synthetic category) apart from any observational facts, and the British Empiricist denial that true knowledge of an 'outside reality' could be obtained by way of the senses, stimulated a number of arm-chair 'theoreticians' who, thinking of themselves as repositories of intuitive inner wisdom, conceived speculative edifices about the nature of Man's life and disease; many of which were no more than variations of a theme already sounded, not only in the preceding centuries, but often even in the ancient world.

In Medicine speculative theorizing reached a feverish pitch, but also there were spectacular empiric advances. John Brown, for example, popularized a version of Themison's Methodist Doctrine revolving around the concept of 'excitability'. For him life was the result of external 'stimuli' acting upon matter. It followed that diseases were either sthenic or asthenic, according to how much 'excitation' or 'inhibition' thereof, was provided by the stimuli, and consequently treatment consisted in the administration of depressant or stimulating medications to counteract the 'excesses' or 'defects' of the stimuli.

We had already seen that Georg Ernst Stahl following closely in the steps of Van Helmont created the theory of phlogiston and, more relevant to the field of Medicine, he expounded a version of animism identifying soul with 'life force'; therefore dispensing with the 'gases' and 'seeds' of his predecessor. Diseases resulted from disturbances in the activity of this soul and depended on the 'tonus' of the blood vessels; again a variation of the Methodist theme of relaxations and contraction of the 'pores'. Johann Kampf championed the so-called doctrine of the infarctus, whereby all diseases resulted from 'fecal impaction'. Accordingly, laxatives, purgatives and mineral waters were his mainstay of treatment.

Astrological lore and magical conceptions of disease were also during this period reintroduced 'formally' into Medicine by Franz Anton Mesmer who, in his doctoral dissertation, defended a thesis of 'planetary influences' in biological bodies; something coming to be known as 'animal magnetism'. His 'magnetic therapy' consisted in the laying of hands upon the diseased parts of the body. The procedure, of course, was not new or revolutionary but he promoted it as an acceptable and reputable medical practice by devising a theory of 'magnetic fluid', which was supposed to suffuse every living body and circulated in the blood, releasing a special 'force' animating matter. Diseases resulted from derangements in the distribution of this all pervading force. Mesmerism could easily be identified as a version of Centro-European animism and was extremely popular among the people (in France the kings subsidized him in the funding of a 'Magnetic Institute').

Finally Christian Fiedrich Samuel Hahnemann formalized into Medicine the conceptions of sympathetic magic with his Homeopathic Medicine, that is to say, introduced the therapeutic fashion of prescribing drugs capable of simulating the symptoms of the disease in question. During this century also the vogue of disease classification, following the successes of Linnaeus and other workers in botany, picked up steam. Naturally, such a task required as a necessary prerequisite the notion that diseases were 'entities' in their own right; something which, as we have seen, had been already claimed by the Cnidian School of ancient Greece and, later on, formed the basis of Van Helmont vitalism.

Elsewhere we have discussed the dangers of equating dynamic processes, like diseases, with 'physical objects', like animals and plants, particularly when the definition of the term 'disease' is an ambiguous one; something that had undergone a significant evolution during civilized history. Sufficiently will be to add here that classificatory urge in Medicine followed the general encyclopedic trend of the age.

But in some respects this century saw significant advances in Medicine, particularly in what respect to the already alluded physiology of respiration, and in the experimental works of Albrecht Von Haller in muscular irritability and nerve conductivity (called by him 'sensitivity'), as well as his studies in the role of bile in the digestion of fats. Spallanzini, the Hunter brothers (who founded the first school of Anatomy in London), Robert Whytt and Luigi Galvani also made significant contributions in the field of physiology. In Clinical Medicine there were great names too, like Auerbrugger, Boerhaave and Giovanni Battista Morgagni who established, with his perseverance and industrious personality, anatomic pathology in a solid basis. Morbid morphologic criteria, since then, came to frequently replace symptomatic denominations of disease; initiating a vogue, as we will see, still prevalent at the present.

Ironically, as it is so frequent in Medicine, two of the most momentous advances of the XVIII Century were the result of keen observations by lay persons. One was the 'discovery' by an old matron of Shropshire of the therapeutic excellence of foxglove in 'dropsy', from which William Withering learned it in 1776. The other perhaps is the greatest single advance in preventive Medicine ever: The successful application of vaccination by Edward Jenner, who learned that cow-pox conferred immunity against small pox from the country people of Gloucestershire. Although not the 'discoverer' of the idea of preventive inoculation (it had been attempted in the Orient for many centuries before) he was the first to apply it consistently and with good results.

Plainly, in these cases, the rationalist hope that 'advances' in Medicine followed naturally as a consequence of well known facts serving as theoretical underlining principles allowing an understanding of 'why and how' an illness comes about, and therefore to approach its cure or prevention 'rationally', just simply was not realized. The usage of digitalis did not followed from a true understanding of what was the 'dropsy' it cured, even less of how 'foxglove' achieved its therapeutic results. The explanations as to its 'mechanism of action' had been A POSTERIORI conclusions. As a matter of fact, when digitalis was first used there was no clear distinction between cardiac, renal and hepatic dropsy; even ovarian cysts were then considered cases of that same mysterious malady.

The same thing can be claimed of the case of vaccination. Although the idea of inoculation as preventive measure was known even in ancient India, its popularization by Jenner and its eventual acceptance by the medical profession did not followed any kind of perspicacious 'insight', or understanding, about the 'mechanisms' of immunity. We need only to mention that the Germ Theory of disease, although a deeply rooted popular belief many centuries before the times of Jenner, took almost another century to be 'proved'. The discoveries of vaccination and digitalis, it has to be emphasized, resulted from keen observations by lay persons and therefore were eminently empiric achievements.

The real difference between the genuine medical advances and the numerous speculative theories and system-buildings of the XVIII Century (as of any other historic period), hinges precisely in the fact that the former were based in empiric evidence (whether observational or experimental), while the latter in indemonstrable illusory categories. Nobody ever identified or isolated the 'anima', 'archeus', 'animal magnetism' or 'tensions', but muscular irritability and nerve conductivity were observed experimentally. It is this capacity to directly ascertain and consistently identify under controlled conditions given phenomena (the objects of study), what separated quackery from Medicine, or any other science. The 'empiric' nature of the Promethean light was perhaps never better realized than during this period when so many speculative and ideological systems collapsed under the weight of their own sterility.

But the search for 'fundamentals', 'causes' and 'explanations' of existing phenomena persisted to haunt Western Man, who continued unrelentingly to deceive himself in the firm belief that pure 'Reason', the deductive demonstrative logic of the Greeks, was capable of providing man with 'true knowledge' and 'understanding' into nature, because this was something divested of deceptive contaminations, a searchlight capable of guiding him thru the chaotic kaleidoscope of sensory experience.

As the technological base of civilization expanded in the post-Renaissance era the domain of man's experiences grew at a rapid pace, demanding integration and tabulation of facts according to the traditional epistemological categories (See Chapter IV) which had served him well in previous cosmic quests. The synthetic and deductive logic of the ancients continued to be utilized in providing 'justifications' and solutions for the new discoveries and findings based in the systems proliferating during the XVIII Century; the vast majority representing nothing but deceptive contraptions designed to assuage man's vanity and exalted ego.

The realization that the 'clinical picture' of a patient had a 'morphologic counterpart', or correlated 'morbid expression', was perhaps the most notorious facet of the century; an expedient, however, conveying the danger of confusing these organic detectable changes, not as other manifestations of an illness, but with 'the disease' itself. Perhaps nothing else could be expected of a positivistic and materialistic emerging class which viewed the biological beings as 'machines' and symptoms as expression of a deranged 'mechanism'. By the end of the century it was clear that the bourgeoisie rationalistic world view of coastal Western Europe had firmly taken the upper hand over vitalistic conceptions of the Germanic lands.

The early part of the XIX Century saw the consolidation of Morbid Pathology as the repository and final arbiter of medical wisdom. Francois-Joseph-Victor Broussais led the way in this direction by rejecting the misconception of considering a group of symptoms and clinical signs as 'a disease' or 'clinical entity' in its own right, emphasizing that only morphologic organic changes deserved such denomination; something essentially representing the replacement of one diagnostic criteria for another. His compatriot Rene-Theophile-Hyacinthe Laennec, one of the master clinicians of all time, inventor of the stethoscope and promoter of the auscultation method, made extensive clinical-pathological correlations, 'explaining' many clinical symptoms and physical findings by the deranged texture and function of diseased organs. These correlations were considered sufficient 'explanations' for the illness in question and a name descriptive of the abnormal organic condition (liver cirrhosis, bronchiectasis etc) was accepted as specifying 'a disease'. The conceptual change was therefore complete.

During this period, however, an approach at the time little noticed but destined to have considerable repercussion in the practice of Medicine the following century first took shape: The utilization of statistical analysis to evaluate prognosis and therapeutic results. One of the instances in which the procedure was systematically applied was by Pierre-Charles-Aleixandre Louis in his refutation that blood-letting was of any benefit in cases of pneumonia.

Yet, it was not until the second half of the XIX Century that momentous events, not devoid of its share of human drama and misery propelled Medicine into a definite modern path. The idea that, at least, some diseases are contagious is perhaps as old as Medicine, but the first serious proponent of this view, Oliver Wendell Holmes in the U.S. and Ignaz Philipp Semmelweis in Austria, were received, for not perceptible good reason except perhaps entrenched dogmatism, with violent opposition mixed with scorn and resentment from their colleagues; in the case of Semmelweis reaching the point of vindictiveness, persecution and ostracism, despite of the fact that this author had significantly decreased the mortality from 'puerperal fever' in his own ward in Vienna's Allgemeines Krandenhaus Hospital utilizing the simple expedient of careful washing his hands between cases.

Antiseptic techniques were first systematically applied in surgery by Lord Lister whose father, faithfully enough, perfected the achromatic microscope lenses, an advance permitting the strides in Histopathology, Microbiology and Genetics that took place in the second half of the century and which gave Medicine a truly modern outlook; a look brought about mainly by the effort and toil of several extraordinarily prolific individuals, some who were not even physicians but rather humble investigators working with relatively modest means.

Take, for example, the case of Louis Pasteur, a man from the Jura region of France and of peasant stock. By profession a chemist, his first significant discovery was that racemic acid represented a mixture of dextro and levo polarized parts resolvable by chemical and biological procedures. Pasteur further studies, in what could be defined today as Industrial Microbiology, brought him to discover the role of microorganisms in fermentation (demolishing the chemical theories of Liebig) and to devise a method to avoid the spoiling of wine that immortalized his name (pasteurization).

He soon was commissioned to investigate the disease then inflicting heavy losses to the silk industry of France, and in time not only discovered the cause and prevention of pebrine but also of another silk worm disease (flacherie), before turning to the field of Medicine, where his studies yielded truly revolutionary results.

Pasteur is credited with the profound remark that 'chance favors the prepared mind' and never, perhaps, was this better shown than in the faithful incident which then, in the last quarter of the XIX Century took place, an incident with an immense repercussion in the field of Medicine. Returning one good day from a short vacation he noticed that some cultures of chicken cholera organisms which had been inadvertently left to decay in his lab, when inoculated into animals were unable to produce the disease, but nevertheless conferred immunity to progressively more virulent strains of the same organism and eventually against the disease itself.

Pasteur deferently called the procedure 'vaccination', in honor to the man who firstly successfully inoculated humans against Small-Pox, but the perspective and potential implications of his discovery were farfetched, as time would care to show. Works with the organisms of Anthrax, Chicken Cholera and Swine Measles, revealed the fact that their 'virulence' could be attenuated or enhanced by successive passages thru suitable hosts or cultured media. This not only immediately brought in rewards in the form of 'vaccines' against anthrax and eventually rabies (a microorganism too small to be seen in the microscope), but also resulted in enormous advances in the field of immunology, which fruits were soon to be harvested.

Roux and Yersin discovery of the diphtheria toxin as the morbid agent in this affliction, a true scourge of the XIX Century, as well as that of 'antitoxins' in the blood of afflicted persons and animals in the case of tetanus found by Behring and Kitasato, soon provided for a prophylaxis of both, diphtheria and tetanus; affording the experimental basis for the explosive expansion and refinement achieved in the field of immunology in the XX Century.

If the life of Pasteur offers an example of 'spill over' genius into the field of Medicine from other scientific disciplines (namely how an insight into chemical observations led, ultimately, to discern the consequences of the growth and reproduction of microorganisms and therefore to unravel the nature of biological processes like fermentation and putrefaction), his contemporary Robert Koch is a dramatic example of how much a single, strong willed and determined individual with modest economic means could accomplish independently in the second half of the XIX Century.

After serving in the Franco-Prussian War Koch settled as a district physician in Woolstein, Germany. It is said that, in order to counteract the monotony and boredom of his placid rural existence he engaged in 'private studies'. Ironically, and perhaps enviably, at that time his 'private studies' represented serious research AT THE FRONTIER OF SCIENCE. The magnitude and importance of his works were understood when one good day he casually reported to the great botanist Ferdinand Cohn, discoverer of the anthrax bacillus, that he had unraveled the complete life history of this bacterium. At an invitation by Cohn, Koch then gave a demonstration of his findings and methods in Breslau to a selected audience, which was extremely impressed with his findings and conclusions that the bacillus discovered by Cohn was truly the 'cause' of the disease, because a pure culture of the organism after growing for a while in laboratory media, was capable of 'transmitting' the affliction to newly inoculated animals.

Koch's private and independent researches were soon published by Cohn and opened for him the doors of fame and immortality. In close succession followed his publications in drying and staining techniques and his studies of microorganisms in wound infections. In 1880 he was appointed to the Imperial Health Department, where he proceeded to develop his techniques of bacterial culture in liquid gelatin and meat broth.

Koch eventually was appointed professor of Hygiene and Bacteriology at the University of Berlin and the achievements of his life-labors are so abundant and well known that they hardly need to be mentioned. Of considerable interest to medical epistemology, however, are the now famous postulates bearing his name and considered as indispensable preconditions for the acceptance of the causative role of a microorganism in a given disease. In summary, they established that the microbes should be recovered from the diseased animal or person, cultured in pure form and finally capable of transmitting the disease in question to an experimental animal, from where they should then be recovered again.

The indefatigable investigations of Pasteur, Koch, and their numerous followers, gave the science of Microbiology a solid foundation, and their studies were not only immensely useful in the fields of Medicine and Veterinary but also of great relevance in industry and agriculture. They were without the slightest doubt true 'advances' of far reaching importance achieved by modest means.

In Medicine, the discovery of numerous disease-related organisms gave a solid 'scientific' support to the ancient idea of 'contagium', and divested it of the superstitious and numinous content folklore has dressed it with by identifying the legendary 'miasmas'. Predictably, and understandably, these marvelous revelations afforded by the novel science had immediate repercussions in the concept of morbidity, in other words, of what really constituted 'a disease', permitting more practical and relevant classificatory schemes. The opinion naturally emerged of disease as a BATTLE between invading forces (the causal organisms) and the 'defenses' of the patient, who ipso facto became the 'battleground'. Man, again maybe unavoidably, was borrowing images of societal dynamics to 'explain' himself.

The technical progress which allowed the development of Microbiology also permitted expansion and elaborations in other fields of the biological sciences, such as Histopathology and Genetics. The perfection reached in optical equipment and staining methods by the second half of the XIX Century, allowed giant strides in microscopic observations and clarification of ultrastructural details hitherto impossible. As we have seen Lorenz Oken, following the speculations of Leibnitz and Van Helmont, proposed that biological beings were composed of invisible and immortal elemental units or mucus-vesicles, which survived the death of the body to reassemble again in a new creature. The 'particulate' obsession of the Nature-Philosophers appeared to be corroborated when Mathias Schleiden and Theodore Schawn, both disciples of Johannes Muller, based in their microscopic studies proposed that both plants and animals were formed of elemental building blocks or cells.

It should then come as no surprise that these new findings set the stage for the works of another disciple of Muller, a man whose multifarious interests, seemingly inexhaustible energies, intense dedication, versatile talents and respectable figure brought him to a pinnacle of fame, notoriety and power, reaching the point of veneration by his contemporaries, who came to worship him as a true 'pope' of Medicine.

Rudolf Ludwig Karl Virchow was unquestionable a great teacher and innovator, generally credited with being the 'father' of cellular pathology, who, with the force of his poignant personality, helped in the consolidation, against the unsupported theorizing of the Nature-Philosophers, of the empiric scientific method in the traditionally mystic Germanic lands. The works of Virchow following in the heels of the discoveries of Schleiden and Schwann led him, ironically enough, to the further elaboration of the vitalistic Centro-European brand of atomism with his formulation of the 'Cell Theory' of disease; perhaps a logical terminus of the cultural tradition he belonged to. According to him, any 'sickness' began as a disturbance of one cell and propagated by its multiplication; in essence a 'neoplastic' conception of disease.

For Virchow 'a disease' was a sort of REVOLUTION in the midst of the society of cells constituting a biological being; a notion strangely reminiscent of the convulsive revolutionary ferment of Europe in the midcourse of the XIX Century. It might also not be a coincidence that he himself was a democratic spirit, openly critical of the policies of Bismarck, and who's reforming efforts resulted in important sanitary changes which took place in his native land during this period. In addition, his works in cranial dimensions helped to discredit the then current belief in Germany about the 'purity' of 'northern races'.

Virchow's contributions to Medicine were many and of great relevance. His notable works in thrombosis and embolism are well known. He studied extensively parasitic and fungus diseases, vascular abnormalities, vertebral afflictions, gastrointestinal disturbances and also introduced a number of pathological terms still in vogue: Like agenesia, ochronosis, cloudy swelling and amyloidosis among others. He was among the first to describe 'leukemia', a disease of the white blood cell, as well as, the 'chlorosis' of young women and the histological patterns of 'tuberculosis'; a malady he stubbornly, and misguidedly, held to be different from 'phthisis'.

As a matter of fact, Virchow descriptions and 'discerning eye' hardly spared any morphological or micro-structural data of the diseased body, but yet I cannot help the feeling that despite of the adulations of sympathetic panegyrists the world over, his awe inspiring charisma popularized medical notions and practicing styles which had a distinct negative influence in Medicine. I am referring specifically to the belief that structural organic changes are not only the final locus and justification for a 'disease process' but ARE IT; thus providing the basis for taxonomic schemes frequently divested of practical relevance, but that nevertheless did appear to represent 'knowledge' thanks to what was already referred to as the 'magic power of words'. The pathologic 'verdict' became a final and unappealing, divinely inspired, utterance transfixing the audience of awe-stricken colleagues who had the good fortune of witnessing the holy pronouncements of the presiding 'authority'. Old ways are hard to die, and still today medical teachings in many places retain a considerable dose of medieval histrionics.

Virchow's achievements despite of originally being of an eminently empiric basis, in many respects resulted in the replacing of one set of dogmatic beliefs for others no less dogmatic, and in many ways casted Pathology into a rigid pedantic straight jacket which still today, in many quarters, it pompously displays. Virchow's cell theory was as much a one-sided view of disease as the notion of 'crasis' proposed by his contemporary Carl Rokitansky of Vienna, one of the greatest pathologist of all time, an unassuming man who the great German Pathologist bitterly criticized.

Virchow's firm opinion that white cells did not wander thru the blood vessels to sites of injury was only disproved by the meticulous research-work of his compatriot Julius Cohnheim, and to the end of his life our good professor opposed with stubborn determination the germ and humoral theories of disease proposed by his contemporaries, despite of belonging to their same cultural and scientific Centro-European lineage. Perhaps one of his most significant and everlasting accomplishments was the realization that each cell derived from another (Ommis cellula e cellula), but even this was only a rephrasing of Pasteur (Ommis vitae e vita). His valiant defense of the right of the working and frequently exploited people maybe, ironically enough, was the catalyst for his cherished and now defunct Cell Theory; one of the final efflorescences of Centro European vitalistic doctrines in the field of Medicine.

Virchow's life work certainly helped in catapulting pathology to the forefront of 'scientific Medicine' but, nevertheless, he contributed to a large extent in perpetuating a rigid dogmatic mold from where Pathology has found difficulty to escape; a mold nurtured and cared for by his followers with the solicitous attention and devotion of high priests of a secret temple who had failed to notice that their precious abode was turning into a withering mausoleum.

The generative power of Nature Philosophy, however, was not exhausted in the battlements of 'cellular pathology'. Indeed a line of inquire which, in a long run, was to prove of far reaching importance in biology, as well as in Medicine, began to be explored in the second half of the XIX Century by the works of an assiduous microscopist and also by means of shroud observations recorded by a most unlikely person: A humble and allegedly uninspired monk who failed to made the grade as a teacher because, according to his examiner, "he lacked insight and the requisite clarity of knowledge". Let us first start with the philosopher and microscopist.

Carl Nageli, professor of botany at several distinguished Centro European universities (among them Zurich and Munich), studied under Oken and Hegel and, later on, Botany with Candolle at Geneva (See also Chapter II). Nageli claimed that plant and animal cells (already established by Schleiden and Schwann to be elemental constituents of all biological beings) were not the true fundamental units of life but, instead, in their turn were formed by ultramicroscopic 'micelles' akin to inorganic crystals(a sort of 'spontaneous generation'). These micelles merged together by strict physical forces and when mixed with water produced the living cells.

Nageli also believed that the impetus for evolution stemmed from a mysterious immanent force characteristic of all life, which produced the development from primitive organisms to more complex living forms; but there was no transformations from one animal species to another, every evolutionary line was a 'monad' of a sort. His opinions only basically deferred from those of the preceding Nature-Philosophers in the view that the evolutionary force in question was not a 'vital' or spiritual entity, but must definitely a physical one.

Nalegi accepted Darwin's concept of 'struggle for survival', but the biological changes upon which selection worked, he thought, were not small variations that when accumulated gave rise to a slow and rather 'smooth' process; instead these changes were large and sudden, true leaps following in general a Hegelian dialectic-type of dynamic pattern. Heredity, then, was mediated by way of particles (micelles) inducing sudden phenotypic transformations. Evolution took place in discontinuous leaps; a theory, as we already mentioned, with strange resemblances to the postulates of another Centro European achievement in the physical sciences: Quantum Mechanics.

Nageli also made another important proposition. Since it was assumed that both parents contributed equally to the heritage of the offspring and that the female gamete, the egg, was much larger than the male, he postulated that only part of the cell could hold the hereditary material; which he called the idio-plasma and, strangely enough, in something we can only define as an anticipatory premonition, he thought it was composed of a CHAIN OF MICELLES.

August Weismann, professor of zoology at Freiberg, where Nageli had also taught for a while, took over his hypothesis of the idio-plasma and elaborated it still further. He began by changing its name to germ-plasma and conceived that all metazoan organisms partook of this essential ingredient (the reproductive germ line), which was immortal because of its passing from one generation to another. According to him there was also a somato-plasma (representing the soma or body), which function was to provide for the nourishment and 'housing' of the germ-plasma thru its successive generations.

Contrary to Nageli Weismann declared that phenotypic variations were not brought about by modifications in one germ-plasma, but as a result of the merging together of the contribution from both parental organisms. Now Weismann had another intuitive genial insight. Because, 'he reasoned', the off-spring could not have double the amount of germ-plasma in the parents (otherwise the germinal make-up would double in each generation), then necessarily, the latter should split in two sometimes before the gametes are formed; a conclusion therefore advanced several years before the actual observation of the phenomena of meiosis by Van Beneden in Liege.

Because already Hertwig and Fol had detected in animals, and Strasburger in plants, that sexual reproduction implied a union of the nuclei of both gametes, and taking into consideration the studies of Van Beneden, Weismann then proceeded to postulate that the hereditary material actually resided in the nucleus; more precisely in the chromosomes seen by the investigators during the course of the mitosis.

The idea of the 'sudden variations', first introduced by Nageli, was further elaborated by Hugo De Vries. Working with the American evening primrose, in what can be defined as an anticipation of 'selective inbreeding', he noticed that some plants differed markedly from the average kind, and from them he obtained further variations. Several other investigators were actually involved in these researches in different countries, and in their work they had detected occasional variations transmissible to the off-springs; what we call today mutations .Searching in the scientific literature for previous work in this field then De Vries and also Hohanse, who had been working with peas, found the material published almost 30 years previously by a forgotten monk from Brno.

Gregor Mendel, after failing to make the grade as a teacher, was nevertheless send by his abbot to Vienna to further his education in Mathematics and Biology; the fields where, ironically enough, he had failed more shamefully and sparking the acid comments of his examiner. It is not well established why and how our good monk became involved in researches with sweet peas, but it is known that after returning to the monastery, and during a period of 11 years (1857-1868), he worked intensely in his investigations and at the same time taught high school students at the local gymnasium, still without having successfully taken his grade as a teacher.

Mendel studied the pattern of inheritance of seven different characteristics and them all yielded identical results. For example, when he crossed long and short plants the off-springs were always long. If then he allowed self insemination of these hybrids to proceed he obtained 25% of true short plants (those which in future generations only gave rise to short plants), 25% of long ones and 50% of new hybrids, which upon further self inseminations would reproduce the same proportions of pure hybrids than their progenitors. Utilizing a flawless, and quite modern statistical approach, Mendel then concluded from his results that each of the characteristics he studied in the sweet peas appeared to share determinants from both parents; one of which was predominant and controlled phenotypic expressivity. Convinced that his findings upheld Nageli hypothesis about the 'micelles' or 'germ particles' he lost no time in sending him reprints of his publications; but the great investigator, apparently without a true appreciation or understanding of the monk's work, dismissed them as 'not rationalistic enough', an impertinence very revealing and typical of the deeply rooted Western epistemological bias.

Mendel's papers were published only in a local journal of Brno and his efforts of 10 years fell into complete oblivion before finally been resuscitated, more than three decades later, by De Vries and others. Soon after concluding his researches Mendel was promoted abbot of the monastery where he worked and his energies were then dissipated in administrative duties until the end of his life. Our venerable monk, despite his undeserved anonymity, is also another clear example of how much persistent dedication and perseverance with modest means could accomplish in science, even in the second half of the XIX Century.

In addition, like with Pasteur before, he was an outsider to the field of Medicine, although his works became the basis for the genetic sciences, of such great consequences for the advancement of the healing arts. Like Koch at the beginning of his researches, Mendel was not a 'professional' or 'academician', but rather a curious and methodic mind who followed the course of his personal inspiration to the very end with a determination deserving, at the time, better recognition. It would be erroneous, however, to assume that he was an intellectually ostracized figure producing his amazing investigations by the sole power of his fertile mind.

In fact, the works of his contemporaries were very well known to him, as shown by Mendel's efforts to allied the support of Nageli and other prominent scientists, but his approach was empiric and original and his conclusions a decisive prove of the fact that in the determination of any phenotypic characteristic partake both progenitors; although often one of them is dominant and the other recessive rather than equal contributors, as many others thought at that time to be.

Mendel's works, when rediscovered, were an indication of how some genetic characteristics, the recessive ones, could remain dormant for generations until a time when they would suddenly manifest themselves again under conditions of pairing with another of equal kind. What then appeared as a mutation was but this expression of a recessive character. De Vries, and other biologists, now pointed out that the behavior of Mendel's traits were similar to that of the chromosomes during the germ formation and union; something supporting the hypothesis of Weismann that these particles carried the hereditary information. As frequently happens in science, both possibilities, mutation and expression of hidden recessive traits, were found eventually to be operative in phenotypic expression.

So it closed the XIX Century, a period when scientific 'advance' in general, and Medicine in particular, quickened in relation to previous ages thanks, above all, to the technical progress achieved by mankind;

the perfecting of instrumentation and techniques allowing what could be considered an 'objectification of knowledge' and also permitting, as we had seen, original and independent research to be carried out, in comparison with today standards, with appallingly modest means and singlehandedly by pioneer and highly original minds, often working outside the stultifying influence of conservative and unyielding academic and professional circles.

Again, medical progress, as in the preceding ages, did not result, as Nageli thought, from 'ratiocinations' into the process of disease or by deliberate 'logical' analysis of 'fundamentals' in order to 'explain' given findings, but merely by relating and tabulating these findings; a process often assisted, as dramatized in the case of Pasteur's works in vaccination, by a great dose of serendipity which a great mind was prepared to seize and elaborate. Medical advances proceeded in a solid empirical basis.

Now, necessarily, we have to come to grips with the XX Century, a period beginning inauspiciously, still with candle lights in many houses and vehicles pulled by animal traction, only to witness a technological explosion without parallel in history, too diverse and well known to need description, but of an scope that simply pales by comparison to even the wildest dreams of our grandfathers.

We live and labor submerged in a thick ocean of 'progress'. We eat, breath, see and hear of continuous spectacular and unrelenting 'advances' sufficiently, I am sure,to bewilder any man not more than 50 years ago, but that today we have learned to accept with a taken for granted, business as usual attitude and even with a touch of indifference.

Medicine, of course, has not lagged behind in this literally unbelievable pageantry, but rather has participated decisively in it. At the turn of the century the physical discoveries, by Wilhelm Roentgen of X-rays and Madame Curie on radioactivity, opened new vistas in Medicine eventually leading to the creation of an entire novel field in diagnosis and therapeutics. The marvels of modern surgery, due to the developments of new instrumentation, techniques and anesthetics, are also well known, as are the discovery of multiple nutritional factors indispensable for health and life itself, giving rise to a remarkable improvement of human diet; at least for those who can afford it. But the most remarkable and far reaching discovery in the field of therapeutics came about at midcentury, in fact shortly before the end of the Second World War: The usage of antibiotics to cure infectious diseases.

The story, however, began in the second half of the XIX Century in no better place than the Koch's Institute for infectious diseases in Berlin, where Von Behring and Kitasato had made their great discovery of 'antitoxins'. A new addition to the staff, Paul Ehrlich, conceived of antitoxins as 'magic bullets' specifically aimed and lethal to toxins and germs. Just as some dyes, he reasoned, had specific affinities for certain tissues or even cellular components or organelles, there should be some compounds with a selective capacity to penetrate and kill microorganisms without necessarily producing deleterious effects on host tissues and cells. Ehrlich was a compulsive and meticulous investigator who systematically began to test different substances for the desired results. After much trying and errors he finally came up with an arsenic compound, Salvarsan (the 606th compound he tested), which proved immediately effective against an old scorch of humanity: Syphilis.

The works of Ehrlich were followed by others in Germany. In 1917 Michael Heidelberger and W.A. Jacobs discovered that an azo dye, sulfanilamide, destroyed bacteria. When Gerhard Domagk discovered the antibacterial activity of another dye, Prontosil, a synthetic product, it was soon found to be of great applicability in severe septic states and, later on, it was discovered that this dye was degraded in the human body into sulfanilamide; the substance already reported by Heidelberger to have antibacterial properties.

But these findings were only appetizers for what was going to come later. It was already known, and evidence continued to mount at a steady pace, that some bacteria, molds and fungi had themselves antibacterial activity against pathogenic organisms. Alexander Fleming, who after graduating at St. Mary Hospital Medical School and at the University of London had become involved in research in bacterial activity and antiseptics, one good day, while working at the hospital with a severe cold, a drop from his nasal secretions fell on a plate with bacterial cultures, and soon he detected a clearing in the colonies precisely where it felt. That was the first clue to the existence of anti-germ substances in human secretions, later on also identified in tears, saliva and milk. In time a proteinaceus substance was extracted and purified from these secretions and found capable of destroying bacterial organisms.

No practical applications came from this fortuitous discovery of Fleming but his luck had not yet completely ran out. While working at the same laboratory in 1928 (the nature and purpose of his investigations are not clear), he had set aside a pile of bacterial cultures (staphylococcus) in a lab bench close to the floor for several weeks during the summer months[7]. When he finally inspected one of the cultures [8] Fleming detected an area of inhibition around a mold. When he sub-cultured this mold in broth, the latter was found to acquire the capacity to kill and dissolve a number of disease-producing bacteria.

As we all know today, Fleming had discovered the first in the expanding list of 'wander-drugs' generically called antibiotics which had revolutionized therapeutics as no previous drug had ever done: Penicillin. His attempts to isolate and purify the substance, however, proved beyond his means and took the work of another investigator (Howard Florey) to effect the necessary extraction and testing of the material, eventually enabling the production and marketing of the drug.

It is therefore clear that in the case of Fleming, like in that of his predecessor Pasteur when working with his cultures of chicken-cholera, the element of chance, working on a prepared mind of course, played a crucial role in the discovery. Were not because it was summer time and cultures had been set aside in a low bench close to the soil where the mold disseminated more efficiently providing thus with optimal conditions for its growth and spread [9], the discovery would not have taken place when it did, and therefore a deliberate search for similar antibiotics would have been delayed considerably.

THE IMPORTANT POINT TO BE EMPHASIZED HERE, AS AT ANY OTHER TIME IN THE HISTORY OF MEDICINE, IS THAT PROGRESS POSSESS AN EMINENTLY EMPIRIC DIMENSION. THE DISCOVERY OF ANTIBIOTICS WAS NOT THE RESULT OF A 'RATIONAL INQUIRE' INTO THE STRUCTURE AND MORPHOLOGY OF BACTERIA AND THE CHEMICAL CHARACTERISTICS OF A PUTATIVE SUBSTANCE CAPABLE OF RETARDING THE GROWTH OR KILLING THESE ORGANISMS, BUT RATHER THE REVERSE.

Any proposed 'mechanism of action', as far as antibiotics is concerned, is only an A POSTERIORI elaboration of the mind to satisfy, soothe and assuage the 'explanatory' compulsion of Western Man, the bias at the root of Greek thought we so often referred to. The credit, however, should be granted to modern technology because it increases enormously the number of facts, or relevant information, available to man and capable of being integrated inductively and constructively into the fabric of human knowledge; that is, what truly represents scientific progress. But many of these 'facts' relate to unseen assumed realities projected inferentially from data collected by sophisticated and, presently, extremely expensive equipments.

We credit these technical advances with the spectacular strides taken in the XX Century by Biology. From studying microorganisms only capable to be 'visualized' by means of the microscopes, this science became 'molecular'; merging therefore with biochemistry and penetrating a realm incapable of being directly ascertainable to man, an unseen terrain 'conceived' by way of models that, like in the case of 'chemical formulas', essentially represent, as it was proposed before, only SHORT HAND NOTATIONS, symbols summarizing THE ENTIRE SPECTRUM OF DETECTABLE PROPERTIES SURMOUNTED BY MEANS OF OUR COMPLEX EQUIPMENTS, that is to say, properties representing a collection of observed phenomena and ascribed to a presumed reality beyond our sensorial reach.

To researches the obvious fact that some of these models had serve to synthesize large biological molecules, like insulin, growth hormone and even DNA itself (as well as the more recent recombinant achievements), is sufficient prove that they are true reproductions of reality, because one certainly has to 'understand' how something is constituted in order to be able to fabricate it, in other words, to reproduce whatever is constructed. If we don't know how a chair or a table 'looks' and how it is made up, it is claimed, we will never be able to fabricate another identical to it. We have to identify its constituent parts and how they are 'spatially arranged'.

When we are dealing with unobservable, and therefore inferential 'things', this analysis, however, is a dangerous comparison. What we are actually dealing with is a concatenation of events detected by instruments[10], which by a conventional SYSTEM OF REFERENCES we have been trained to relate to a characteristic chemical model based in 'images' borrowed from our cosmic level of existence. I contend that the synthesis of a chemical compound, no matter how complex, do not need of any 'visual' understanding, but solely of a highly structured design of sequential steps in keeping with the known properties of the compound we want to synthesize; therefore exactly what the chemists do but without the purported 'visual' interpretation of their results. (See also Chapter II)

A chemical substance, hence any biological compound, is the SUMMATION of all its properties AND NOTHING MORE. Yet, prizes are prodigally awarded for 'elucidations' of architectural designs, or otherwise, for 'producing images' which we proudly parade as 'unraveling' hidden secrets of the ultra-microscopic 'objects'.

The insistence for 'explanations', 'causes' and 'mechanisms' by Western Science, this misunderstanding of the true meaning and purpose of the scientific effort capable in some occasions to hinder progress, can hardly be more notorious than in Medicine. A typical example is the reluctance to accept Chinese acupuncture on the basis that no plausible or discernible 'mechanism of action' is found. Those who place such unjustified demands hold an unrealistic and, as could be inferred from our brief perusal of historical highlights, mistaken position based in a confuse view as to what is truly the aim and method of Science.

CHAPTER VI

A quite difficult and characteristic problem in medical science is the confusion immanent in something apparently as obvious as to what the term 'disease' refers to. The vexation is not only semantic but also epistemological. A 'disease', it was pointed out before, in itself is a process evolving over time. Such an entity is represented ordinarily by a group of symptoms and physical findings associated with radiologic and laboratory data and also frequently accessible to specific therapy; which usually add to the process of identification.

But the situation is not always that simple. The 'causes' and 'etiologies' of many afflictions are not known, and symptomatic, morphologic and therapeutic findings vicariously substitute in the diagnostic process; which essentially consist in ascribing a 'name' to a putative derangement of health. If to that is added that in many cases there is an overlapping of 'findings' between groups of 'maladies', it is not difficult to understand the bafflement and ambiguity that often arises.

Part of the problem, of course, resides in the fact that prior to any therapeutic effort there is a need to render, or at least to attempt, a categorization of the condition suffered by a patient. The situation is complicated by the vagaries of classification and definitions of 'disease entities', as well as, the frequent mystifications and free interchange of terms, like 'syndromes' for 'diseases' and vise versa.

The greatest danger, of course, is in the assignation of names to imaginary 'conditions', that is to say, to invalid categories. Because no specific criteria are known as to how morbid entities are to be defined, such a possibility is a real one. It is precisely in these shaky grounds, particularly in those instances when no etiology is known, that the temptation materialize, if for no better reason than the 'pressures' and urgency to administer treatment, to PRODUCE a name. This decision often has the magic power of dissipating uncertainties and doubts because of the aforementioned mysterious enchantment of 'words' which is based in the generative power of human language, and the convincing influence of emphatic repetition.

Artificial arbitrary denominations based in fashionable and glamorous medical 'theories' are so prevalent that it hardly becomes necessary to mention them. Dogmatic criteria, with no practical relevance, are 'common place' in Medicine despite of the purported excellence of modern 'advances' in this science.

The problem can be traced to the historic evolution of the concept of 'disease' itself. Originally this term was applied to disruptions of the state of health to which common people assigned various 'folks' names in accordance to the wit, imagination, superstition or taste of a given social group. We had already seen that Paracelsus and the Iatrochemists were the first to conceive, in the Western World, of diseases as 'entities' in their own right, although such a concept was intuitively believed by the populace since antiquity and was also held by the Cnidian School of ancient Greece. It is very likely that the idea of a 'morbid process' evolved from the evidence of 'spread', in other words, from the transmission of diseases from person to person. Contagiousness, when divested of any numinous content, can certainly be 'explained' only as a passing from person to person of some basic generative 'agent', that is to say, of some primordial ingredient or 'essence' of the disease itself.

Vaguely conceived as 'miasmas' in practical medical lore, speculations of this kind were forerunners of the germ theory and the ultimate acceptance of nosological entities as 'realities' capable to be apprehended and studied by the human mind. Undoubtedly, the concept that health disturbances were specific entities is a very old one. When somebody, in antiquity, did call excitedly on his neighbors to warn them about 'lepers coming down the road' it immediately conjured disquieting visions of deformed and repulsive human derelicts with variable degree of visible mutilations. People 'knew' what a medieval physician meant when he claimed that somebody was suffering from bubonic plague, typhus, tetanus, epilepsy, ergotism, etc.

The un-rationalized conclusion that diseases were 'entities' was, of course, reasonably justified by the similarities of symptomatic pictures exhibited by some sick people. Patients with 'consumption', or 'phthisis', did cough persistently, often produced bloody sputum and wasted away. Those suffering from 'San Vito dance' displayed peculiar jerky motions of the extremities and a characteristic gait. The catalog of ancient diseases with a quite specific group of identifying features could be long indeed, from the mutilations of a leper to the prostration and stupor of 'typhus'. Well defined and recognizable symptomatic clusters and physical signs is what constituted 'diseases' for the ancient, medieval, and even quite modern societies (practically up to the time of popularization of morbid anatomy in the XVIII Century). As it was mentioned, physicians, up to then, were in fact merely people more knowledgeable in 'identifying' these findings, and also versed in the art of healing and cure which was firstly practiced, as the historic record shows and the studies of contemporary primitive societies demonstrates, by priestly classes and 'witch doctors'; because of the common notion that maladies were 'caused' by 'bad spirits' or otherwise constituted the results of 'evil' influences upon the state of health.

As a matter of fact, the early confusion of syndromes with 'diseases' appears to be behind intriguing historical facts like, for example, the apparent decline of leprosy in Europe in the XV Century, after 'syphilis' was firstly 'identified' by Girolamo Fracastoro in the years following its purported appearance (as Morbus Gallicus) in Italy during the siege of Naples, in 1495, by the armies of Charles VIII

It is puzzling, anyway, that leprosy up to that time was considered as highly contagious and transmitted by sexual contact. The possibility that many manifestations of tertiary syphilis were attributed to leprosy, and vise versa, is therefore a good one. Sudhoff, who in 1912 made an exhaustive study of the subject, concluded, after dismissing the until then popular hypothesis of the Indo-American origin of syphilis, that not only leprosy but also possibly psoriasis as well as other exanthematous and venereal conditions were originally confused with this scorch of humanity.

With the dissemination of the practice of autopsies in the XVIII Century the 'clinical' picture, the symptomatic complexes and 'physical findings', came to be correlated with Morbid Anatomy findings (firstly attempted, as we have seen, in Hellenistic times) which were equated with 'the final answer' and definitional characteristics for health disorders; which in fact BECAME the 'disease'. With the shifting of emphasis new names came to replace old terms, and gross morphologic findings were the basis for medical nomenclature and classifications. (See also Chapter V) For example, 'dropsy' was replaced by 'liver cirrhosis' in some cases, 'nephritis' in others, etc. Physicians congratulated each other in the conviction that 'now we know better' what these diseases 'really are'. OBVIOUSLY THE ANATOMIC PENETRATION INTO THE HUMAN BODY CAME TO SYMBOLIZE AN EQUAL PENETRATION INTO THE UNDERSTANDING OF DERANGED HEALTH, in other words, into the 'pathogenesis' of these conditions. The new denominations were more 'accurate' because man could then 'see' the disease itself.

Human capacity for self deception nears infinity and Medicine has not been an exception. The replacement of one group of terms by others claimed to be more truthful or exact is an old compulsion of the human mind, of which we see frequent examples in practically every taxonomic denomination, Medicine being typical in this regard. It is hardly surprising that humans, being essentially visual animals, began then to label morbid conditions with names descriptive of the morphologic alterations in organs then coming to DEFINE a 'disease'. For example, the nodules seen in the lungs in cases of 'phthisis' became known, in the morphologic era, as 'tubercles' and the malady became 'tuberculosis'.

A revealing fact is that throughout history, and certainly up to the XIX Century, many workers who exerted great influence in the medical field were outstanding taxonomists. Theophrastus, the first acknowledged botanist, and later on Celsus, were greatly influential in Medicine. Among the great systematizes of the XVIII Century, Haller, Stahl (the proponent of the phlogiston theory), and Linnaeus, were not only true 'medics' but also botanists. Notwithstanding the great difficulties inherent in the task of organizing medical information in a meaningful pattern, the compulsive urge to equate Medicine with Zoology and Botany brought in its throes the insane follies of the Natural History School in Germany during the XIX Century. Even today the confusions brought about by those well meaning individuals who desired to render order from the apparent chaos by 'inventing' names to apply to obscured and often imaginary maladies, is real and unfortunately poorly understood by the medical profession.

The uncertainties and vagaries as to what constitutes a 'disease' were not resolved, to say the least, by the introduction of the microscope into Medicine. Predictably, new terms were proposed in generous profusion by the histopathologists and, as frequently happen with new technologies, a 'new' theory of disease based in the 'wonderful instrument' crystallized with Virchow. Histopathology replaced 'Gross morbid Anatomy' as the repository of ultimate truth.(See Chapter V)

Theories and hypothesis in Science, based in 'modern' fashionable technologies, are often dressed with an irresistible glamorous mystique, and Medicine is far from been an exception in this regard. Within the medical specialties Pathology (in the European tradition of Morbid Anatomy and Histology) bears the dubious distinction of being among those contributing the most, in modern times, to the type of grandiloquent dispensations of idle terminology and arbitrary theorizing still so prevalent in contemporary Medicine.

A seemingly unending stream of pedantic labels studded with Germanic, Latin and later on, French pre and suffixes, for old and new maladies, began to plague the medical literature; very often without practical purpose, but representing the results of new investigations and discoveries 'visualized' with the aid of the marvelous optical portents which did introduce a 'profound' dimension into medical research. Most fittingly, a child of this revolutionary methodology was the already alluded 'Cell Theory' of disease, a natural derivation from the 'infusorial' speculations of Oken', whose mystic insights allowed him to foretell the existence of these biological units before the microscopes first identified protozoa and other unicellular organisms. From there to the affirmation that cells constituted the uncontestable irreducible biological essence (the multicellular organisms representing only 'societies' of the original unities), as Virchow claimed, was only a small step, and the understanding of disease as 'a revolution' of the cells a logical follow up. In fact, so much infatuated was Virchow with the recently discovered beautiful cells that he adamantly, and persistently, refused to accept the revelations accruing from the works of Pasteur and his own compatriot

Koch, despite of overwhelming empirical evidence in their favor and the rigorous experimental works of the latter.

Although much solid and useful work has been undeniably done (above all in the histological appearances of neoplastic disturbances and in the study of tissue inflammation and repair) Pathology did become, perhaps because of its early dramatic successes, an stronghold of settled beliefs, with their practitioners always ready to place 'a label' into any conceivable microscopic abnormality and more than eager to 'explain', based in their marvelous microscopes and techniques, the 'mechanisms' of disease and the 'causes' of sickness and death. By 'looking', whether by gross inspection or visual aids, they claimed to be able to answer every question and dissipate all doubts. For the early pioneers admission of ignorance was frequently disgraceful, a personal shame and even a cowardice. Few self respecting pathologists ever intimated in front of his peers even the shadow of a doubt, and,when asked, always had to be ready with a prompt and categorical answer. Hesitation was deemed a sign of weakness unworthy of the profession. If the esteem of other physicians was to be maintained it was thru courage, determination and forceful promotion of the self ('hard selling' would be called today); RENDERING A DIAGNOSIS WAS NOT ONLY A NECESSITY BUT A MATTER OF HONOR. By substituting the myth of symptomatic diagnosis for the one of morphologic definition of 'diseases', Pathology, despite many positive contributions to Medicine has, sadly enough, been a major influence in the entrenchment of dogma; and today counts among its ranks some of the worst offenders in this respect. The speculative streak bore by the specialty since its inception still runs hot in our veins.

Be it as it may, the new 'visual' morphological and structural search into the 'deranged states of health' meant an undeniable advance upon previous external 'appearances'; although couple with it there was introduced into Medicine multitude of new names and terms difficult to equate and relate to previous ones, adding in many ways to the increasingly perplexing state of medical nomenclature. Many previously existing categories were divided and subdivided while others were lumped together; something still active today in all fields of the health sciences.

Not that there were lack of attempts to systematize medical terminology. During the XIX Century took place the subdivision of 'disease processes' into inflammatory, to which the suffix 'itis' was added; degenerative, when the corresponding suffix was 'osis'; neoplastic and tumorals, suffixed 'omas'; followed in later times by many other categories and subcategories not needed to be enumerated in here. Nevertheless, considerable obfuscation has remained as to the taxonomic place, and even identity, of many morbid entities.

As in the case of Gross Pathologic Anatomy, the high hopes that Histopathology was going to provide for a definitive diagnostic answer in all cases, were crashed against the bitter reality. Although man was, at least it appeared to be, 'penetrating' more and more into the secret abode of morbidity, the final 'truth' eluded him. Yet, the pressure was on; in fact the expectation that 'Pathology' would render the definitive diagnosis was so high that the practitioners of this 'science' found distasteful in the extreme degree a failure to render it. After all, didn't they possess in the microscope, a marvel capable of unraveling the most recondite secrets of the human body?

Parallel to the development of histopathological techniques, which enthralled physicians for many generations, there proceeded a new and spectacular advance in Medical Sciences: The discovery of microorganisms (also by microscopic techniques), and the dramatic prove of their causative role in many morbid conditions. (See Chapter V). From these findings finally stemmed a truly convincingly useful approach to the nomenclature of health derangements. For the first time in medical history a rational approach to classification, this time based in ETIOLOGY, was possible. Knowing the cause of a disease it was then possible to search for a cure in a more methodical and 'logical' manner. Any substance, or group of substances, capable of 'killing' or altering in some form a microorganism, was potentially a curative drug for the 'disease' it gave rise to. Because of their prognostic and therapeutic implications it was generally agreed that, whenever a cause for a malady was discovered, it should form the basis for classification and for naming a health disorder; which came in that way to be finally defined and characterized.

But this discovery not only was of major importance in what concerns therapeutics, it also permitted a new 'insight' into the morbid process itself, clearly demonstrating that numerous disparaged and hitherto different clinical pictures were, in actuality, 'caused' by the same organism; in other words, the protean manifestations of diseases was discovered. Likewise, in time it was shown that similar clinical pictures, and even histopathological findings previously considered to be the same sickness, were in fact totally different afflictions and therefore responsive to different 'cures'.

These revelations in the domain of infection diseases should have alerted physicians to the inconsistencies and limitations of classifications based in clinical and morphologic determinants but, instead, during the latter part of the XIX and the entire XX Century, the sacramental assignation of names to clinical and morphologic findings, if anything, accelerated at an astronomical pace, bombarding the medical literature with eponyms and synonyms of all sorts. The term 'disease' is at present equated variously either with a collection of symptoms (more properly denominated a syndrome but often utilized loosely interchangeably with it), morphologic or histopathologic features as well as etiologic determinants. Even a test or groups of tests can occasionally define and categorize a disease. [1].

The ambiguity arises because such a denomination should be exclusively reserved to processes, like an infection, represented by a typical constellation of symptoms and signs, a more or less characteristic evolution in time, either favorable or unfavorable, and an identifiable specific etiology, that is to say, to a totality of features associated with a given morbid disorder. To ascribe a name to a symptom, morphologic abnormality, laboratory or radiologic finding, and subsequently proceed to equate such a name with 'a disease' is a dangerous practice enmeshed in such definitional vacuum.

For many, I am sure, these considerations probably represent a sort of worthless nomenclatural platitudes lacking in practical value; again also a dangerous conclusion. It is precisely this failure to understand the dynamic nature of morbid states, the fact that they constitute processes rather than structural alterations or 'abnormal findings', what insidiously had permitted the introduction of names in Medicine devoid of etiologic support and practical worth whatsoever, helping only to confuse the issues; a disservice to the 'art' of Medicine. Typical in this regard are the numerous dermatological conditions 'baptized' with eponyms serving only as a cover up for ignorance and perplexity, like for instance: Lichen in all its varieties, granuloma faciale, alopecia cicactrisata, chondrodermatitis nodularis helicis etc. The list of sundry conditions, even in our times, in all fields of Medicine is great indeed (in fact it is increasing thanks to the marvelous new diagnostic procedures we avail ourselves with).

When analyzed carefully the fact seems inescapable: Although classificatory activity, the ordering of information about the world, is mandatory for any scientific enterprise, there is the clear danger of grouping the facts into imaginary categories to soothe the fancy of a given 'investigator', but lacking any practical value in guiding action which, after all, in the final analysis is the ultimate purpose and justification of Science. Perhaps, and because of its peculiar nature, such a mistake becomes more prevalent in the field of Medicine where entrenched, inaccessible, academic dogmatism is, still in our times, as rampant as ever.

There are obscured areas on the medical sciences where the lack of concrete evidence allows speculation to deceive the imagination of investigators into thinking that they 'truly' have discovered a 'new' disease. This situation usually arises when the 'causes' of sickness are not known. Then is when the tendency to delude oneself by arbitrary groupings of signs and symptoms, morphological findings etc. is more powerful, and the illusion of 'discovering' a new entity is more vividly manifested in the assignation of a name that seems to have the magic power of 'clearing the horizon', and 'dissipating' all doubts as to what the condition is. The point to be made is that any terminology in Medicine not firmly supported in etiology should, at least, have a DEMONSTRATED prognostic or therapeutic value instead of being based in arbitrary characterizations. Admittedly, there are difficult cases and even impossible ones, but it is preferable to concede ignorance than to believe that God bestowed upon us the divine grace of 'generation by the Word'

In summary, the effort to organize in an intelligible manner the constellation of findings in deranged states of health met in Medicine with the intrinsic difficulty of having to deal with processes rather than objects, with a sequence of temporal events rather than phenomena. Because of the limited symptomatic and morphologic expressivity of a living organism in response to injurious agents or causal determinants, over the ages there has been a pernicious tendency to equate symptomatic complexes and later on, with the development of Morbid Anatomy, of morphologic and/or histopathological features with what constitutes a disease process. Perhaps in Medicine, of all sciences, is where the 'alluring' power of words, this generative property of language, becomes better manifested. The justifiable eagerness of man for 'identifying' its worst 'natural enemy' (lack of health) has frequently catapulted him into an epistemological trap, provoked by his failure to produce a distinct definition of what constituted this enemy. (See also Appendix III)

As I see it the confusion as to what 'a disease' is frequently results from a distorted understanding of the term, a misrepresentation deeply rooted in Western thought and in the nature and dynamics of language. NAMING SOMETHING ONLY CONSTITUTES KNOWLEDGE WHEN WHAT IS NAMED CORRESPONDS TO A CLEARLY ASCERTAINABLE EXPIRIENCE WITHIN AN ESTABLISHED CATEGORICAL FRAME, AGREED UPON BY COMMON CONVENTION. It will be erroneous to give a leg, eye or mouth an animal name, in other words, TO CONFUSE A PART FOR THE WHOLE. Likewise it is a mistake to misrepresent a symptom, sign, or laboratory finding etc, for a given disease. Substituting a morbid process for a name with no clear therapeutic or prognostic value only serve to retard true progress in Medicine. Over the years this attitude, not excluding our present marvelous advanced technological age, has sadly resulted in misdiagnosis, as well as, over and under treatment to suffering legions of humans.

APPENDIX I

It is only fitting now to ask ourselves a question increasingly important for modern man, a question that perhaps only a few decades ago would have been even irrelevant. Is it there any foreseeable limit to that 'progress'? Two different aspects of the question should be distinctly differentiated and separately considered. One is, of course, the possible existence of a limit to 'material' advance; the other refers to the biological potentiality of that fundamental characteristic of man, what we think distinguishes us from the rest of the Animal Kingdom: The human soul, the spiritual substratum of our intellect, of how much it is still capable to keep striving for increasing perfectibility and excellence.

The first aspect of the question, the possibility of a limit to technological progress, has been answered by some with qualifications. Although no limit is envisaged at the present time, they contend, it is reasonable to assume that there is one which we are, by the way, approaching at a vertiginous speed, at an ever escalating geometric pace. There have been numerous attempts to quantify human achievements, many 'parameters' had been used in this line of inquire: Like world population, energy consumption, rapidity of travel etc. According to this view, if it is granted that these 'magnitudes' have an upper attainable limit, it will be reached in a very short span of historic times.

What all these 'theories' lost perspective of is, however, the difficulties inherent in a general definition of what true progress consist of and relate to. Let us take as example world energy consumption. Could we assume that if such consumption declines or stabilizes necessarily would imply a PARALIZATION of progress? Can we equate such 'parameter' OBLIGATORILY to 'advance' in general? I do not believe so. If improvement in the standards of living and increase control over the environment are considered the indispensable ingredients of this 'progress', at least in the material sense, they are definitely conceivable even with stabilized energy consumption, world population, or any other indicator of material progress that our fancy or imagination could produce. The fact remains, therefore, that despite the vertiginous rate at which the technological explosion is proceeding the end is not yet in sight, and it will be idle to speculate as to a potential limit.

If progress is going to cease in the near future, we have to conclude, the reasons for that will have to be search elsewhere, namely in the human soul. For this we are going to lack objective measurable parameters to go by in our evaluation, and instead would have to rely in indirect signs reflected in societal characteristics whose change over time will give us inkling as to what is going on (things like religious and moral outlook, customs and cohesiveness of the human group).

The task, therefore, is obviously not easy, mainly because different people will attribute to such changes different meaning or no meaning at all. As a matter of fact, there might be people who even would deny that changes had taken place. Understandably, the difficulty here is the finitude and shortness of the life span of man when compared to social groups, and consequently the impossibility of acquiring 'first hand' personal information about historical changes. Here then the necessity to trust in the perspective of other men who, to make things even more difficult, lived and toiled in other epochs and perforce did have a dissimilar 'outlook' to the present one.

But dark clouds are crowding the horizon of science. The tendency to dogmatize had been related psychologically to anxiety, alienation, and low self-esteem. In Science it has its first historical manifestation in the Dogmatic Sect of physicians and it seems to relate to a human urge to 'share in settle beliefs' usually if the beliefs are accepted and promoted by the conventional wisdom or preconceived notions from which a person seek acceptance. This need to participate and endorse cultural points of view, attitudes and rituals stems from the basic makeup of man as a social animal and the need to depend on the group, originally for sustenance and protection and, as society became more complex, also for acceptance and promotion.

It is logically assumed by many that with the improvements in education and the enormous advance in communication humanity had witness in the last century, that Man today will be better informed and therefore freer in all ambits of human endeavors. Yet, sadly, the opposite is happening. Manipulation of facts and news by The Establishment is rendering us in many ways cultural illiterates and Science in general is not the exception. Dogmatism in science is as rampant as ever and frequently unproved hypothesis are accepted as established facts. Scientific publications, government and corporations are largely to blame for the creation and perpetuation of concepts and poorly documented conclusion that becomes institutionalized paradigms. Any proposals that contradict the pronouncements of the egregious authorities do not have the slightest chance of being accepted or published in reputable journals or any other lines of communication. The examples are many in all fields of Science. Sadly, the present situation provokes an enormous waste in resources, time and efforts which do not bade well for any branch of Science.

APPENDIX II

An intriguing, and, I believe, very revealing fact is what appears to be, as J. Campbell expresses, an ulterior transformation of this powerful symbol, in view of the fact that in more recent myths the serpent from being a supreme deity becomes the personification of satanic forces; the incarnation of evil, the malevolent incubus which seduced Eve and prompted the 'Fall of Man'. Several myths contemporaneous with this surprising inversion of meaning perhaps give a clue as to what has happened. Zeus vs. Typhon, Tiamat vs. Marduk, Vitra vs. Indra, all sound the same theme: The account of the triumph and overpowering by a 'solar' and glorious deity of dark, subterranean and wild powers represented by monsters-dragons who tyrannized the Earth before being vanquish in the final confrontation with the shiny irons of the heroic god-saviors.

The themes, curious by their similarities and disseminations, are the same among the diverse Levantine cultures, ancient Greece, and Indus Valley mythical lore. They all lend credence to the view that an old generation of chthonian, earth-bound, ancient divinities related to the fertility cults of early agricultural matriarchal societies, was eventually replaced by a pantheon of masculine, luminous deities; those extolled by Homer in his immortal poems and sung in the Indian sutras as early as the VII Century B.C.

Elsewhere (See Chapter I) it was suggested that early philosophy and speculative thought, the forerunners of the 'scientific spirit', originated among the Ionian descendents of the Aegean Bronze-Age civilizations uprooted by Indo-European nomadic invaders, which descended upon the Eastern Mediterranean basin early during the Second Millennium B.C. Similar irruptions, somewhat earlier, in the Indus Valley created equivalent demographic disturbances in the Punjab, triggering an exodus of the native population toward the Gangetic Valley where, intriguingly enough, appeared about the VII Century B.C. and approximately simultaneously with the dawning of the philosophical spirit among the Ionians, those religions WITHOUT GODS represented by Sinkhaism, Jainism and Buddhism.

Are men subjected to similar conditioning by environmental circumstances, although widely separated geographically and culturally, prompt to behave in like manner? Are defeated and uprooted people prompt to 'castaway' the gods who seemingly have betrayed them? Is this psychosocial circumstance what influenced the Ionians to 'seek for truth' outside nature and in the case of the Indian sagas to adopt the opposite (introverted) attitude of taking refuge in themselves and search for revelation by way of the 'inner light'? Of course we will never know the answer to such complex questions but there are perplexing facts (exemplified upmost in the scientific-religious hybrid sect of the Pythagoreans, whose concepts and speculative ideas are partially expressed in Plato's Phaedo and Timeus) that certainly seem to represents an early manifestations of a new inquiring spirit toward nature, a questioning devoid of divine allusions and explanations; and yet, theirs was a religious sect whose orphic rites were poorly disguised remnants of the fertility ceremonies, the wild Dionysian festivities and orgies of their bronze-age forebears.

The Akousmata, a body of superstitious precepts, hardly seem to proceed from the same source as the beautiful concept of the natural number and the 'melody of the spheres' from where the Pythagoreans gained their widely and deserved renowned. On the other hand, their belief in the transmutations of the soul strongly evokes quite similar doctrines to the Indian ascetics in the Gangetic forests, and appears to be a manifestation of a widely held conviction among bronze-age Levantine societies, embodied in the orphic rites of Ancient Greece.

─────────── APPENDIX III ───────────

Modern Medicine, besides its obsessive preoccupation with causes, mechanisms and explanations, is afflicted by some very specific epistemological pitfalls, some of them actually representing 'carry-overs' from previous ages but others distinctively new and precisely the consequences of our marvelous technology.

Nowhere perhaps has the impact of these changes been more notorious or apparent than in the attitudes of the physician. Because increased societal demands for more and better servicers, ever more pressing regulations from government, medical organizations, hospitals and agencies of all sort, besides the need to keep abreast in their professional field of expertise, the modern doctor, with little time for anything else, is taught to 'store' information in their brain cells and never to question sources.

This mass-produced conformism, as much a by-product of modern technology as the much more emphasized 'de-humanization' and depersonalization of medical services, certainly has not helped the development or sustenance of a critical spirit in Medicine. As a matter of fact, there is substantial and significant evidence that despite the paradoxical explosion of medical literature during the past few decades, there is, and had been for a while, a progressive decline in quality. For example, Robert and Suzanne Fletcher (News England Journal of Med. Jul 1979, P. 180) in a review of 612 randomly selected articles from original publications in the three leading journals for general clinical audiences in the English literature (JAMA, Lancet and the New England Medical Journal), found an increase in research methods of less sound scientific credentials: Like uncontrolled clinical trials an cross-sectional studies

(25% to 44% and 13% to 21% respectively), while there was a notable drop in the more solid cohort type (from 59% to 34%).

There might be several reasons for this already alluded 'mass production mentality' which has permeated the academic establishment today. 'Quantity at all costs' is a post-industrial cry heard in all fields of human productivity and creativity. Elliot M. Berry, in an article in the New England Journal of Medicine, pointed out the fact that from the years 1964 to 1972 the journal coverage in the Science Citation Index grew from 600 to 2400. Wondering about the presumptive causes of such a proliferation of journals and publications during this time-period Dr. Berry, after citing the growth of new specialties and Science in general, mentioned undue delay in publications by established journals, selection forces and political reasons as important factors in this regard. Further on, in the same article, Dr. Berry points out that whereas in the past an applicant for an associate professorship listed an average of 18 papers, at the present the candidates ordinarily present three to five times that number of bibliographical entries.

The logical corollary of this situation is, of course, an obliteration of the spirit of dissent (by no means confine to Medicine but widespread in Science). Conclusions are frequently drawn from ill-conceived protocols designs and /or faulty, unwarranted interpretations of the results by which, nevertheless, the authors find not only easy access to the publishing media but also instant recognition; especially if they are well known 'authorities'. Before long the research 'findings', without much further elaboration, sediment as 'knowledge' in text books, continuing medical education courses and 'workshops'. As a matter of fact disagreements and controversy are often actually frown at and had become more of an oddity, limited basically to studies where conflicting economic interests are involved.

Admittedly the problem is extremely complex and plagued with difficulties. Because of the statistical nature of much of the medical evidence the adequacy of sampling methods is of paramount importance; as it is the manner of conducting the investigation and the way of collecting and interpreting the generated data. More often than not editorial boards of journals (usually the first and more important 'distillers' of medical information) lack the screening capability, whether because of lack of expertise, time or desire, to weed out or reject unworthy manuscripts. Sadly to say, frequently enough, publications are awarded more on the bases of 'reputation' or 'prestige' of the authors than on intrinsic merits of the work itself.

When dealing with subtle changes of some characteristics under investigation (say for example, the response of patients to drugs), it would be in some occasions very difficult to arrive at a definitive conclusion. Concrete answers, therefore, are only possible in cases when the biological changes resulting from the studies are obvious and uncontestable in all respects. In fact, in some instances, there is hardly a need for a controlled prospective study of any kind.

Take for instance the miraculous case of the results obtained in the early works with antibiotics. Penicillin produced consistently such spectacular cures of hitherto frequently lethal and crippling infections that it hardly needed any expert, even less controlled testing, to prove its efficacy. The great worry was with potential deleterious (toxicity and/or hypersensitivity) effects, but no one did ever dreamed of questioning its therapeutic merits.

Unfortunately, and unavoidably, results of medical trials are evaluated probabilistically and interpreted as 'statistically significant' or not, depending on whether the value of P. (the probability function) falls within a defined limit of 0.05, which is a way to express that the achieved results had a 95% possibility of being correct; an indication that still there is a 5% possibility of the results not being so. Therefore, even assuming the impeccability of experimental design and execution, still chance cannot dismiss entirely the falseness of a positive result. The larger the populations included in the tests the more reliable the results will be and the more uncertainties will be dissipated. Yet, however, practical considerations limit the number of participants and the number of times a given experiment could be repeated.

Again a most significant possibility was pointed out by Harold M. Schoolman et. al. (Statistics in medical research: Principles versus practices', Volume 71, No. 3, P. 257). Commenting on researches assessing the efficacy of specific treatment protocols in a given disease, they emphasized that in most occasions if the results between treatment and placebo are not significant, they are not publish. This will give rise to multiplication of effort in view of the fact that the negativity of effect will not be reported. It is easy to surmise the degree of waste in resources and time that this omission will give rise to.

But this is not all. Because if an experiment is performed often enough there is an increasing possibility that significant outcomes will be obtained by chance alone, whoever has the bad luck of achieving these unlikely, but entirely possible, results will most probably publish them and there will be no way to detect the error, in view of the fact that none of the negative instances would had been so reported. For example, if a positive result has only one chance in twenty to be obtained by chance alone (with the usual traditional confidence limits of P .05) the investigators will conclude that a given treatment is efficacious when in reality is not (Type I error), because in the other 19 occasions when the therapeutic study in question was attempted by other investigators and no significant effect found the results were not published.

The chance of arriving at wrong conclusions, based not even in mistaken designs or statistical pitfalls, but in customary reporting patterns by those who failed to report negative findings on the assumption that they are irrelevant, is a real one. Conversely, if the project is terminated too soon there is a risk that treatment be dismissed as inefficacious when in reality it is not. (Type II error).

What all this amounts to is the realization that even in the best design protocols, if the medical and biological changes under investigation are subtle enough, there always will remain a lingering element of doubt inseparable to the results; practical considerations might force us to dismiss them but, nevertheless, it is an ever present component. If this holds true in the best of cases, what then when the experimental design has not been as meticulously planned and/or executed? We can only surmise the consequences. Unfortunately many works in the medical field today lack the necessary rigor and objectivity to be accepted as relevant.

In an article in the British Medical Journal ('Misuse of statistical method: critical assessment of articles in the B.M.J. from Jan to March 1976-1977, 1, 85-87) Sheila M. Gore, Ian G. Jones and Eilif C. Rytter concluded that from 62 papers and originals in 13 consecutive issues, 32 were afflicted by serious statistical errors, falling in six different categories listed as follows: Inadequate description of basic data, disregard for statistical independence, errors with Student's test and with X^2 tests. These investigations, it should be added, according to the authors pertained only to the statistical manipulation of the submitted data and were not concerned with a critical evaluation of the design or implementation of the research project. Although the authors of this article promptly emphasized that only 5% of the errors gave rise to mistaken conclusions, it is difficult to dismiss the seriousness of the situation; particularly when it is taken into consideration that the British Medical Journal is one of the most prestigious in the field and that, as the authors also stated, the studies were limited by the 'ease' of how researchers disguised the data they analyze, so suspicion or error could not be proved.

The reasons, therefore, for faulty conclusions accruing in modern medical research are multiple. Some pertain to the intrinsic difficulties inherent in medical and biological phenomena, others depend on either errors in design and implementation or in defective statistical manipulations of the generated data; even, in some cases, do to failure in reporting negative results or, on the contrary, forming premature conclusions.

A particularly knotty problem is when the investigation is design to discover possible causal association in disease. Because the difficulty of utilizing prospective controlled longitudinal studies in this area researchers are forced to content themselves with retrospective studies, in other words, to begin with the gathering of cases where the disease HAD ALREADY OCCUR and also to procure a matched group of controls before proceeding with the investigation of presumptive etiological correlations (case-control studies).Often the problem here is precisely HOW THESE CONTROLS ARE SELECTED. Many different type of bias (susceptibility, surveillance, detection, early death and, above all, protopathic bias) threaten the reliability of results and are difficult to guard against.

Sadly enough, the possibility of identifying these inaccurate results, poor researches, or even worse, of exposing accidental distortions and fabrications, becomes ever more remote because of the complexities and difficulties inherent in such monumental tasks; which often would require the repetition of prolonged, involved, costly and complicated experiments. If to that is added the ever increasing conformism and loss of critical spirit we can commence to surmise the mounting wastage of efforts and resources characteristic of modern medical research. [1]

Central to the lack of discriminating spirit is the compartmentalization of medical studies with the consequent development of narrow outlooks and interests which, like in any other field of human endeavor where such divisions take place, give rise to jealousy, secretiveness and mutual suspiciousness, ultimately provoking a break in free communication, trust and collective action when more critical to tackle difficult problems. It only needed to be mentioned the numerous debates during the first half of the XX Century between the advocates of surgery or radiation in cancer therapy, with each side parading 'convincing' evidence for the primacy of one or the other treatment modality; invariably the surgeon rallying to the side of Surgery and the radiologists to radiation.

Contrary to what we will like to believe, scientific inquire is not the impartial pursuit of an objective truth by careful design of experimental methods. (See Chapter II). On the contrary, dogmatic unproven beliefs often not only are the basis of therapy but because of their emotional content are defended AT ALL COSTS, stifling honest initiative and tainting with their bias research projects designed to prove their validity. There are many examples in Medicine and Biology of mere 'hypothesis' which are confused with 'established' knowledge but this obfuscation could not be explained solely on the basis of compartmentalization of the research effort.

Thomas R. Dawber, from the Department of Medicine of Boston University School of Medicine, in an address to the Massachuset Medical Society placed, I think, the finger squarely in the sore spot. Professionalization of the research effort, he claimed, the development and consolidation of a class whose survival depends on 'productivity at all costs' and of approval by peers in government and granting institutions, is another important factor. In addition, the control of assignments of research funds, as Dr. Dawber states, are often 'moved by narrow interests' and, I may add, also by distorted views which not always can be explained on rational basis. (New England Medical Journal. Volume 299, P.452.)

In other issues, as for instance the case of tonsillectomies in the prevention of upper respiratory infections (mentioned also by Dawber in his address), a possible pecuniary incentive appears more plausible; particularly when it is remembered that until recently, as he noticed, approximately 800000 procedures per year, at a cost of $150 millions of dollars, has been preformed. In his perusal of the voluminous literature the above author, however, could only find ONE PROSPECTIVE STUDTY IN THE SUBJECT, and that was in 1930, carried out with a very small group of controls. Later views by J. L. Paradise ('Why T&A remains moot' Pediatrics 49: 648-651, 1972) and Shaikh W., Vayda E. and Feldman W. Pediatric 57: 401-407, 1976) had found the reports of superior results with tonsillectomy wanting in statistical rigor and reliability.

We could go on with a seemingly inexhaustible list of important, unproven and poorly documented beliefs in Medicine which nevertheless form the basis of serious therapeutic decisions, while millions of dollars are poured into investigations of relatively rare but glamorous conditions (for example, congenital enzymatic pathways deficiencies), justified by the premise that discovery of their causes and care will provide 'marvelous insights' into morbid processes. Admittedly, in many cases, long prospective trials are marred by enormous difficulties and the practicing physician is under strong psychological pressure to utilize the latest available technique or drug in the treatment of his patients. Even when their purpose is evaluation of a drug the protocols are not devoid of intrinsic difficulties like, for example, changes of response by a microorganism to a given anti-microbial agent because of the emergence of resistant mutants that, with time, will alter the results despite of unassailable design and flawless implementation of the projects.

Once these limitations are accepted still remains a large body of dogmatically endorsed beliefs not being submitted to serious investigations. No doubt, among other things, the foul-up priorities in research deriving from the creation of a class of professional investigators with vested interests in narrow projects and 'easy results' (and often the deliberate evasion of the great controversial issues), has been an stultifying factor in medical sciences and instrumental in the proliferation of worthless literature. Perhaps, as Dr Dawber suggests, the practicing physician should have a 'much louder voice' in research planning. Yet, I believe, it is precisely the apathy and absence of a critical spirit, the willingness to accept unproven hypothesis and, I suspect, the failure to discriminate between established knowledge and mere opinion, what is characteristic of the busy practitioner of today. The peculiar dichotomy, rooted in history and almost unique to Medicine, between the investigators and practitioners, has certainly been a major contributory factor in the entrenchment of dogma in this most humane of sciences. This could not be better illustrated that in the history of the approach to treatment in cancer of the breast.

Anatomically an easily accessible tumor it has been traditionally considered as amenable to surgical approach and potential eradication. Until the times of Halsted, nonetheless, all the approaches met with failure. This surgeon, in 1889, based in contemporary theories of cancer biological behavior (the belief that carcinomas spread firstly by way of lymphatic channels to regional lymph nodes representing a 'barrier', or natural sieve, from where it eventually disseminated throughout the body) devised his radical mastectomy procedure including, besides the total extirpation 'in block' of the breast and underlining chest muscles, also a meticulous dissection of the axillary lymph nodes.

The operation, originally performed in large bulky tumors, significantly improved the survival of patients, and soon commenced to be used in all cases of breast cancer irrespective of tumor size and degree of clinical involvement of axillary nodes. In time it was found, in accordance with the theory and premises in which treatment was based, that those patients with smaller tumors and absence of axillary metastases did have a better prognosis; in expert hands even reaching the encouraging figure of 50% survival at 10 years after surgery. The 'radical mastectomy', as the procedure was to be called and as any physician of our generation knows, became enormously popular and the unquestioned treatment of choice in breast cancer.

For over half a century, and despite of the attendant rather considerable morbidity and ugly mutilation, nobody ever dared to question its premises or rationality, nor even vaguely entertained the possibility that a more limited procedure, even much less any alternate therapeutic avenue, like radiation therapy for instance, could meet with similar or identical success in certain subpopulations of cases (notwithstanding existing evidence that it might have been assisted, at least, with as good a survival as surgery). Furthermore, nobody ever questioned whether such extensive surgery really was necessary in all cases until the decade of the sixties, when the

Cooperative Breast Cancer Project (the National Surgical Adjuvant Breast Project Group) to study alternative therapeutic modalities picked up steam, and finally concluded after years of studies that more conservative surgery couple with radiation to breast and axillary areas produce similar results. An early enlightening article in this subject by Vincent T. De Vita from the National Cancer Institute addressed one fundamental problem with modern medical research when he claimed that: "investigators find it difficult to set up therapeutic experiments without a bias toward their own background and training." ('The evolution of therapeutic research in cancer', New England Journal of Medicine Volume 298, P. 907)

It is hardly a secret that in our nation deliverance of health care had become a multimillion dollar industry of colossal proportions, beset by wastage, bloating inefficiently and staggering costs, catapulted by inflation, lack of foresight, bureaucratic entanglements, greediness and the inroads into Health Sciences of modern 'space' technology with its mechanical devices and computerization at every level, which allows an enormous output of services offered, more often than not, at exorbitant prices to the clientele of patients. The hospitals, more and more, happen to be large business enterprises managed by armies of non-medical administrators whose central interest, curiously enough, is to 'accrue a profit' in this traditionally most typical devoted and humane profession.

As a corollary to this professionalization of the research effort there naturally has followed its manipulation by granting institutions, whether governmental or private agencies. There is an element of danger in this, the possibility that research will become in the best of cases divorced from the public interest, and in the worst that conclusions be tailored to suit the interests of the sponsoring agencies. Notorious examples are the research activities financed, directly or indirectly, by pharmaceutical companies. Product advertisement based in, hypothetical or real, poorly carried out and planned experimental designs has not been, to say the least, unknown to Medicine. More recently, subtle influences upon the medical profession are exerted by the increasing sponsoring of continuing medical educational programs by such organizations. Naturally, survival depending in the capacity for 'selling' their products, it will be naive to assume they would patronize somebody with negative views in the matter. The propaganda efforts, however, are usually soft and often even surreptitious, almost imperceptible, except for those who keep an alert deliberate search for the positive evidence. A casual remark here, a pamphlet given away at the conclusion of a lecture, a sign or mention prominently displayed at the entrance door of the lecture room is sometimes all that can be discovered. The psychology of advertisement techniques knows that it is more than enough. The manifested 'prime mover' of a capitalistic society is the profit motive, which constitutes the original purpose of a business enterprise. Research or educational activities financially supported by them run the risk of becoming bias, retarding true progress in Medicine.

But there are even more ominous black clouds darkening the medico-scientific horizon. Because of recent reductions in research outlays from governmental agencies and a new and dangerous, difficult to explain, commercialization of the scientific 'enterprise', investigators and universities alike had been entering in increasing numbers into partnership arrangements with industrial companies; a marriage that, although at first appears to be beneficial, is nevertheless fraught with potentially devastating consequences for society and science. In a recent article Charles Seife, professor of Journalism at New York University commented about the increasing association with, and financing by the pharmaceutical industry of 'independent' medical researches doing work that relates to the drugs these companies are marketing (Scientific American Vol. 307, Number 6. Dec 2012)

The author proceeds to document the close association, not only of the pharmaceutical industry with speakers at meetings and researchers but, even more ominous, with granting institutions and approving government agencies including the NIH, which allocates billions of dollars every year to investigators.

If to that is added the direct saturating propaganda efforts by drugs companies to the lay public using every avenue of communication at their disposal, and the almost daily sensationalistic reports of new miraculous products (research by 'press release'), we perhaps might commence to understand the waste of resources and potential distortions of the evidence, with the attendant increase in cost to the Health Industry and danger to the public, implied in such practices.

Besides the above described peculiar epistemological problems, in the field of Medicine as in science in general, the XX Century had brought in its throes not only the glorification of modern technology, the God who so assiduously we all worship, but together with its marvels also the demise of the amateur-scientist, like Mendel, who instilled their highly refreshing personal vistas to bear fruit in far reaching accomplishments of great use to humanity from outside the scientific establishment of the day.

The need for highly complex equipment and expensive research protocols has brought with it that unavoidable need for substantial economic resources and, therefore, the necessity of resorting to grants by governmental or private institutions, which then obviously control the type and direction the investigations will take. Evidently, because these granting institutions have a stake in the work to be done, they measure the results in PRODUCTIVITY, whether financial or scientific, with the ultimate aim also being financial.

Because of the complexity brought about by modern technology into the medical field there is often an attendant obliteration of personal initiative that deprives science of one of its more precious fountain-heads. By emphasizing quantity rather than quality of output it also prostitutes the scientific effort that becomes then banal and superficial, tending also to create and perpetuate dogma and mistaken notions which turn into unassailable beliefs because of the impracticality, and often impossibility, of disproving them in view of economical and institutional constrains that render such tasks out of question.

To repeat, besides the build-in incertitude inherent in any statistical conclusion, something unfortunately central to any conceptualization in medical sciences, there is a whole group of potential mistakes stemming from pitfalls in design, performance and/or interpretation of results which deliberately, or unintentionally, frequently distort biomedical conclusions. The present situation is further compounded by excessive compartmentalization of the scientific effort and pressures to 'produce' with attendant sedimentation of entrenched dogmatism, and by the peculiar dichotomy academician-practitioner, which often renders the average physician incapable to judge the merits of the received information. If we add to this the basic conceptual difficulties in the understanding of what constitutes and represents a 'disease' we can begin to appreciate the colossal difficulties that modern man need to face and tackle in this most important field of human endeavors: The Health Sciences.

——————— APPENDIX IV ———————

In fact, as many of the early quantum physicists never tired of telling us, and as we had already quoted in the cases of pioneers like Heisenberg, the infra-structure of matter is too far removed from our senses and too radically different from what we know and had ever 'observed' to allow the semblance of a 'visualization' by our minds. The atom, they emphatically stated, can only be defined by a series of differential equations, in other words, by abstract mathematical formulations RELATING variables like position, momentum, time, waves and frequencies, as well as, mysterious atomic unimaginable powerful and complex 'forces'.

Furthermore, because of the intrinsic limitations of 'wave mechanics', the position and momentum of infra-atomic 'particles' could not be ascertained simultaneously (neither their counterparts time and frequency). As a matter of fact, many great minds, like Einstein himself, never reconciled themselves to accept the notion of 'physical incertitude' which they interpreted as stemming from our 'lack of knowledge' of some fundamental parameters, only to be resolved once these parameters be 'discovered' (an opinion caustically explained in Einstein's cryptic comment that "God doesn't play dice").

Time appears to have tilted the balance of truth in favor of quantum physicists, something which categorically imposes an obstacle, truly an ABSOLUTE limitation, to our capacity to determine at the same time the different characteristics of subatomic particles, and so appearing to 'eradicate' from them those properties necessary to establish a comparison using the traditional categories we ordinarily resort to in our universal neighborhood. In fact, Quantum Physics had found very useful to interchange the concept of 'forces' and 'particles' in the microcosmic world with the result that energy, matter, and forces, all are viewed as essentially interchangeable notions, modes of 'viewing' and ways of conceiving or depicting the same thing.

The point could be cogently argued as to the inappropriateness, or invalidity, of keeping or maintaining concepts such as 'particle' and 'wave' in reference to subatomic phenomena, and some authorities had even suggested the advisability of replacing them with noncommittal, perhaps more sincere, denominations like 'events'. Could it be then that the infra-cosmic 'indeterminacy' results from a conceptual bias of the human mind? If we address Nature with preconceived notions, couldn't we expect 'incertitude' giving rise to absurdities like the so-called 'Schrodinger cat'? If we ask where 'the particle' is, and there is not such a thing, couldn't we expect a crazy answer? Is it possible that subatomic phenomena simply do not SIMULTANEOUSLY have position and momentum? Whatever the response to these questions there is something reasonably clear and undeniable: Visual 'models' BASED IN NOTIONS ACCESIBLE TO OUR UNDERSTANDING and capable of inspiring 'general laws', of the type that the inductive method had accustomed us in the Western World, SIMPLY ARE NOT VALID in the microcosm and therefore stop serving a useful purpose. To assign 'a name' to unknown phenomena represents a commitment to a 'line of enquire' towards where we are dragged by the semantics of our language, and by that analytical and individualizing precondition of Western knowledge and communication.

The reductionist approach of Western rationality, the search for 'simple' constituents or elements in phenomena which, once identified, by the method of 'induction' would allow us to 'discover', and perhaps manipulate, the hidden rules of creation, the 'reasons' why things ARE in the way they are, is only a chimerical dream that has to be abandoned. Our analysis, which proceeds by 'dismantling' and 'singling out' the individual constituents of complex phenomena, presupposes, maybe again because of man's cognitive limitations, JUST THAT, in other words, the existence of these 'basic units' of phenomena (a menagerie of colorful microcosmic particles 'discovered' by the works of our marvelous 'particle accelerators', which scientists had arranged in a glamorous family array of progressively heavier corpuscles of same kind they called 'The Standard Model', including evanescent members that mysteriously and suddenly materialize and dissipate out of existence). What truly are being observed are traces of discrete events in the recording apparatus interpreted as specific decaying cascades of presumptive elemental 'particles'.

In an attempt to understand the microcosm Man, after the discovery of quantum effects, resuscitated the old 'atomic paradigm' of the ancient Greeks which has resulted, thanks to the wonderful modern instrumentation at our disposal, in the proliferation of subatomic particles presently arranged in the above alluded 'Standard Model', proposed to represent matter and forces(fermions and bosons), which interactions are suppose to explain the conformation and stability of our Universe.

But quantum mechanics laws had given rise to unpredictable consequences to this cozy model, which potentially would have created imbalances incompatible with the present stable state of the Universe. To explain the inconsistencies and preserve the vision of a harmonious Cosmo particle physicists postulated that fermions and bosons do possess super-partners, which imply an exuberant proliferation of 'elemental' units by requiring that the known particles couple, with still not discovered, counterparts.

Another example is the postulation of 'String Theory' which instead of particles proposes the existence of microcosmic strings which patterns of vibration explains their properties, that is, of the particles they are assumed to replace. The theory arose in an attempt to achieve 'the grand unification' in Physics, the possibility of a merging all the known 'forces': The strong, weak, electromagnetic and gravitation (which so far has avoid integration with the others).The theory happily accepted the supersymmetric scenario which avoided the uncomfortable notions of a 'fine tuning' of cosmological constants by postulating a cancelling out of destabilizing quantum effects into the fabric of the Universe, but this theory still lacks predicting value, the prerequisite for any practical scientific postulate. .

These attempts to unravel the universal 'grand design' points out to an important characteristic of human behavior : The elaboration of hypothesis based in interpretations of physical observational and experimental evidence incorporated in a working model, is modified according to the needs in accommodating new facts. More often than not there is great resistance by the investigators to abdicate their cherish conceptions which often crystallize in dogmas (comfortable beliefs that assuage our souls with the illusion that we 'are in the right track'), a reassuring feeling of our self-worth and importance often defended at 'all costs', a dangerous and ancient proclivity of humans.

The desire to visualize and render intelligible The Microcosm, the urge to discover why the laws of nature are the way they are (the amazing fine tune of universal parameters), the ultimate truth behind the 'veil of appearances' is in essence a religious urge, a search for God, a futile and very expensive quest. Speculative theorizing base in conceptions borrowed from our cosmic neighborhood are not the answer. We might be formulating the wrong questions to Nature.

As a matter of fact, the evidence accruing from the sustained studies of subatomic structures are having a sobering effect in our preconceived, taken for granted, assumptions as to the architectural conformation of Nature. Fundamentalism in physics had been actually put in serious question by some 'off the main track' philosophical inclined physicists (the bootstraps theorists) who consider futile such a 'search' for the simple and basic. According to this view all phenomena are truly complex, and in actuality form an INTERPENETRATED WEB from which no 'elemental units' could be extricated; (something also supported by the already quoted Piaget's studies to the effect that living creatures conceptualize perceptual input in meaningful constellations of events). ('The Tao of Physics', by Fritjof Capra. Bantam Books.1975,P. 276.)

APPENDIX V

The conception that progress in the physical sciences is the result of well thought elaborations of theoretical studies is easily discredited by the history of the great inventors responsible for ushering the industrial era. The cases are too many to be mentioned in their totality but few well known examples should suffice to illustrate the point.

Take, for instance, the case of a sickly boy from Greenock in Scotland, a son of a carpenter and shipbuilder who from an early age wanted to be an instrument maker. James Watt formal education although it included some basic mathematics, was never the type that would granted him a professorial position although his recognized abilities allowed him, eventually, to set up a shop in the grounds of the University of Glasgow. His independent discovery of the 'latent heat' of vaporization inspired his development of the separate condenser for the Newcomen Engine, which ultimately permitted the construction of workable and reasonable efficient steam motors. The further development of these devises consisted of further refinement and perfection of the seminal invention of Watt, such as the Roebuck-Watt and Boulton- Watt engines which added another invention of Watt: The translation of the linear motion of the piston to rotary motion.

Enlightening in this regard are also the works of Carnot. Born into a distinguished family he had a solid background in Mathematics and became an army engineer. After the final defeat of Napoleon he somehow survived the political turmoil and joined the General Staff. His basic work in thermodynamics took place more than a century after the design of a workable steam engine and 50 years after the contributions of Watt.

Carnot was primarily concerned with the efficiency of the steam engines and his main contribution to the subject was the creation of a model based in the essential features of the apparatus, whereby he was able to conclude that efficiency depended solely in the temperature gradient between the main constituents or reservoirs of the motors and not on any consumption of an esoteric agent, which was fashionable at the time to call 'caloric', and thought by many workers in the field, to be burned during combustion.

Carnot framed his findings in fairly simple mathematics, not going beyond elemental calculus, and his conclusions were utilized by Lord Kelvin and Clausius to further conceive the second law of thermodynamic and introduce the important concept of entropy. In this case also the theory and mathematical formulations of thermodynamics in no way preceded the experimental evidence and practical accomplishment of the inventors; on the contrary, it was an a posteriori elaboration that disclosed the hidden relation between the different components of the combustion process.

Alessandro Volta hardly needs any introduction. His name is immortalized in Physics and Chemistry in expressions such as Volt and Voltaic pile (a primitive kind of battery and in fact an early version of an electrolytic system). His early educators in a Jesuits school described him as a talented young man and soon he developed great interest in electrical and chemical studies then in vogue. Yet, his education did not include advanced mathematics. Volta became professor of Physics at the Royal Academy of his native Como were he devised a machine called 'electrophorus' to produced static electricity. One of his early achievements was also to isolate the gas methane. Later on he was named professor at the University of Pavia where he remained for the remaining of his active life. One of his greatest discoveries was the description of what is now call 'electrical capacitance' and the development of the concept of electrical potential and charge, revealing that they were proportional. One interesting caveat was his de- mystification of what Luigi Galvani called 'animal electricity', showing that the legs of the frogs he used functioned both as electrical conveyors and detectors by the mere expedient of replacing them with brine soaked paper, an indication that biological phenomena had a physical origin; a revelation very much in keeping with the 'mechanistic' conception of the world then in vogue.

Among his numerous contributions to Physics was the perfection of an instrument called eudiometer to measure the composition of gases. Volta also was a child of the prolific XVIII Century and Napoleon ultimately pay him tribute for his work by naming him count in 1801.

Take also the case of the prolific genius Michael Faraday, a man of humble origin and one of the pioneers in the field of Electromagnetism. His research of magnetic field induction around a conductor of direct current, and his observation of the effect of electric fields in light propagation, established the basis of this science and serve as a foundation to Maxwell equations years later. He invented a prototype of rotary electric motor which was to revolutionize transportation and industry. Faraday is reputed with receiving only basic education in Science and Mathematics and in many ways was a self-thought man who, thru observation and experimentation, reached the enormous importance he has in history.

But the works of Faraday were not brought into existence out of thin air. Shortly before his research and inventions a casual incident triggered his interest and enormous accomplishments in the field of Electromagnetism. Hans Christian Orsted preparing for a lecture in 1820 noticed that a magnetic needle, which was part of his lecture's material, deflected from the magnetic north when an electric current from a near-by battery was turned on. If the dictum that chance events working in a prepared mind leads to great discoveries and scientific advances needs any corroboration, none better than this. His subsequent researches proved the principle of magnetic induction by electric currents, leading to a cascade of events including not only the works of Faraday, but also of Ampere (See below), and the inventions of the telegraph, originally by the works of Friedrich Gauss(one of the greatest mathematicians of all time), Wilhelm Weber and of Samuel Morse; a painter who, after the unexpected death of his wife, became interested in 'rapid remote communication', which eventually inspired by the work of Thomas Jackson, originated the concept of single wire telegraph, followed by the creation of the code that bears his name.

Another case in point is Andre Marie Ampere, a child of the Enlightment. His father was a successful business man who admired, among other things, the philosophical conceptions of his contemporary Jean Jacques Rousseau. So infatuated was him with the predications of the latter that he then decided to follow scrupulously the recommendations of the famous social scientist and declined to enroll his son in a traditional school education; deciding instead to provide for the necessary upbringing by exposing the lad to 'direct contact with nature'.

To this effect, the good father provided his son with an ample and well stocked library where he avidly learned directly from the masters of the time; being exposed to the works of such towering figures as Diderot, Leclerec and d'Alambert among others, including the best mathematicians of the age. He appeared to have been a sort of genius and by the age of 18 seemed to have mastered the advanced mathematics available at the time. Ampere was versed and interested in many other topics beyond his main areas of expertise: Including Philosophy, Religion and Literature. After a difficult period during the French Revolution he finally secured a job as professor in Physics and Chemistry at the Bourg-en-Bresse Ecole Centrale.

Ampere is widely known for his popular Ampere's law, which establishes that the mutual action of two current-carrying wires is proportional to their lengths and the intensities of their current. Not surprisingly his interest with electrical currents and magnetism was also triggered, like in the case of Faraday, by the observation of Orsted about electrical induction of a magnetic needle (See above). Ampere devoted much of his efforts, because of his background in Mathematics, to search for explanations and correlation of his experimental findings, like his discovery that wires carrying electrical current attract of repulse themselves according to the direction of flow of the current. This ultimate led to the formulation of his famous law, and finally to the publication of his memoir which, significantly, he titled 'Memoir on the Mathematical Theory of Electrodynamic Phenomena, Uniquely Deduced from Experience', which I believe is a recognition and tribute to the eminently empiric nature of scientific enterprise in general.

A pivotal figure in the field of electromagnetism was without question James Maxwell. From early childhood the lad displayed great interest in the Physical World and Mathematics, which resulted in some early works in the properties of ellipses. In Edinburg he experimented with chemical, electric and magnetic contrivances and did some research in the polarization of light. He is also reputed to have discovered the principle of photoelasticity. In Mathematics he introduced the term 'curl' for the vector operator defining rotational derivatives in a tridimensional vector field.

While at Trinity College he worked in the properties of light and with a contrivance called 'spinning tops', invented by Forbes, proved that white light was a mixture of different shades of color; in essence an anticipation of the spectroscope. While at Marischal College at Aberdeen he amazingly anticipated that the Saturn Rings were formed by small particles, concluding that if they were formed by a rigid material they would be unstable and, if liquid, they would rapidly dissolved into globs. He is, however, mostly remembered for his theoretical accomplishments in Mathematical Physics with his famous equations in Electrodynamics.

The case of J.W. Gibbs is also similarly enlightening. He was roughly contemporary to Maxwell with whom he corresponded. He was a studious, dedicated lad who graduated(with honors) from college at Yale at the early age of 19. He subsequently was granted the first P.H.D. degree in engineer given in U.S. and became a tutor at Yale. Following a long sojourn in Europe, mostly in France and Germany, he accepted an honorary position as a Professor of Mathematical Physics at Yale, where he remained for the remaining of his professional life. His solid knowledge in Mathematics and Physics allowed him to make important contributions in both sciences and is reputed with being one of the fathers of statistical mechanics,as well as, being instrumental in the founding of physical chemistry as a scientific discipline.

Gibbs works in practical subjects were few, including a railway brake(which he patented) and a governor for a steam-engine motor, but his theoretical contributions to the physics of thermodynamic phenomena and their application to chemical systems were considerable. In Mathematics he was one of the fathers of vector calculus and coined the term 'del' for the gradient of a scalar field. His vector analysis permitted him to simplify the descriptions of the physical behavior of multi-phase chemical systems (conceived as large assembles of 'particles').

Notwithstanding the mathematical talents of Maxwell and Gibbs I think it is fair to state that their achievements would not have been possible without the experimental basis created by their predecessors, which is an indication of the empiric source of this science. The works of these investigators are a clear example that mathematic formulations in Physics represent nothing else BUT A REVELATION OF CORRELATIONS BETWEEN PARAMETERS which permits predictions to be made and 'explanations' to be given, allowing the formulation of relational Laws valid at OUR COSMIC DIMENSION OF EXISTANCE because of the regularities of unfolding events at our universal proximity.

In the case of Maxwell the equations are only approximations to be replaced by Quantum Electrodynamics at microcosmic dimensions, where traditional conceptions failed to incorporate short distances perturbations and microcosmic oddities like quantum entanglement. Actually phenomena like the photoelectric effect, or any other physical disturbance conceptualized as discrete photons, could not be explain by his equations which conceive electromagnetism as a wave phenomena.

Following in the steps of Maxwell was the son of a wealthy senator of Hamburg who displayed early talents in Science and Language. Years later after graduating from the University of Berlin he accepted a position there, before becoming full Professor of Physic at Karlsruhe University. Heinrich Rudolph Hertz has been credited with the conclusive proof of the 'wave' nature of electromagnetic radiation which it was found to move with the speed of light, a fact anticipated by Maxwell years before.

Hertz radio-wave generator consisted of an induction coil and a spark gap. The receiver was a circular piece of cooper wire with a brass sphere at one end. The presence of an oscillating current in the receptive wire was to be detected by sparks between the brass sphere and the other end of the wire, indicating the existence of surges of spatial oscillating perturbations between the two parts of the apparatus. He subsequently prove that the speed of these ethereal 'waves' was the same as light.

Hertz contributions to Physics and Electromagnetism were many to be enumerated in detail here. Suffice is to say that they served as a basis for further work in radio, telegraph and for wireless communication. He also contributed to the field of photoelectric effect, and demonstrated that radio waves traveled thru some materials and no others. His work help in reaffirming that electromagnetic perturbations,including light, have a periodicity which allow them to be considered and described as part of the same physical phenomena we denominate as 'waves'.

Another pivotal figure in the field was Guglielmo Marconi. Early in his life he became very interested in the works of his predecessors and otherwise had a good round education. In many ways he was a fairly typical prolific inventor. In the attic of his house in Italy he commenced his experiments with wireless transmission of telegraphic signals with the help of his butler. The first apparatus was a crude contraption consisting of an oscillator, a piece of wire, a coherer receiver, an operating key and a register.

Many other inventors had tried similar systems but unsuccessfully. Marconi slowly improved in his device achieving progressively larger reach in his detections by using longer antennas. Although his work originally found a poor reception in his native country he eventually was welcomed in England, where he obtained the material help and acceptance necessary to proceed with his work, which finally attained international recognition. Marconi was able to effect long distance wireless transmission, ultimately achieving the portentous feat of transatlantic communication from a base in Nova Scotia.

During his late life Marconi became a prosperous business man and was the recipient of many awards, including sharing the Nobel Prize in Physics in 1909. He was also honored with the title of marquees by King Victor Emmanuel III in 1929. If anything his life is a proof of how much a man with solid but not advanced formal theoretical education could achieved in the cause of progress.

The history of the development of Radio-communication discloses a similar pattern to that of Telegraphy. Like in the case of the latter there were many independent contributors, like Julio Baviera, Reginald Fessenden, Harold Power and Edwin Armstrong, among others. The technical advances, including the use of crystals, the development of amplitude modulation, and the introduction of vacuum tubes for amplification revolutionized radio-reception, followed by the introduction of transistors and 'color tubes'. In the case of radio, like in other cases, the advances and refinements were granted by the successive accumulation of technological achievements permitting the perfecting and refining of the different aspects of radial transmission and reception.

A paralleled course to Radio was the invention and perfection of the Telephone. The urge of Man to talk to somebody else at a distance farther than could be reach by the human voice is almost as ancient as humanity. In fact rudimentary contraptions consisting of diaphragms interconnected by an intervening piece of string has long been a toy of children. Both Gauss (the prolific genius) and Eduard Weber are reputed to be the first who designed electromagnetic apparatuses for the transmission of telegraphic signals.

As in the case of Radio there were numerous inventors who contributed to the final perfection of the telephone. It is therefore not surprising that quite a few patent claims, counterclaims and law suits, not only by individuals but also by corporations, accrued during the process of its development. Work by men like Grafton Page, Manzetti, Bourseul, Antonio Meucci and Johann Phillip Reis, among others (the list do not pretend to be all-inclusive), culminated with the achievement of Alexander Graham Bell and modern telephonic. Reis is reputed to have design in 1860 a crude electromagnetic device capable of transmitting mostly indistinct speech which he coined with the term 'telephon', and shortly thereafter it is assumed to have invented a way to achieved an induction loading of telephone wires, although he failed to patent it in US.

Meucci, however, is credited by many to be the inventor of the first electromagnetic apparatus to detect the human voice. The vicissitudes of his life and his frustrated attempts to find recognition for his discovery are beyond the scope of this book. Suffice is to say that the American Congress in 2002, belatedly, gave credit to Meucci for the invention of the Telephone, further stating that if he would have paid a 10 dollar bill to maintain his patent after 1874, Bell would have not been able to be granted one for his apparatus.

Now, Alexander Bell is also known to have been a shroud and influential business man who certainly did have had an advantage in expediting recognition for his work. Bell was professor of 'Vocal Physiology', his main work consisting in teaching deaf-mutes how to speak using an apparatus design by Leon Scott to record speech vibrations. He engaged early in Telegraphy using a design already discovered by others, essentially consisting of current interrupters with vibrating steel reeds which generated pulses of current to a distant electromagnet activated receiver, which in its turn made a tuning fork to vibrate. In an occasion when the receiver steel reed failed to respond Bell told his helper to remove it, thinking it had stuck to the pole of the receiving magnet, but to his surprise he was able to hear in his end of the apparatus a clear reproduction of the plugging sound at the other end.

After more experiments he concluded that it wasn't the current from the battery of his transmitter what was causing the vibration of the receiver, but that it was the magnetic perturbation induced in the magnet by the electric current of the battery what caused the vibration of the receiver pole. This is another instance (if more are needed) of how chance in a prepared mind often triggers a chain of events provoking momentous advances in the field of Science and Technology.

This inside in the nature and potentialities of electromagnetic effects gave rise to the construction of the first telephonic machine, which consisted of a diaphragm with an attached armature of magnetized iron capable to vibrate in front of an electromagnet in circuit with the line. Bell's Telephone was perfected in following years and the first transatlantic transmission took place in 1876. Significantly, the Italians still today give credit to Meucci for the invention of the Telephone. Others, like Manzetti, who claimed that Bell stole his ideas, and Elisha Gray, who invented the 'water telephone', engaged in controversy and claims of precedence in submitting patents for approval

The case of the development of the Internal Combustion Engine is also illuminating. Cranks with connecting rods mechanisms had been known to exist since Late Antiquity. In 1780 Alessandro Volta devised a system to provoke a combustion of air and hydrogen triggered by an electric spark giving rise to a sudden explosive expansion of gases, a principle used shortly thereafter in the first prototype of internal combustion engine by John Barber; essentially a turbine capable of generating motion for metallurgical operations.

During the latter part of the XVIII and first part of the XIX centuries there were many contributors to the development and perfection of the Internal Combustion Engine. Men like Niepse, Isaac de Rivaz, Samuel Brown, William Barnett (the first to use intra-cylinder compression), Barsanti, Matteucci, Otto and Langen, helped to perfect the design and the transition from steam to gas driven motors. Joseph Etienne Lenoir built a practical prototype of the system and Nikolaus Otto was the first who manufactured a marketable four-cycle engine.

A detailed chronology of the development of the Internal Combustion

Engine is beyond the purpose of this work. Suffice is to say that it was the result of efforts by dedicated inventors and engineers based fundamentally in the increasing practical knowledge accumulated thru the ages. Mathematical and physical formulations were essentially a posteriori conceptions (relating the different physical parameters like, heat, work, gas expansion and contractions, mechanical action etc.) to 'explain' why things worked the way they did.

The history of the development of electrical powered devices and electrical based lighting is also fairly typical of the true dynamics of inventions.

A quite interesting case was that of a brilliant, ubiquitous but erratic genius, a colorful unconventional personality who was son of a Serbian Orthodox Priest and once ran away from being conscripted by the Austria-Hungarian army; a restless man but a great inventor. Nikola Tesla graduated from the Higher Real Gymnasium of Karlovac and is reputed with finishing his studies in fewer years than the curriculum demanded. Subsequently he enrolled in an Austrian polytechnic school, but soon after an argument with a teacher left without concluding his studies.

Tesla then for a while lived a dissipated life becoming a heavy gambler and dropping out of sight. Subsequently he is known to have become Chief Electrician to the newly open Budapest Telephone Exchange where he claimed to have made some improvement to the equipment, including an amplifier which he never patented. His wandering life landed him in France and later on in New York, where he worked for Edison after a harrowing experience in a ship, when he nearly escaped being thrown overboard.

In his new job Tesla claimed to have made significant improvements in Edison equipment but ultimately left the association in disgust following some differences with his boss. After some difficulties he finally set up the Tesla Electric Company where he worked in an AC induction motor based in a rotating magnetic field, although others were working in similar devices. His patent was finally licensed by Westinghouse for use in his companies and he even contracted Tesla to work for him. In following years Tesla continued to improve in his electric instruments and even worked in the development of X-ray equipments. His work in radio communication is also notorious. He developed the 'Tesla coil' and became a pioneer in radio-waves control, also experimenting with high voltage gadgets attempting unsuccessfully to transmit wireless transatlantic messages, being also credited with patenting a design for a plane that took of vertically; a concept very advanced for his time.

Tesla inventions were many and in multiple fields but some of his claims were exaggerated. He was a flamboyant character but a man of undeniable talents. Some of his high flying projects like the Wardenclyffe tower and later The Telefunken, which he hoped will transmit electric power trans-oceanically, eventually failed to achieve the promises of their founder. Toward the end of his life he struggled financially despite of his many lucrative patents.

Another notorious case that deserves to be highlighted in this brief exposition is that of a versatile inventor and businessman, who acquired early mechanical skills working in the shop of his father manufacturing agricultural machines. George Westinghouse dropped out from college a few months after obtaining his first patent: A rotary steam engine.

Westinghouse, could fairly be stated, was a visionary in business and technology. He had a rare ability to rapidly obtain patents for his inventions, seizing then the opportunity to found companies to commercially exploit his achievements. He was an early proponent of alternating current, which at that time (late XIX Century) encountered great opposition because it was considered dangerous. Undeterred he proceeded to set up the Westinghouse Electric Company, finally finding general acceptance after providing the electric lightning for the Chicago Columbian exposition of 1893. His invention of the transformer permitted to carry electricity to great distances, which allowed the harnessing of the water power of Niagara fall where his company was contracted to build three huge electrical generators, the first of their kind. His great skills as a business man was proved when shortly after opening his company he acquired the exclusivity of Nikola Tesla's for his system of alternating current.

Among his other inventions, it should be mentioned, an effective air brake for locomotives and later on he was majorly instrumental in introducing the electric locomotive. He also designed a system for safe gas conveyance and invented a system of compressed air springs for automobiles. During his life Westinghouse obtained a total of 361 patents.

His was another example of how much a man with modest theoretical education could accomplish in the field of Science and Technology.

We cannot conclude this brief exposition without mentioning the achievements of a man who can be define as a prototype of what I am hoping to highlight. Thomas Alba Edison does not need introduction. Edison was of humble origin and he dropped out of school after three months of formal education, subsequently being informally thought by his mother. His proclivities as an experimenter came early in life while working as a telegraph operator when he devised one of his early inventions in the baseman of a friend's house: A stock ticker.

Edison first novel and practical invention was the Phonograph which soon became a resounding success, eventually one of far reaching importance. The machine recorded in tinfoil around a rotating grooved cylinder. With the proceeds for the selling of his phonograph Edison founded the first laboratory to research and produce industrial products in Menlo Park New Jersey. He also was keen enough to surround himself with capable people able to help in his researches and designs. Interesting for us is his employment of Frank Sprague, a mathematician, to work for him in the application of mathematical analysis to the production process by determining, for instance, the optimal conditions for the manufacture of products, serving therefore an eminently practical role.

It is a common error to credit Edison with the discovery of the light bulb, which was the product of the labor of many pioneers like Volta, Humphry Davis and Henry Woodward, to mention just a few. What he did was to design the first commercially useful incandescent bulb using carbon filaments. He also design the first commercial fluoroscope and was credited, together with his photographer associate K L Dickson, with the development of the film camera, which he called Kinetograph.

Edison was also a shroud business man, one of the originators, with Henry Ford, of the mass-production process. He founded several successful companies, like Edison Electric Light Company and Edison Illuminating Company (which was the first public own electric utility).

We can carry on and on with examples of what I am intending to prove. Suffice is to mention Eli Whitney, the inventor of the 'Cotton Gin' of such enormous importance in the industrialization of America, Samuel Colt who design a hand gun with a revolving chamber, John Fitch the inventor of the Steam Boat and the Wright brothers, who design and built the first 'flying machine', those initiating a revolution in transportation. In fact, many of the complicated machinery which helped propel the Industrial Revolution were the result of efforts by multiple inventors, who frequently added upon their predecessors. Needless to say, and as happens so frequently in history, many of these men did not obtained the credit they certainly deserved.

When the process of the so-called 'Industrial Revolution' is analyzed the evidence seems to me indicative that advanced theoretical mathematic and physical knowledge was not necessary for its historic onset, growth and progress. With few exceptions the main actors were men of relatively limited knowledge of these sciences, frequently having no more than a practical notion of them which, nevertheless, was sufficient for their multiple inventions. Mathematicians of the caliber of Maxwell, Gauss or Gibbs were non-existent in this group of discoverers.

Mathematics, it should be emphasize again, besides a practical role in calculations, serve only the purpose of REVEALING HIDDEN RELATIONS BETWEEN PHYSICAL PARAMETERS AND/OR TERMS OF AN EQUATION, which nevertheless serve the useful purpose of allowing predictions to be made and correlations to be 'discovered' AT OUR COSMIC NEIGHBORHOOD. If so, this science has to assume the validity of a world where causality and induction are real categories. This is not surprising given the fact that its entire imposing edifice is an elaboration of the human mind, a very successful product of biological evolution which has permitted our marvelous adaptation to our hierarchical level of existence, but a device which might prove inadequate in its present form to challenges at more remote Universal Realms.(See the Conclusion).

FOOTNOTES

CHAPTER I

1   Whoever entertains the idea that mathematical postulates are unassailable ignore the stormy history of this discipline. Suffice is to mention the emotions elicited relatively recently by the transfinite theory of Georg Cantor, which arose so much animosity in the late XIX and early XX Century. The conceptions of Cantor were passionately denied by Leopold Kronecker from Berlin University and by the great French mathematician Henri Poincare, who once referred to it as "a disease from which later generations would regard themselves as having recovered", while the prominent David Hilbert commented that "No one shall expel us from the paradise which Cantor has created for us"

2   Indeed such an insidious transformation of the significance of a term certainly is not without precedent in the history of language, but rather is often the rule; as we can see in the semantic evolution of many words in practically all modern languages.

3   Historically, classifications are of two types: 'Artificial' or based in one single characteristic, like Linnaeus ordering of plants based in reproductive organs, or Malpighi taxonomy based in complexity of respiratory organs. 'Natural' are those classifications supported in multiplicity of perceptual similarities or differences, as is the case in our example.

CHAPTER II

1   There is a popular belief, among historians of Science, to the effect that mechanistic inclination has its origin in Calvinistic Protestantism, while the vitalist outlook arose with Luther's Reformation. There is no doubt that the collapse of the medieval Catholic-Aristotelian 'world order' (with its stratification

of angelical beings) effected by the Protestant Reformation, was a precondition for the revolution of human thought crystallizing in the downfall of the geocentric dogma with Copernicus; but we have already seen that both, rationalistic and animistic world views had ancient and profound roots in the West.

2   Yet, his procedure was not full proof as he failed to perform THE measurement capable of disqualifying his hypothesis, namely the weighing of the added water which was much less than the increase in weight of the bush. But perhaps it was a good thing he didn't because it would have led him to conclude that matter could be created out of nothing!...After all, the discovery of photosynthesis was several centuries away.

3   Kekule, for instance, thought, before the acceptance of Avogadro's ideas, that the laws of equivalent weights and volumes were not sufficient to chemistry. He wrote in 1861:

"Besides the laws of fixed and multiple proportions of weights, and in gaseous bodies also of volume, chemistry had as yet discovered no exact laws... and all so-called theoretical conceptions were merely points of view which possessed probability or convenience" (S.F. Mason 'A History of the Sciences'/ Collier Books. 1968, P.461)

Clearly, Kekule needed visual models in order to 'understand', and fittingly one night he dreamed about the mythical Uroborus (the self-devouring serpent), an experience which 'revealed' to him the 'shape' of the benzene nuclei.

4   There has been, however, a deliberate attempt to compare Harvey's works with that of his contemporary counterparts in physics, especially by some medical historians. Garrison in his 'History of Medicine' tell us that Harvey's importance was not so much the discovery of blood circulation but rather it's 'quantitative mathematical demonstration'.

Now, without the slightest desire to subtract any merits from the works of the great Englishman, to anyone who REALLY is acquainted with 'De motu cordis' it would appeared that Garrison's claims in this regard are not only totally unfounded and unwarranted but also betrayed a great and widespread misconception as to what constitutes ' the scientific method'. In the first place, Harvey's observation as 'to the quantity and velocity of the blood', although certainly in keeping with the vogue of physical measurements, did not represented more than a rough approximation and in no way even a conventional type of 'mathematical demonstration'.(See also Chapter V)

5   Posthumously Einstein, also in a late and generous homage to his predecessor, commented: "Apparently Mach would have arrived at the theory of relativity

if at the time when his mind still had the freshness of youth the question of velocity of light had already engage the attention of the physicists".(Cf. Vasiliev 'Space, Time and Motion', P. 206-207)

6   In this regard it is interesting to note that the definitive formulation of differential calculus by Cauchy in the XIX Century was only possible after an algebraic (abstract) approach substituted for the traditional geometric, then visual, conceptions of his predecessors; thus accomplishing the final emancipation for the search of 'sensorial' fretters which although heuristic, retarded the evolution of this branch of mathematics for over two millennia and had plagued the works of many predecessors, like Archimedes, Cavalier, Fermat, Roberval, Gregory of St. Vincent, Torricelli and even Newton and Leibnitz (See Carl B. Boyer 'The history of the Calculus and its conceptual development'. Dover Edition. 1959, P. 309)

7   Superficially 'empirical attitudes ' such as those held by traditional British empiricists appeared opposite to those of the Oriental mystic with his renunciation of the World. Yet, when 'explored' more closely, both views converged. They equally reject the idea of an independent ascertainable 'objective' or external reality. The difference is this: For the Indian saga truth was only reachable by meditation AFTER REJECTION OF 'SENSORY DATA', which he thought were only 'illusions' referable to nothing real and independent of human consciousness itself.

The British empiricists, on the other hand, not only believed that these 'sensations' WERE THE ONLY SOURCE OF KNOWLEDGE but also asserted their non-correspondence to any purported 'outside reality'; something they conceived as a redundant hypothesis. From this it follows that sensations are something personal, and a belief in them represented A FORM OF INSTROSPECTION. The ancestry of these notions, in a still crude unelaborated form, are found in the Greek sophist Protagoras who believed that 'man is the measure of all things'.

Strict empiricism, with its radical denials, was and is of course, a fruitless philosophy as far as scientific usefulness in concern. It is intimately related to solipsism and the impossibility of positing the first mandatory 'a priori' premise of any scientific endeavor: The existence of such a thing as a 'physical world' accessible to human consciousness or 'intellect'. On account of this sterile position the meaning of 'Empiricism' has reversed to the original Greek position and taken to mean that the senses are the only acceptable source of 'knowledge' from a posited 'external truth'; which is taken for granted if scientific activity is going to be possible at all.

8   An extreme position in this regard, certainly bordering with solipsism, was expressed by Edmund Husserl who doubted the validity that sensations referred to any outside reality and that the only things 'real' were these sensations and the emotions evoked by them ('phenomenological reduction'), therefore refusing to accept the recovery of the world effected by Descartes with his 'cogito'.

9   Erwin Schrodinger's was the last grand attempt to divest 'particles' of any substantiality. (A.D'abro 'The rise of the new physics'. Dover Edition. 1952, P. 726). Eventually Schrodinger's ideas became untenable when it was obvious that his 'packets' of de Broglie monochromatic waves, as the experiment of Davisson-Germer indicated, would rapidly disperse in space-time. At the end, then the Bohr-Heisenberg synthesis giving microcosmic events a wave-particle dual character had become generally accepted, something having the unfortunate consequence of preserving terms (waves, particles) with strong sensorial connotations borrowed from our immediate cosmic neighborhood.

10   In fact, and quite predictably, the 'fundamentalist' urge of the Western mind had already, in order to cope with the exuberant 'proliferation' of types of quarks, postulated the existence of even smaller elemental units of matter; the pre-quarks, and a new range of basic 'forces'. (See 'The structure of Quarks and Leptons', by Haim Harari. Scientific American, April 1983; P. 56)

More to the point is the present expensive and emotional charge successful search for the notorious Higgs boson, an anxious quest with religious connotations (it has been called the 'God particle'), which we are now assured had been detected as cascading decay patterns in the recording instruments and successfully disentangled from the prodigious torrents of related events. The legions of researches recruited into the effort and the billions of dollars spend should give an idea as to the magnitude and passion of the effort.

Man, it seems obvious, considers enormously painful to depart from the 'particle paradigm' as source and explanation for the origin of the Cosmo. It didn't matter that the works in the 'Large Hydron Collider' have not, and probably will not in the near future, be reproduced by any INDEPENDENT group of researches and therefore lack CORROBORATION (the cornerstone of the scientific effort).It didn't matter either that the work at present have no perceptive practical value. Millions of dollars had been spent and Nobel prices need to the prodigally adjudicated!

CHAPTER III

1   Evidence from other researches seems to point out that the process of associative learning in primitive invertebrates is mediated by changes of non-synaptic

neuron membrane permeability, giving rise to increase inflow of Calcium and decrease outflow of Potassium associated with enhanced cellular excitability (See 'Learning in a Marine Snail' by Daniel L. Alkon, Scientific American Vol. 249, Number 1, July 1983)

CHAPTER IV

1   Another is the efforts spend in applying the kinetic-molecular theory of gases as an 'explanation' for the Second Law of Thermodynamics. Very revealing in this regard are the justifications of authors in text books for this expensive and exhausting enterprise. It was considered 'very profitable' to find a molecular interpretation of entropy. Evidently, the 'profitability' does not refer to a tangible useful value, but as a devise to perpetuate the validity of a presumptive 'model' of reality: The atomistic dream of the ancient Greeks which we think is our duty to defend and preserve at all costs. (See Gordon M. Barrow 'Physical Chemistry '. McGraw-Hill. 1961. First Edition, P. 144)

CONCLUSION

1   If it is claimed that it is the 'force' of gravity what produces the space-time curvature, it can be argued the opposite; in other words, that it is precisely the curvature what gives rise to the collection of matter representing the celestial bodies where they are. To assume otherwise is to introduce into the argument assumptions based precisely in conceptions borrowed from naive 'common-sensical' causality.

2   I believe it is significant in this regard that according with the works of Mathew D. Scharff, from Albert Einstein College of Medicine ('The genetics of antibody diversity' By Philip Leder, Scientific American, May 1982, p. 102) with clones of mature lymphocytes, there is a mutational rate in these antibodies producing cells of $1/100000$ per generation, a remarkable fact indeed, indicating an unusual degree of genetic transformation activity reflecting the high antigenic pressure these cells are known to be subjected to and with which it seems to correlate.

If mutations are random phenomena independent of any other influence, how such high mutational rate in this critical area for survival could be explain? And why these mutations are mostly concerned with the genes encoding the variable portion of inmunoglobulins from where antibody specificity ensues?

There appears to be a mysterious mutual interdependence and complementarities between proteins and polynucleotides. Why an experimental design to study (perhaps by a process of reversed translation and transcription) the possibility that some mutations are the guided result of environmental induced changes in the genome never had been attempted?

CHAPTER V

1   In fact, according to some modern scholars, for instance, the Oath is the ethical canon of the Coan School. All other portions of the Corpus appear to be of dubious procedence, and even some tracts have been attributed a Cnidian source; like 'On internal affections' and 'On diseases'.

2   As a matter of fact, even among theories of disease there appears to be obvious contradictions within different portions of the writings. For instance, in 'On regimen' a disease theory of fluxions, of which seven are described, is advanced offering clearly an entirely different genealogy than the 'Disharmony of the humors' already mentioned.

3   Of the other schools products of the Greek mind the Methodists believed in the existence of 'pores' whose constriction and relaxation caused the diseases. It was founded by Themison, a follower of the great Asclepiades, after rejecting the doctrine of the 'four humors' that had tyrannized Greek thought for many centuries.
      Finally the eclectic mind, so characteristic of human endeavors, could have not failed the 'maiden of sciences'. Apparently evolving from the pneumatics they did not subscribed to any of the existing schools, but applied whichever modality was necessary in a given case. According to Galen one of the best representatives of this school was Archigenes who distinguished himself above all in surgery, particularly in amputation techniques.

4   Besides the example of Bagdad, the Hohenstaufen Emperors of Sicily forbade anyone to practice without a passing examination and a long period of formal studies in Logic, Medicine and Surgery.

5   The man who designed a clinical thermometer, a pulse-clock, a hygrometer and diverse surgical instruments.

6   See Castiglione's 'History of Medicine'. Jason Aronson Inc. 1975, P. 522

7   Some even claim that the plates were there because the cleaning lady had neglected to throw them away.

8   According to a version while complaining to a friend about the cleaning lady neglect.

9   And perhaps even the apathy of the cleaning lady and the visit of the friend.

10 For example, a peculiar absorbance pattern in a spectrophotometer (resulting from a 'chemical' reaction taking place when some 'specific' reagent, or reagents, are mixed in given proportions) which we have learned to identify with the presence of certain 'aminoacid'.

CHAPTER VI

1   Example of the first is, for instance, 'eclampsia', a name that addresses itself to a symptomatic complex, and of the second 'pulmonary emphysema' which gross morbid picture forms the basis of the denomination. In the third category there are numerous notorious newcomers into medical literature, like 'macroglobulinemia', 'heavy chain disease' and 'amylopectinosis', among many others.

APPENDIX III

1   Above and beyond the possibilities of the unintended structural error there is the more ominous specter of deliberate distortions of data, which, being a flaw of the human soul, no degree of expertise by presumptive reviewers will be able to guard against, ultimately requiring cumbersome and expensive repetitions of trials by other workers in the field; something only performed rarely, usually in those areas where conflicting economic or legal interests play an important role.

   A notorious example of how a clever swindler can deceive the academic community and work his way up the ladder of success by indulging systematically in fraud, even in respectable educational and research centers, is provided by the 'Darsee Affair' (See J.A.M.A., April 1983 Vol. 249, No. 14, P. 1797.)

INDEX